The Pyramid Approach

The Pyramid Approach

A Framework for Raising Student Academic Achievement

George Woodrow Jr.

ROWMAN & LITTLEFIELD
Lanham • Boulder • New York • London

Published by Rowman & Littlefield
A wholly owned subsidiary of The Rowman & Littlefield Publishing Group, Inc.
4501 Forbes Boulevard, Suite 200, Lanham, Maryland 20706
www.rowman.com

16 Carlisle Street, London W1D 3BT, United Kingdom

British Library Cataloguing in Publication Information Available

Library of Congress Cataloging-in-Publication Data

Woodrow, George Jr.
The pyramid approach : a framework for raising student academic achievement / George Woodrow Jr.
pages cm.
Includes index.
ISBN 978-1-4758-1350-0 (cloth : alk. paper) — ISBN 978-1-4758-1351-7 (pbk. : alk. paper) — ISBN 978-1-4758-1352-4 (ebook)
1. School management and organization—United States. 2. Educational leadership—United States. 3. Teacher participation in administration—United States. 4. Teacher effectiveness. 5. Academic achievement—United States. 6. Educational change—United States. I. Title.
LB2805.W58 2014
371.200973—dc23
2014026376

∞™ The paper used in this publication meets the minimum requirements of American National Standard for Information Sciences Permanence of Paper for Printed Library Materials, ANSI/NISO Z39.48-1992.

Printed in the United States of America

Contents

Acknowledgments

I would like to thank, first and foremost, my entire family, above all my parents. Gratitude goes to all of the educators, students, and parents I have had the honor of working with over the years. In addition, I thank Sheryl Santos-Hatchett, Doug Shouse, Kay Forsythe, Juanita Simmons, Robert Malzahn, Claudis Allen, Johnetta Hudson, Richard Fossey, Joseph Brew, and Jay Cummings. I have learned much from them, and continue to learn more. Finally, appreciation goes to organizers and presenters at the Harvard Graduate School of Education Principals' Center, chiefly Mildred Blackman and Jeff Howard.

Introduction

> Synergy is the interconnectedness of the whole, which produces an effect that is greater than the sum of its individual effects.

The Pyramid Approach shares contemporary educational research that hones in on what makes effective schools work. It was written for anyone who seeks to understand why American schools are not performing better and what can be done about it. Further, it illuminates clearly the connections among a quality education, a promising future for young people, and a thriving economy and nation.

Simply put, because we live in an ever competitive and interconnected global community, a quality education is more essential than ever before. This book attempts to make a convincing case that there is an urgent need for a systematic approach to strategically guide our professional practice in schooling. This research-based approach, the pyramid approach, may well be the missing link between mediocrity and excellence in schools.

Further, the purpose of this book is to call attention to a pressing need for an educational framework that guides educators' professional practice. It is needed to replace the guesswork and frequent fads that have proven to be unsuccessful in the past. *The Pyramid Approach* was designed to provide this type of guidance.

The Pyramid is also needed to supplant the many ineffective business models that were hatched in the corporate community and borrowed by educators. I am confident these concepts proved successful for the purpose in which they were designed. However, the problem is that parents are not customers. They are partners. And students are not commodities, products, or widgets. They are children and they are our future. Therefore, educators need a comprehensive yet simple paradigm or framework that was developed specifically for advancing achievement in education. The Instructional Leadership Pyramid is such a framework.

A few topics examined include: (1) the latest international test rankings and an analysis of these test data; (2) the negative impact poverty can have on children and some possible ways to minimize its effects; (3) the use of student feedback and effective classroom management methods; (4) the pros and cons about merit pay as well as induction programs; and (5) the educational systems of some high performing countries like Japan, Finland, Poland, and Korea.

CAN YOU HANDLE THE TRUTH?

This book is based on the most current research as well as more than twenty-five years of experience, during which I have provided leadership at the campus and district levels and worked as an assistant professor teaching educational administration courses. Additionally, this book emanates from two central and vital questions: One, how do educators effectively apply what we know to improve all students' academic achievement level? And two, why hasn't this knowledge been applied effectively across the educational system so far?

The Pyramid Approach will pull the cover off and expose the "bare facts" regarding these questions and shine light on a comprehensive synergistic approach that exposes misconceptualized and misapplied professional practices. The bare facts are those issues that are many times the least discussed, yet they are largely responsible for clogging real and lasting progress in the daily work of educators.

Each chapter will conclude with some relevant bare facts. This exposure will provide a catalyst to confront the bare facts head-on. In the movie *A Few Good Men*, Jack Nicholson is on trial. At the end of the movie, Tom Cruise, the attorney, asks a series of questions designed to elicit the truth (bare facts). Nicholson replies, "You can't handle the truth!"

The Pyramid Approach is written on the premise that we can and must handle the truth. Ron Edmonds, a Harvard professor, declared in the 1980s that we already know more than we need to know to educate all students successfully. And he questioned why we haven't done it so far. This question by Edmonds in no way implies that the motives, intentions, and goals of educators are not honorable and noble, because they are indeed; however, good intentions have been trumped by fragmented and inconsistent application of what works in schools.

This book takes a profound position. *It is not that we don't know; it is that we don't believe what we know.* And those who do believe current research concepts and methods find it difficult to apply that knowledge school-wide in a framework that is not centered in a synergistic culture. These issues are tackled in this book. As you continue reading, you will begin to see more clearly the relationships among and between methods, research, and processes that naturally lead to significantly improved professional practice and student proficiency. At this point, I should define a frequently used term in this book: research-based belief system. It is simply possessing self-efficacy and believing all students, through applying effective effort, possess the capacity to demonstrate proficiency with rigorous curricula.

You may be tempted to reason, as you read this book, that "I already know this." While in some instances you may be correct, the thought I would like you to hold in the forefront of your mind as you read is: To what degree do I currently apply this knowledge? Most would concur with the adage that we learn from our experiences. I submit that we learn even more from reflecting upon those experiences.

A wise saying, generally attributed to the American writer and futurist Alvin Toffler, asserts: The wrong answer to the right question is more important than the right answer to the wrong question. Thus, the impact this book will have on each one who reads it will to a large degree depend upon how the information is internalized, and whether it is fully embraced; hence, at the end of each chapter, I will attempt to ask the "right questions" in the hope that you reflect and truly begin the process of transforming your thinking about human capacity and daily practice. This book is unique in that at the end of each chapter, a section is provided for you to record your reflections. I encourage you to use it. Then begin a process of inquiring and thinking about your thinking.

REFLECTIVE THOUGHTS

What are your thoughts and beliefs regarding the following statements and how are they manifested in your daily practice?

- How do you personally feel about change?
- Do you consider yourself a leader?
- Can you handle the truth?

BARE FACTS

- Common sense is not so common.
- Good intentions are trumped by fragmented and inconsistent application of what works in schools.
- We in education too often don't believe what we know.

REFERENCES

Collins, Jim. (2001). Good to great. New York: HarperCollins Publishers Inc.

Covey, S. M. R. (2006). The speed of trust. New York: Free Press.

DuFour, R., and Eaker, R. (1998). Professional learning communities at work. Bloomington, IN: National Educational Service.

Fullan, M., and Hargreaves, A. (1996). What's worth fighting for in your school? New York: Teachers College Press.

Hanushek, E. (2014). Why the U.S. results on PISA matter. *Education Week*. Vol. 33, Issue 15, pgs. 20–21, 24

Indicators of School Crime and Safety. (2007). U.S. Department of Education, National Center for Education Statistics. (NCES 2008–021).

Lloyd, S. C., and Swanson, C. B. (2014). Equity in achievement, funding a hurdle for states amid progress. Education Week. Vol. 33, Issue 16, pg. 34.

Sergiovanni, T. (1996). Leadership for the schoolhouse. San Francisco: Jossey- Bass.

Whitehead, A. N. (1957). The aims of education. New York: Macmillan Publishing Co.

REFLECTIVE THOUGHTS

ONE

Culture of the Organization

We tend to think we can separate strategy from culture, but we fail to notice that in most organizations strategic thinking is deeply colored by tacit assumptions about who they are and what their mission is. — Edgar Schein, professor, MIT Sloan School of Management

SYSTEMATIC FRAMEWORK AND KEY TERMS

Administrators and teachers often use different methods and strategies to improve students' learning at school. While all are aimed at the same outcome, the problem is that their methods and strategies do not always work together. They do not build on and support each other. Too often, transforming the campus culture so that student learning flourishes is expressed in idealistic terms; it needs to be framed in the real world of schooling (Fullan and Hargreaves, 1996). *The Pyramid Approach* does it this way; it is not a quick fix or philosophical panacea detached from the real world of everyday school challenges. *The Pyramid Approach* organizes and applies critical research-based educational principles in a comprehensive and comprehendible way. Throughout the book, I will use several analogies and metaphors in an attempt to clearly demonstrate how the Pyramid Approach works.

1

It provides educators with a framework, involving others in the school community, for a systematic approach that will advance the teaching and learning experience in schools as well as provide a platform for all students to experience academic achievement at high levels. In other words, the Pyramid Approach offers a process that will more efficiently allow instructional leaders to realize the goals they seek.

Further, it is grounded in systems thinking. This kind of thinking cultivates an appreciation for analyzing the whole rather than any individual part. It is a framework for seeing interrelationships (Senge, 1990). It calls for a new way to think about improvement. Inherent in this kind of thinking is a concern for and commitment to the whole organization not just one part of it. Instructional leaders begin to move beyond reacting to the present and begin to focus on shaping the future—they feel empowered. Embracing systems thinking causes everyone to share responsibility for failures and successes within the organization. Thinking in this way improves decision making and it galvanizes positive action for improving professional practice and schools.

At this point, I should clarify the use of several terms: the pyramid approach (PA) and the instructional leadership pyramid (ILP). They are terms that can be used interchangeably. The instructional leadership pyramid is the specific framework or model for improving student achievement and schools, while the pyramid approach is simply a reference to the ILP. The term instructional leader (IL) is any individual with instructional responsibilities who fosters students' learning and has direct contact, in some form, with students. Because of the importance of this concept, and of how often the term will be used in this book, I will often refer to it by the acronym "IL." The term "campus instructional leader" will often be used to identify the principal; "classroom instructional leader" will refer to instructors; and "instructional leader" will be used interchangeably to refer to both administrators and those who instruct in the classroom.

Some educators refer to principals as head teachers. The primary responsibility of principals is to protect and enrich the learning environment in such a way that it ensures students demonstrate academic proficiency with challenging curricula. Every decision they make should be made with the goal of student proficiency in mind. It naturally follows that campus administrators are indeed instructional leaders. Research clearly shows, however, that teachers are the most important factor in this endeavor. They too are instructional leaders. Others observe them daily, including students; hence, they lead by their example. They lead students, parents, and community stakeholders to seek and experience continuous improvement. They do this through leading professional learning communities, professional development activities, students' curricula and co-curricula activities, as well as leading followership. That is, they embrace and follow the organization's vision to attain excellence.

They assist with shaping group norms; hence, they lead the development of campus culture and promote organizational change. They are leaders, even if only of themselves.

"Instructional leader," therefore more accurately describes effective educators than the honorable and endearing, yet incomplete, terms teacher and principal. While essentially there is not a difference between the two terms, teacher and instructional leader, there is indeed a significant distinction between them in the following discussion. Teachers may merely follow lesson plans and guidelines, while instructional leaders will always follow a noble organizational vision that seeks to cause a sea change in the achievement level of all students. Some teachers may reason, "I taught it, they just didn't get it." On the other hand, all instructional leaders will reason, "Until students demonstrate proficiency, the right conditions for learning have not been put in place."

Some have suggested that the term instructional leader has perhaps out served its usefulness because its focus seems to be on instruction, not learning. I make just the opposite case. Instruction is still an indispensable science and art. Alexander the Great owed his prominence to Aristotle, Aristotle owed his academic prowess to Plato, and so it is in the classrooms of today. Standing by the side of successful learners are successful instructional leaders.

When students are not learning, it is, notwithstanding all other impediments, either because quality instruction is not present, or an appropriate learning environment has not been created. Good schooling is a combination of quality instruction and quality learning. Confucius himself declared, "The process of teaching and learning stimulates one another." It is not an either-or situation—both are essential. And, of course, just because one is an instructor does not mean that one no longer learns. Instructional leaders understand and appreciate the significance of lifelong learning. As the old saying goes, "The best way to learn something is to teach it."

Thus instructional leaders model learning for students and parents by fully embracing the notion of being "learning leaders" themselves. They understand effective learning is a collaborative process that involves students, parents, and the larger campus community. If one person cannot, by herself, accomplish the task of ensuring all students on campus learn, then it only stands to reason one person cannot independently deliver all of the leadership required to achieve success for the school.

Leadership density is the model that research consistently demonstrates is most effective in this regard (Sergiovanni, 1996). The key principle is for instructional leaders to create and embrace a shared vision. Applying the term instructional leader to both principals and teachers embraces the goal of leadership density and facilitates the advancement of that same objective. The term instructional leader thus suggests that those it is applied to carry an awesome amount of responsibility and expertise. This term connotes difference makers—they understand, once again, that they are not following the wishes of a single individual leader but of a lofty and noble organizational mission.

To cultivate this kind of thinking and action, I coined a new term: *collective instructional leadership*. Its focus is on achieving high quality instruction and learning for all through united efforts. *The Pyramid Approach* attempts to underscore the significance of collective instructional leadership. The notion that one charismatic leader rides around campus atop a white horse to save the inhabitants is a myth that even Hollywood is reticent to promulgate. It just does not exist.

This is why in this book the reader will be encouraged to embrace the notion that only through collective instructional leadership will schools begin to move up the pyramid. However, it should be noted that just as the classroom instructional leader makes the most dramatic impact on student learning, the campus instructional leader (principal) is the one most responsible for orchestrating the collective efforts of the other instructional leaders, students, and parents. Just as a symphony's conductor ensures everyone is in the correct seat performing at his peak level, so does the campus instructional leader. She is the straw that stirs the drink.

THE BARE FACTS

Before discussing the relationship between organizational culture and the success of its mission, let's first examine some "bare facts" regarding the state of affairs for education in the United States and briefly highlight the five levels of the pyramid.

In 1966, the United States Office of Education published the "Coleman Report" (nicknamed after James Coleman, its primary author), which essentially concluded that if one knew the zip codes of a given set of students, he would then know their aptitude. That is to say, schooling has little effect on student academic achievement. The official title of the report was "Equality of Educational Opportunity Study" (EEOS). At the time it was one of the largest studies in U.S. history, including more than 150,000 students in its sample.

In 1983, the secretary of education released a report, "A Nation at Risk," which asserted, "We have, in effect, been committing an act of unthinkable, unilateral educational disarmament." Now, decades after the "Coleman Report" and the "Nation at Risk" report, we are still wrestling with the complexities of our educational system.

For example, a barometer used to gage education progress in the United States is *Quality Counts*. It is a K–12 report that has been published by Education Week since 1997. The report assesses each state's performance against a broad set of eighteen separate indicators, including the National Assessment of Educational Progress, high school graduation rates, and scores on Advanced Placement exams. Unlike some score cards on student achievement, it analyzes results across three critical dimensions: current state performance, improvements over time, and equity as measured by poverty-based achievement gaps. In 2014, the nation as a whole received an overall score of 70.2 or C-minus for the 2013 school year.

The Trends in International Mathematics and Science Study (TIMSS) is an international assessment used to measure the achievement of fourth and eighth grade students in math and science. It is administered every four years. In 2011, mathematics students in ten countries scored higher than U.S. fourth grade students. Eight countries scored higher than U.S. students in eighth grade mathematics. There was a one point improvement in U.S. eighth-grade mathematics scores from 2007 (508) to 2011 (509).

Furthermore, the National Center for Education Statistics reported the results of a well-regarded international benchmarking tool: the Program for International Student Assessment (PISA). The PISA was first administered in 2000. Every three years fifteen-year-olds take this global assessment in reading, math, and science. PISA not only examines how well students can reproduce what they have learned; but it also attempts to determine how well students are able to apply that same knowledge in unfamiliar settings.

According to its designers, PISA has a high correlation with the Common Core State Standards for Mathematics (CCSSM). Most states have adopted Common Core as their state mathematics standard. In 2012, the percentages of U.S. students scoring in the "top performers" category were: 8 percent in reading, 7 percent in science, and 9 percent in math.

And the percentages of U.S. students performing below the proficiency level were: 17 percent in reading, 18 percent in science, and 26 percent in math. In part, here are a few countries that overtook the United States in math on the PISA: Poland, Vietnam, Ireland, Latvia, and Luxembourg (see table 1.1). In Shanghai, China, students attained a mean score in mathematics of 613. This means these students scored nearly three years above the average scoring countries. And the U.S. students scored below average.

Some have questioned these results. They assert comparing Shanghai, China to the United States is like comparing apples to oranges. Shanghai is a Special Administrative Region of China, and America is a large country. Further, they claim, if the scores of disadvantaged students were excluded, U.S. students' scores would spring to the top. That explains it. There is only one problem: the "bare facts" do not support these claims.

(1) Shanghai, China	(19) Australia
(2) Singapore	(20) Ireland
(3) Hong Kong, China	(21) Slovenia
(4) Taiwan	(22) Denmark
(5) Korea	(23) New Zealand
(6) Macau, China	(24) Czech Republic
(7) Japan	(25) France
(8) Liechtenstein	(26) United Kingdom
(9) Switzerland	(27) Iceland
(10) Netherlands	(28) Latvia
(11) Estonia	(29) Luxembourg
(12) Finland	(30) Norway
(13) Canada	(31) Portugal
(14) Poland	(32) Italy
(15) Belgium	(33) Spain
(16) Germany	(34) Russia
(17) Vietnam	(35) Slovakia
(18) Austria	(36) United States

Table 1.1. Program for International Student Assessment Math (PISA) Results from 2012

According to the 2009 PISA results, students in Shanghai, China, not only scored above America's top math scoring state (Massachusetts), they also scored higher in math, science, and reading. When comparing our most affluent students' math scores to economically similar students in other countries, the United States ranked eighteenth. And comparing our most needy students' math scores to economically similar students in other countries, the United States ranked twenty-seventh.

That is, affluent students in these countries exceeded the performance of our affluent students and students living in poverty outperformed our students living in poverty. Following is a list of a few countries that produced successful math students who scored above our students at both ends of the socioeconomic ladder: Canada, Korea, Slovak Republic, Finland, Poland, Japan, and Slovenia.

Still, skepticism regarding the worth of these international benchmark tests remains. Keith Baker (2007), who worked at the U.S. Department of Education, studied these assessments and concluded they are essentially worthless. We are committing the "ecological correlation fallacy," he asserts. It is a mistake to assume what is good for an individual (high test scores, for example) must be right for a nation as a whole.

Baker did not find a strong relationship between high test scores and improved economic productivity of nations. Maybe it is, maybe it isn't. He believes the jury is still out. Diane Ravitch (2013), a research professor of education at New York University, concurs that international assessment comparisons are not relevant. She states, "Trying to raise America's test scores in comparison to those of other nations is worse than pointless" (p. 72). But she adds, "I do not contend the schools are fine just as they are. They are not" (p. xii).

Then there is Eric Hanushek (2014), a senior fellow at the Hoover Institution of Stanford University. He and his research associates demonstrated that indeed long-term economic growth of nations is closely related to the skills measured by assessments such as PISA. He concludes that the United States has the world's strongest economic systems and institutions, and this may have protected us from some deficiencies in our educational system. Hanushek makes two final points: the U.S. economic system rewards high-level skills and other nations are emulating the U.S economic system while at the same time producing improved human capital.

Robert Compton, in his groundbreaking documentary, "Two Million Minutes: A Global Examination," paints a similar picture, one that is congruent with *Quality Counts* and international achievement data. He points out that China and India, two potentially formidable economic competitors, are devoting more time and effort than the United States to preparing their students in high school for the twenty-first-century global economy.

To be sure, some politicians, policymakers, parents, and many other non-educators are not absolved from their responsibility in this matter. No reasonable person denies inequality permeates the educational system in the United States. And that if poverty and what amounts to a dual education system were fully redressed, all students would benefit. In spite of this reality, rather than debate the validity of international academic benchmarks and who should shoulder the primary responsibility for students' outcomes, I recommend ILs borrow methods that have universal success and reject those that are unproven or appear to be harmful. Doing it this way provides the best opportunity for all students to experience success.

It seems that national studies and reports succeed each other but the conclusions remain the same. K–12 students are not performing to their full academic potential. These disappointing and unacceptable results persist notwithstanding overwhelming research that has definitively highlighted what works and what does not work within the school setting. Why, if we know what works, do approximately 15 percent of white students fail to graduate high school within four years while minorities (Hispanics and Blacks) fail to graduate at an even higher rate during that same four year period, roughly 30 and 25 percent respectively (National Center of Education Statistics, 2011–12)?

In my view, these numbers are misleading because the actual dropout rate is unknown. For instance, there are multiple methods used to calculate students' attrition rates in school: specifically the status dropout rate, event dropout rate, adjusted cohort rate and average freshman graduate rate. One attrition rate measures a single year dropout rate while another measures the dropout rate between ages sixteen through twenty-four. And even worse, some attrition rates count General Education Development (GED) recipients as graduates (Heckman, 2013; National Center of Education Statistics, 2011–12). So why are some educators and students undermotivated and underperforming? In "Two Million Minutes," Compton frames it this way:

> The simple fact is global education standards have passed America by. When it was Finland who was winning, it wasn't such a concern. But now that our K–12 students are being outperformed academically by China and India—the two highest populated countries in the world with the fastest growing economies and with cultures that embrace intellectual challenge—it is cause for serious concern. (Compton, 2007)

Many will agree that we in education know what to do but have not yet applied our knowledge sufficiently to reap the benefits of it. Libraries are replete with research articles; journals and books are filled with information espousing how to enrich learning so students are inspired to attain their full academic potential. So what is the problem? The problem is that too many educators refuse to face the "brutal facts" (Collins, 2001). In addition, some are too slow to shift their focus from just the acquisition of knowledge to the implementation of it. Alfred North Whitehead, in *The Aims of Education*, crystallizes this truism. "Education is the acquisition of the art of the utilization of knowledge" (1957, p. 4). He continues:

> You cannot be wise without some basis of knowledge; but you may easily acquire knowledge and remain bare of wisdom. Now wisdom is the way in which knowledge is held. It concerns the handling of knowledge, its selection for the determination of relevant issues, its employment to add value to our immediate experience. (p. 30)

The Pyramid Approach is a conceptual framework that not only targets research that works but also goes one-step further: it provides a synergistic process that clearly and precisely reveals the interconnectedness of effective instructional leadership. For instance, when it was reported the German army was developing the first submarines, Great Britain was concerned that these submarines would neutralize their naval advantage. The British decided to offer an international prize to anyone who could develop a strategy that would render the submarines impotent. Mark Twain wired a solution that recommended boiling the ocean. He then requested his prize. When questioned about more specific details regarding his recommendation, Twain replied that he had generated the idea. It was the responsibility of the leaders of the navy to provide the specifics (DuFour and Eaker, 1998). The Pyramid offers fresh ideas and specifics about how to more effectively apply what we know works in education. It was not written to participate in the "blame game." That is, blaming educators for most of society's ills. An industry for that purpose appears to already exist.

THE FIVE LEVELS OF THE PYRAMID

Offering a concept as a solution to a challenging issue without a framework to apply that concept, as Twain did, is analogous to laying out the ingredients for a five-star meal without providing a recipe. The recipe reference is not intended to suggest the Pyramid is to be applied identically on all campuses. It does provide a framework that should be applied consistently; however, within the Pyramid, flexibility should be used to tailor strategies and approaches to the unique needs of each campus. The Pyramid embraces professional reflective practice, and ILs are expected to ponder, rethink, reassess, adapt, and modify their practices within its structure. This insightful process allows us to use our *collective wisdom*, consideration, and reflection.

The Pyramid specifies these simple but critical steps for instructional leaders, and underscores their interconnectedness as it relates to the process of ensuring all students achieve at a high level. The recipe analogy can be applied again to illustrate how flower, sugar, eggs, and milk can produce something—a cake—greater than the sum of its ingredients.

Likewise, the collective levels of the Pyramid transcend their individual levels. Moreover, the concepts offered in the Pyramid are here to stay, unlike some of the gimmicks we are accustomed to seeing promulgated in education. For example: campus culture, instructional strategies, a research-based belief system, galvanizing students' effective effort, and finally, ensuring the academic success of all students, are the essential components found on successful campuses.

And now, the Pyramid offers a pathway for all campuses to celebrate this type of success. It was developed from my own experiences as an instructional leader, the most current research, and the Educational

Leadership Policy Standards," published by the Interstate School Leaders Licensure Consortium (ISLLC) 2008. Each level of the Pyramid will be developed fully in the first four chapters of this book, while chapter 5 will explain in detail the way the entire Pyramid works as an interconnected whole. This is a brief outline of each level of the Pyramid:

1. Create a safe, caring, and trusting team culture.
2. Develop, implement, and monitor effective school-wide instructional strategies that reflect data analysis.
3. Select and develop master teachers who possess a research-based belief system.
4. Significantly increase all students' academic effort.
5. Reap the benefits of high student achievement that flows from realizing the previous steps.

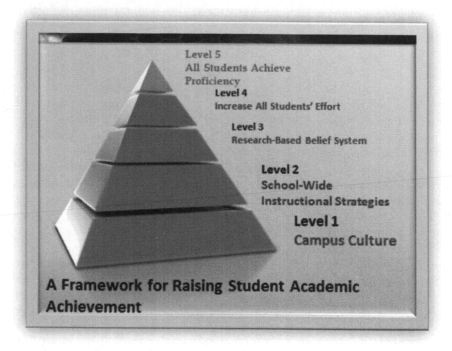

Figure 1.1.

SAFE AND CARING CULTURE

Instructional leadership that advances the teaching and learning experience does not just focus on data collection and pedagogy. While both are essential, the mistake too many educators make is not devoting sufficient attention to first establishing a safe, caring, and trusting team culture. Good organizational culture is an essential prerequisite for creating a successful teaching and learning environment. Sergiovanni states, "The heart and soul of school culture is what people believe, the assumptions they make about how schools work, and what they consider to be true and real" (1996, p. 3).

This one statement, supported by overwhelming research, strikes at the core premise of the Pyramid: beliefs matter. Notwithstanding all of our diligent strategic plans to reorganize and restructure schooling, we are doomed to fail without first solidifying a cultural foundation on which to build the organizational mission. This will not be accomplished overnight, but it is the place to begin our journey toward ensuring all students, staff, and instructional leaders are thriving.

There is substantial research that clearly emphasizes that, while important, reorganizing and restructuring alone will not deliver the desired outcomes. That is, innovative beginning and ending times for schools, block schedules, schools-within-schools, and the like are beneficial. However, it is only thorough reculturing that we begin to see dramatic progress in achieving the mission of schooling, which is ensuring that all students experience academic achievement at high levels.

School decisions should be centered on what we know is best for students, employing those methods that promote their physical, social, academic, and moral maturation (Sergiovanni, 1996). Reculturing is a way of thinking and acting. Simply stated, one of the most effective ways to improve teaching and learning is to first improve the campus culture. Research of higher achieving countries supports this view (Stigler and Hiebert, 2009).

ILs' experience and credentials are important; however, their commitment to collective instructional leadership, their professional beliefs about human capacity and effort-based learning are even more important to the academic success of students. The campus culture shapes these beliefs and effort-based methods. ILs learn to teach from their own school experiences and from observing colleagues; this is why changing ILs will not necessarily improve results in the classroom. ILs must strive to alter the culture in which effective teaching is learned and taught.

PERFORMANCE AT THE GROUP LEVEL

Three research studies underscore this point. David S. Wilson and William Swenson (2000) grew a fast growing plant in small flower pots. The soil in each pot was sterilized except for six grams of unsterilized soil that was injected into each pot. The unsterilized mixture was developed by mixing unsterilized soil with sterilized water in a kitchen blender and setting the dial on high. As mentioned, the researchers inserted six grams of the unsterilized mixture into each sterilized pot of soil. At this point, because of the inserted mixture, each flower pot contained many millions of microbes. Thus, the variation among posts was insignificant.

Wilson and Swenson grew all plants under the same controlled conditions. At maturity, they divided the pots with the largest plants from the pots with the smallest ones. Instead of selecting the plants themselves to grow the next generation of plants, they extracted soil separately from pots of the largest and smallest plants to make future mixtures of soil rich microbes for the next group of controlled plant seeds. They were selecting at the whole microbial ecosystem level—teams, rather than at the level of individual plants. Remember this distinction. We will return to it later.

In other words we could say they focused on performance at the group level instead at the individual level. In effect, each pot developed its own complex biological system. The difference among systems was manifested by plant growth. So by selecting the soil from beneath the largest and smallest plant pots over many generations, they demonstrated that selecting at the microbial ecosystem level (the group level), plants became large or small. In essence, these researchers were able to separate effective teams of microbes from less effective teams of microbes.

A similar study was conducted by William Muir (2010), a professor at Purdue University. Muir's research involved the production of eggs. Hens raised to produce eggs for market are generally housed in cages, eight to ten in a cage. This is standard practice in the poultry industry. Muir wanted to identify a method that significantly increased egg production.

He began by employing two different methods of selecting hens to produce eggs. For the first method, he selected hens based upon their individual productivity. For the second method, he selected hens based upon their productivity as a group. That is, in the first method, he selected individual hens that produced the most eggs and put them in the same cages. And for the second method, he selected the most productive cages of hens—some produced many eggs and some produced very few eggs.

Using these two methods, hens were bred for six generations. The total number of eggs were calculated for both groups of cages—super chickens and super groups. It might appear at first glance that the first method would be more productive. After all, the most productive chickens were grouped in the same cages—the best of the best. So why not directly select the best individual chickens and house them together to increase egg production? Why select at the group level when some chickens are super and others are mediocre? Muir's findings answer these questions. The former method caused egg production to drastically decrease while the latter method significantly increased egg production 160 percent. What happened?

The former method produced mean and selfish chickens. They made egg production a zero-sum game. In other words, these super chickens possessed alpha personalities; they had to succeed even at the expense of the other cage inhabitants. Muir had literally produced psychopaths who pecked and murdered to establish dominance. In some of these cages, Muir discovered only a few chickens left standing. Conversely, the second group socialized more effectively thereby functioning more as one unit rather than individual units.

What is the point? While it is problematic to generalize from these studies to education, I do think, however, there is a lesson to underscore for educators—culture matters. The outcome of these two studies highlights that effective teamwork, on any level, is essential for maximum organizational success. These experiments also raise important questions about what counts as an individual trait.

For example, egg productivity seems like an individual trait because you can count the eggs produced by individual hens. However, upon closer examination the experiment reveals that egg productivity is in fact a highly social trait that depends upon the composition of one's group, not just the individual's characteristics. This example has profound consequences for how we think about human traits that seem individual but in fact are highly social.

Take for instance a third study lead by the U.S. Department of Education's Institute of Education Sciences (IES). It contracted with Mathematica Policy Research to examine the effectiveness of an intervention that was designed to recruit high performing ILs on high performing campuses to transfer to low performing schools. These accomplished or super educators were offered a stipend of $20,000 over a two year period to transfer to a low performing campus. At the same time, high performing ILs already teaching on low performing campuses were offered a stipend of $10,000 to remain at their current location.

The initiative was launched in 2009. It is known as the Talent Transfer Initiative (TTI). According to the study, multiple states have attempted programs similar to TTI. While the results of the study were mixed, the researchers reported that overall (combining elementary and middle school scores) "The combined benchmark-team impacts were not statistically significant." The initiative was not broadly successful.

This is why we, in education, are not "Waiting for Superman" or for Wonder Woman. We are waiting for effective teams. These teams embrace the notion of collective instructional leadership. For these types of teams to flourish we must transform the campus culture—reculturing.

Every classroom deserves and requires high quality instruction; but we cannot examine just individual traits when planning intervention strategies. We must consider group norms and how to shape them, yet hyperbolic comments such as "fire all of them" and "close the school" continue to make headlines. Are these methods practical approaches for reform? To date, school reform on steroids has not worked.

To illustrate, in 2008 a large 9–12 high school was rated "low achieving" by state officials in Texas. District policymakers approved a recommendation to close the school—remove all educators and students. Students were transferred to nearby campuses. That community was in shock. The school was reopened the following year with a new staff and ninth grade students only. Each year thereafter another grade level was added until it became a four-year high school again. Currently, that same school is considered "low achieving" again. This ill-conceived practice has been applied in many districts across the country. And it should be replaced with a research-based approach that is more practical and effective—reculturing.

The kind of reculturing needed in today's schools is to build a collaborative winning attitude within the school that embraces the importance of effort and perseverance. The process never ends (Fullan, 2001). Reculturing requires that people both individually and collectively move from something that is familiar and significant to something unfamiliar and potentially more significant (Sergiovanni, 2000).

Some of the goals of reculturing include: encouraging the use of active listening skills; promoting a safe and orderly organizational environment; creating an atmosphere of trust; acknowledging the importance of counselors, the school nurse, the student intervention team, and parents; making students feel connected to the school; developing a team concept; and establishing a vision for the school. These are just some of the ingredients of a culture that will lead to success. Reculturing is a natural progression that leads to successfully restructuring the organization of schools.

EMPLOYING ACTIVE LISTENING SKILLS

The Pyramid Approach is grounded in the firm belief that successful instructional leaders understand and embrace the importance of acquiring and maintaining effective active listening skills. Active listening is listening with your senses, particularly with your ears and eyes. Many times a person's emotions will reveal more than his words disclose. The goal of active listening is to resist a rush to judgment while acquiring as much credible information as possible. The worst position an instructional leader can be in is not knowing that he does not know. If one listens objectively without immediately drawing conclusions, he is more likely to acquire a new insight (Sample, 2002).

In this regard, Steven Sample recommends, "Artful listening is important for maintaining the contrarian leader's intellectual independence. It enables him to see things through the eyes of his followers while at the same time seeing things from his own unique perspective—a process which I like to call 'seeing double'" (p. 22).

We spend 80 percent of our waking hours communicating; 45 percent of that time is devoted to listening (DuBrin, 1984). Research studies indicate that we remember from one-fourth to one-half of the information we receive; hence, ILs should recognize that improving listening skills takes practice. A commitment to this kind of professional practice will yield extraordinary dividends. Below is an active listening model that works well for me. Pay close attention to step five. Most of us, at the very least, would just like to be heard.

Active Listening Process

Listen with your eyes and ears.

- Pay attention to what is stated verbally and physically. Many times body language reveals as much as conversations.

Listen with your body.

- Present a positive listening posture. Establish positive eye contact. Nod your head to indicate, I hear you and I understand.

Listen to understand.

- Make sure you accurately understand the information you receive. Periodically ask, "Did I hear you say . . . ?" "When you say . . . what do you mean?"

Listen without judgment.

- Consider the speaker's point of view. Minimize interruptions. Do not plan your next comment while listening.

Listen for a solution.

- If you have a solution, offer it at this time. If you don't, ask, "What would you like me to do?" At this point, think win-win. There might be a compromise solution. Two other critical points should be remembered. At times, the best solution is to decide not to decide. If time will allow, defer your decision. Finally, it has been my experience that many people feel better just because they were allowed to express their thoughts. Sometimes having an opportunity to be heard is as important as the solution.

SAFE AND ORDERLY ORGANIZATIONAL ENVIRONMENT

Research has made it clear that in the absence of a safe and orderly classroom environment, true learning cannot occur. National polls continually reflect that discipline is one of the main concerns of classroom ILs. The first and most important responsibility of instructional leaders is to plan for and prevent distractions so that a safe, caring, and trusting team culture flourishes.

Feeling safe is paramount if an appropriate teaching and learning environment is to exist. I am referring to both physical and emotional safety. For example, aggressive students bullying other students must be stopped. This includes students with a high status, such as cheerleaders, athletes, or any other group of students if they engage in activities that adversely affect the campus climate. The most common types of bullying are verbal, social isolation, intimidation, and cyber bullying.

In 2005–2006, 86 percent of public schools reported that at least one crime or theft occurred on their campus; 8 percent of students in grades 9–12 reported being threatened or injured with a weapon in the previous twelve months; and 25 percent reported that drugs were offered to them on school property. Twenty-eight percent of students ages twelve to eighteen reported they were bullied within the previous six months (National Center for Education Statistics). In 2013, the NCES reported after nearly two decades of steady decline, the total nonfatal victimization rate at schools increased from thirty-five to forty-nine victimizations per one thousand students for ages twelve to eighteen years old between 2010 and 2011. The victimization rate away from school increased from twenty-seven to thirty-eight victimizations per one thousand students over the same period.

Given these data as a backdrop for schooling, it should be noted that the appearance of the physical grounds and building play an important role in establishing perceptions and behaviors of students and staff. Gladwell, in *The Tipping Point*, labels this phenomenon the "power of context."

A cracked window, unkempt grounds or cafeteria, and unattractive classrooms or offices may appear to be minor issues but can push a situation past a tipping point to an adverse teaching and learning environment. Physical appearance matters greatly. Because of aging buildings and depleting resources, some large districts and campuses are confronted with real challenges in this regard.

Fully understanding and embracing the power of context, instructional leaders should regularly interface with the maintenance department, campus custodial staff, parents and community stakeholders to ensure that the appearance of the entire campus is a shining beacon in the community. This kind of campus ownership is everyone's responsibility.

The tipping point is the instance of critical mass, the threshold, the boiling point (Gladwell, 2002). The central point is that little things can make a significant impact. On any given campus, 80 percent of the disciplinary referrals may be written by 20 percent of classroom instructional leaders; 20 percent of students may be responsible for 80 percent of campus infractions, or 80 percent of parent complaints may be filed by 20 percent of parents. This is what economists refer to as the 80/20 principle.

With regard to safety, parents will forgive instructional leaders for many shortcomings, but failing to ensure the safety of students and staff is not one of them. Hence, instructional leaders and other appropriate personnel should plan accordingly. Follow these guidelines:

- Anticipate and develop plans to prevent possible interruptions or distractions to quality schooling.
- Minimize crowded areas.
- Minimize recidivism by seeking to identify and redress the root causes of potential threats to the learning environment.
- Establish campus routines that are effectively communicated and enforced.
- Encourage broad input and support for school and classroom rules.
- Accept responsibility for the campus environment beyond your classroom boundaries.
- Become an effective campus IL by being a walking and looking leader.
- Develop a culture of civility and politeness by modeling appropriate actions.
- Encourage all students to become connected with the campus; for example, by joining clubs and organizations.
- Develop and communicate consequences for violations of rules.

SIGNIFICANCE AND ELEMENTS OF A CARING CULTURE

We cannot mobilize staff or students without first establishing trust, which we will discuss later. Care, however, precedes trust. Think about it; the people we know who care the most about us are the same people we trust the most. "The motive that inspires the greatest trust is genuine caring" (Covey, 2008, p. 78). Before I develop the need to care for others in schools, I should caution ILs to care for themselves first. We can only care for others to the extent we are functioning on all cylinders. In short, the nature of caring can be exhausting. ILs will do well to sleep, eat, play, and socialize well. They should pay attention to their own personal wellness. The point is that one must take care of himself before he can adequately meet the needs of others.

Once this is accomplished, ILs can promote a caring environment by manifesting care through their own behavior. For example, when we ask, "How are you doing?" Do we wait for and listen to the answer? How many times do we ask this question in a cursory manner never waiting for nor hearing the response? Every time we act in this manner, we communicate the very opposite of our intentions. Building a caring environment, or its opposite, is largely within our control. We can transmit positive feelings and emotions to others just by what we say and do. We should remember that our interactions with a few impact the feelings of many others.

For example, when we witness someone cringe from accidentally stomping his toe we also cringe as we vicariously feel his pain. When others smile at us, we smile back even if it is barely noticeable. Again, the point is that small things matter. Hence, "Never believe that a few caring people can't change the world. For, indeed, that's all who ever have," says Margaret Mead.

Instructional leaders have the power to infect the entire school with their own positive, winning attitude. It has to start somewhere and with someone. Those who possess this ability to transmit their feelings to others are referred to as "senders" (Gladwell, 2002). No group of students, or staff, for that matter, relishes being in an uncaring environment. Nor do we produce at our full capacity in such an environment. Teaching cannot just be a profession; it must become a mission filled with a caring, passionate determination to make a difference in the lives of students. Effective instruction cannot exist in the absence of caring educators. Therefore, we must transform schools into safe, caring communities. This is critical for helping students become good learners and good people (Kohn, 1998, p. 78).

"People do not care how much you know until they know how much you care," declares John Maxwell. His comment is particularly true of students' regard for instructional leaders. On its website, the Centers for Disease Control and Prevention (CDC) highlights this point: "The belief by students that adults and peers in the school care about their learning—as well as about them as individuals—is an important protective factor."

Abraham Maslow developed a hierarchy of human needs. When relating these essential human needs to schooling, it is apparent how aptly they apply. When students are distracted, regardless of the reasons, proficiency suffers. The premise of Maslow's hierarchy is that physiological and safety needs must be met before higher-level needs such as belongingness, love, esteem, and self-actualization needs are likely to be realized. Given the many physiological, safety, and belonging concerns many students come to school with each day, caring ILs recognize these impediments to learning and plan accordingly.

The Pyramid Approach stresses that these issues are real and that ignoring them exacerbates the problems involved in fully educating students. For example, while pregnancies for teenage girls have decreased at record numbers, approximately 8 percent, still in 2012, the Center for Disease Control (CDC) reported that a total of 305,388 babies were born to teenage girls between ages fifteen and nineteen years old. In that same, year girls within this age group had a birth rate of 29.4 per one thousand. Black and Hispanic teen birth rates were more than two times higher than that of white students. Moreover, the U.S. teen pregnancy, birth, sexually transmitted disease (STD), and abortion rates are much higher than those of other western industrialized nations.

Teens from socioeconomically disadvantaged homes, of all ethnicities, had the highest birth rates. And teens from minority homes comprise almost 60 percent of all teen births. The CDC stresses that childbearing at such an early age adversely affects the academic performance in school for the mother and later for her children (Center for Disease and Control, 2014; Singh, 2000).

The international organization Health Behavior in School-aged Children (HBSC 1998) has conducted a comparative study of teen behaviors among twenty-nine countries since 1985–1986. Since then, more countries have participated. The purpose of this study is to better understand the health characteristics of adolescents. The United States began participating in these studies in 1989. The study focuses on eleven-, thirteen-, and fifteen-year-olds. The United States is among the countries ranked near the bottom, whose students believe they play an insignificant role in establishing school rules.

The U.S. Department of Health and Human Services, Administration for Children and Families, Children's Bureau, indicated there were 4.5 million reports of suspected child abuse in 2002. Classroom ILs reported 16 percent of these cases. No demographic is immune from this abuse.

By 2013, the National Child Abuse Statistics revealed that children are suffering from a hidden epidemic of child abuse and neglect. Every year more than 3 million reports of child abuse are made in the United States involving more than 6 million children (a report can include multiple children). The United States has one of the worst records among industrialized nations—losing on average between four and seven children every day to child abuse and neglect. The vast majority of child abuse cases are classified as neglect followed by physical and sexual abuse.

In 2013, the National School Lunch Program provided low-cost or free lunches for more than 30.5 million children. In 1998, it also began providing snacks to afterschool educational and enrichment programs. Notwithstanding, caring ILs should ensure students' essential requirements are addressed once they arrive on campus.

In 2014, news outlets reported allegations of some students being publicly shamed because their parents had unpaid meal accounts. Some reports suggested parents just forgot to send payment with their child. And in one highly publicized incident, school officials were accused of allowing children to go through the lunch line, select their food, and then after exiting, the food was thrown in the trash. A few of the states, where similar incidents have been reported, received national attention also.

There are no statistics on matters like this. However, this issue is widespread enough to have attracted the attention of the U.S. Department of Agriculture. It is currently reexamining its procedures and guidelines regarding school meals (Bald, 2014). In the meantime, having children go hungry or sending them home with embarrassing reminder notes attached to their clothes seems unacceptable in a caring campus culture.

Eating lunch should be routine, given some of the more perplexing challenges some students experience. The National Center for Statistics and Analysis, for example, reported that after accidents, homicides and suicide were the second and third leading causes of fifteen-to-nineteen-year-old mortality. These daunting statistics amount to a plea for collaborative teams of ILs, counselors, nurses, psychologists, parents, and stakeholders to work in concert across the nation to bring to bear all available resources to ensure the social and academic success of students.

PERCEPTIONS ABOUT POVERTY AND LEARNING

Further, according to the National Center for Children in Poverty, the possible deleterious effects poverty has on quality learning should not be dismissed. For example, in 2010, there were 72 million children younger than eighteen years of age; 22 percent lived in poverty. In 2013, the percentage of impoverished children remained unchanged. Some of these children move from community to community while others have parents who themselves are not high school graduates.

In 2012, the federal poverty level (FPL) was $23,050 for a family of four. Notwithstanding 22 percent of America's students live below this level, another 22 percent are considered near poor and an estimated one million children are homeless. Near poor means living just above the official poverty level. All states have economically disadvantaged students in approximately equal proportions even though the south has slightly more. In addition, students of all ethnic backgrounds are living in poverty.

While there is no relationship between poverty and ability there is clear evidence that poverty can be a risk factor for learning (Ravitch, 2013). For instance, Education Week Research Center (2014) reported between 2003 and 2013, the combined poverty achievement gap for fourth and eighth grade math on the National Assessment of Educational Progress widened in thirty-three states. And of the remaining states, not one narrowed the poverty achievement gap by more than 5 percentage points.

Further, Betty Hart and Todd Risley (2004) demonstrated in their research that by age three or four there is a 30 million word gap between students living in high-poverty families compared to those students living in high-income families. The former group hears fewer words, and as a result develops smaller vocabularies. They hear a ratio of two encouragements to every discouragement. Conversely, children from high-income families hear a ratio of six encouragements to one discouragement.

In addition, Bjorn Carey (2013), a Stanford researcher discovered that this "achievement gap" in language processing skills can begin as early as eighteen months for children living in low-income, less-educated families. In essence, ILs are playing catchup with many of these students by the time they enter school. This is why quality prekindergarten and kindergarten programs are essential for children coming from many low-income families. Generally, students who participate in prekindergarten perform at least one grade level above students who have not had a similar experience.

So, other than excellent early childhood programs, what can caring ILs do in regard to learning gaps that many disadvantaged students arrive with by the time they enter kindergarten? There is a hint in the following picture. Do you see two different animals within the same image? Can you train your mind to see either by choice? I recommend all educators do the same when developing perceptions about disadvantaged students—change their perceptions.

Figure 1.2.

These disadvantaged students can be found in the vast majority of schools in American and in most classrooms. Some are experiencing tremendous success and others are not. The obvious question is why? What makes the difference for these students? For starters, consider Robert Bjork's (2013) research at the University of California, Los Angeles. He is a cognitive psychologist who has labeled the results of his work "desirable difficulties."

He makes a distinction between learning and performance. Performance is the ability to retrieve or use information at an efficient level immediately after its introduction or practice. As time passes, in the absence of follow-up, this same level of competency dwindles. Whereas learning is the capacity to effectively utilize knowledge at a point in the future. Bjork espouses that by having a shorter introduction time for content to be learned, followed by periodically revisiting the same information over time, appears to be more difficult. Yet this difficult approach was more effective than the less difficult method of devoting an extended time period for study without follow-up sessions.

Specifically, he believes that the right type of difficulty enhances long term learning. For instance, introducing variation into the learning of a new task improves mastery. It forces the learner to engage in higher-order thinking. Discovering similarities and differences among a particular task to be learned is an example. Note that his findings are counterintuitive. That is, as difficulty increases, to a point, so does comprehension and competency. He demonstrated that difficulties can have a redeeming effect.

Similarly, Gladwell too (2013) offers a different perspective on this notion about difficulties and who should be considered disadvantaged. To illustrate his point, he discusses a research study conducted by J.T. MacCurdy, a psychiatrist. MacCurdy studied the emotions and behavior of Londoners during the horrendous bombing of Britain during World War II.

Beginning in September of 1940, Germany bombed the city of London for approximately eight months. At one point, they were bombed fifty-seven consecutive nights. Parts of the city were pulverized. MacCurdy's study revealed that the survivors of these very difficult times were divided into two distinct groups: near misses and remote misses.

Near misses were people who saw the deaths close up. Perhaps they even felt the shock of the many blasts or were even wounded. They were horrified, shocked at what they had witnessed. These experiences left them emotionally scared. On the other hand, remote misses were people who heard the bombs but they were at a distance. The bombs fell in their neighborhood but not next door or across the street from them. As a result the remote misses develop a different perspective of the bombings. The bombs had an unintended effect. They produced people who were more resilient.

Both groups were living in the same city, in many instances the same neighborhood and all were living in very difficult times. Yet the near misses were left scared while the remote misses were left more determined, committed, and energized.

What lessons can caring ILs draw from MacCurdy's and Bjork's findings? Not all difficulties are equal. Not all disadvantaged people feel the full weight of their circumstances. Some become stronger and resolute to prevail: They are remote misses.

While no reasonable person would wish that challenging life experiences and hard times befall anyone; it is a fact, however, that these types of experiences are inescapable. Take Steve Jobs for example, the cofounder of Apple Inc., one of his closest friends explained: "Steve always had a kind of chip on his shoulder. At some deep level, there was an insecurity that Steve had to go out and prove himself. I think being an orphan drove Steve in ways that most of us can never understand" (Chua and Rubenfeld, 2014, p. 27). Steve obviously was a remote miss.

In short, Bjork's and MacCurdy's findings confirm what many have experienced personally—tough times can produce tough and determined personalities. Yet, within the culture of education, too often this fact is not fully appreciated.

So given that students from disadvantaged backgrounds are in our schools and classrooms, what options are available to caring ILs? Educators are left with essentially two choices. Choices similar to the couple caught in the middle of the street when the traffic light changed unexpectedly. They could stand still, lament their circumstance or they could take control of their situation and act constructively.

I encourage ILs to act: first by thinking differently about children living in disadvantaged communities. Second, help students experiencing difficulties, to understand that, in one sense, challenges are "desirable difficulties." And third, guide their thinking so that they will understand "desirable difficulties" can be transformed into opportunities. That is what remote misses do.

One cautionary note, I am not recommending the use of these terms, near and remote misses when identifying particular children. I am, however, suggesting that educators embrace the concepts advanced in these research studies.

Further, Poplin and colleagues (2011) studied the traits of highly effective classroom ILs working in high poverty schools. These ILs had the highest percentage of students moving up a level on the reading and math state standardized assessment. Clearly, they were doing something differently from the other faculty members on campus.

The researchers observed methods utilized by these high performing educators for three or four years and cataloged what made them so successful. They were strict, focused on high academic achievement, moved around the room offering feedback, and they didn't use students' backgrounds as a reason for not learning. Below are other recommendations for ILs when working with disadvantaged students experiencing difficulties. Students will benefit from:

- Quality early childhood education
- Access to social services

- Applying consistent guidelines
- Exposure to advance placement curriculum
- Teaching phonemic awareness, vocabulary, grammar
- Providing a positive vision of students' self-image
- Participating in high-quality summer learning programs
- ILs examining the school culture and their own attitudes and beliefs
- Understanding that not all difficulties produce negative outcomes
- Knowing that educators care

Appropriate resources and effective policies are essential; however, the perceptions students form about their daily lives are equally important. Some children explain previous challenges as their predominant reasons for failure while others use these same experiences as reasons to persevere and succeed. Encourage students to reject the former and embrace the latter mindset regarding difficult and challenging experiences. Caring ILs should teach their students how to prevail—remote misses and "desirable difficulties." Remind them of the child who found a cocoon for a butterfly. Out of curiosity, he kept the cocoon. After several days, he noticed a small opening in it. The child sat and watched the butterfly for a couple of hours as it struggled to wiggle and squirm its body through the little hole in the cocoon. Then it seemed to stop making any progress. It appeared stuck.

The child felt sorry for the helpless butterfly so he decided to help it. He ran in his house, got a pair of scissors and cut open the cocoon. The butterfly then emerged easily; but something was strange. The butterfly had a swollen body and shrunken wings. The boy watched the butterfly hoping it would fully develop and fly but nothing changed.

The butterfly stayed the same. It was never able to fly. By not understanding the benefits of overcoming difficulties the child did not realize that the butterfly's struggle to get through the small opening of the cocoon is nature's way of forcing fluid from the body of the butterfly into its wings so that it would be ready for flight.

Again, help students acquire a positive mindset about challenges in their own daily lives. Just like the butterfly they too can turn life's struggles into remote misses and "desirable difficulties." This type of thinking will be developed further in subsequent chapters. For now, the bottom line is, all children need a caring environment in which to study and learn rigorous curriculum.

The Role of Counselors in a Caring School Community

School counselors play a significant role in fostering a caring school community. Lindwall and Coleman (2008) highlight the attributes of these caring school community (CSC) counselors: CSC counseling is founded on a core set of components. These components build upon counselors' campus experiences to make decisions about how to implement CSC efforts and strategies.

They also share philosophy that guides their CSC practice. Moreover, a caring school community promotes a sense of belonging in students. This connectedness that students feel in a caring environment cannot be overlooked or underestimated. It is the glue that keeps students in school and heightens their motivation. Maslow, Comer, Epstein, and others support the premise of CSC.

I am confident that when students perform at high levels, it is because of the contribution caring school communities play in their development. The more than 262,300 educational, vocational, and school counselors in the United States can contribute to that end (Bureau of Labor Statistics, 2011–2012). These counselors collaborate with parents, psychologists, ILs, school nurses, and others to provide services that address the needs of students.

One of the most effective tools counselors can offer distracted and underperforming students is hope, a belief that there is better day ahead. In addition, the counselors can help the students develop willpower and pathways to achieve the goals they set once they have hope. The belief and the reality when it is done right, is that because of these interventions, students will be better prepared to devote their full concentration on becoming more successful.

ILs should appreciate and utilize the complete array of skills and talents counselors bring to campuses. As of yet, not all do. Principals' perceptions may not always be congruent with the American School Counselor Association (ASCA) role standards. Research on the extent to which principals endorse these counselor role standards has produced somewhat inconsistent results (Kirchner and Setchfield, 2005).

In defense of campus ILs, the standardized assessment era has exerted pressures that too often cause campus ILs to make decisions that are not in accord with research-based practices. For instance, it is not uncommon for counselors to lead and supervise campus standardized testing programs. Many times this is done in lieu of focusing on student support programs. Given these types of complex tradeoffs, the campus IL should consistently explore creative ways to address the very real social issues that permeate the lives of students. She realizes that because some of these physical, social, and psychological needs of students are under met, they are very likely to manifest themselves as poor academic performance.

The Pyramid Approach asks this question: Have these types of core students' needs been addressed? If not, focusing primarily on collecting standardized assessment data without first doing so is analogous to looking for a paperclip in one's tool kit. We will never find the solutions we are seeking as long as we continue our search in the wrong place.

Nurses Have a Role

In 1902, school nursing began to reduce the absenteeism rate of students by interviewing students and their parents regarding health issues. The responsibilities of the school nurse have expanded over the years but the central focus has remained unchanged, to promote appropriate health and safety behaviors that facilitate effective student learning (National Association of School Nurses, 2009).

The nurse attempts to connect the efforts of family, health care providers, and ILs. Many nurses are able to tap into a wealth of health services provided by state and federal agencies as well as nonprofit organizations. For example, eye, dental care, and general wellness services are routinely provided to students. Obviously, these types of campus services support students' learning.

Student Intervention Team

ILs would do well to seek models that attempt to concentrate the collective efforts of vital individuals (parents, counselors, nurses, and social workers) to support their student needs. James Comer, a professor at Yale, developed such a child-centered model in 1968. The Comer model focused on the collaboration among parents, school personnel, and students.

The goal of this model is to develop a comprehensive school plan that addresses many of the same basic human needs Maslow identified, so that students are more able to achieve their maximum potential. There are three teams: parents (involved at every level of school activity), school planning and management (plans school activities), and students' staff support (address school-wide prevention issues). Assessment and staff development are used to support the school plan. Finally, the Comer model is grounded in three guiding principles: consensus, collaboration, and no-fault (Barbour, Barbour, and Scully, 2005). By contrast, ineffective ILs seek out a fall guy. Obviously, this type of leadership stifles collaboration and appropriate action.

Parents Collaborating with Schools

Joyce Epstein at Johns Hopkins University, has worked more than twenty years to demonstrate the benefits of parents and schools working together to improve the learning experience for students. To this end, her model for parent-school-community partnerships embraces the notion that "family-like" schools and "school-like" families promote student learning (Barbour, Barbour, and Scully, 2005). Other community organizations would do well to strive to attain family-like structures as well.

Some ILs use the term family when discussing their campuses. For example, "the Magnificent Middle School family ensures all students experience success." As with Comer, Epstein (2002) identifies key members from school, home, and the community to collaborate in making decisions and implementing programs for student academic improvement. Epstein also lists six types of involvement:

1. Parenting: Help parents improve parenting skills.
2. Communicating: Ensure that effective school and home communication exists.
3. Volunteering: Encourage and support parent volunteering.
4. Learning at Home: Assist parents with supporting their children's learning at home.
5. Decision Making: Value parents' opinions when making school decisions.
6. Collaborating with the Community: Interface community resources in the schooling process. When analyzing student data, it should not just be assessment data that is studied. Data concerning the following important areas should be considered as well:

- Students with attendance issues
- Students with excessive discipline referrals
- Students who do not feel connected to campus

ILs should not underestimate the importance of students' connectedness. Students' behavior improves when they feel connected to the campus. For instance, when students report they "like school"; they are more likely to resist engaging in bullying, sexual risk taking, and experimenting with alcohol, tobacco, and drugs (Health Behavior in School-aged Children, 2010). Table 1.2 underscores the importance of students' feeling they have a place in their school.

	11-year-olds		13-year-olds		15-year-olds	
	Boys	Girls	Boys	Girls	Boys	Girls
Students are satisfied with their school when:						
They take part in setting rules at school	***	***	***	***	***	***
They get support from teachers when needed	***	***	***	***	***	***
They feel supported by other students	***	***	**	***	***	***
Expectations by teachers and parents are high	*	*	**	**	**	**

Table 1.2. Factors Associated with Student's Perception of School. Strength of association (Pearson Correlation): None (below 0.15) = *; Medium (0.15-0.25) = **; Strong (above 0.25) = *. *Source*: The International Health Behavior in School-aged Children (HBSC) U.S. Department of Health and Human Services.**

It is well documented that students and schools need the support of parents. A modification of an African proverb illustrates this view: "It takes an extended family to fully educate all students." However, do ILs really want parents more involved in the participation of daily schooling activities? This question should be asked and explored on every campus, particularly campuses that have significant student populations that are not performing well.

There is evidence that too often ILs publicly state their desire to significantly increase parent involvement while privately lamenting that some parents seem to get in the way and that some seem more interested in documenting rather than supporting the school. This happens in many instances because parents and ILs do not receive appropriate training to support such initiatives. If family engagement is needed for student success, then ILs need to be prepared to do it well. To some extent, this has been a challenge because of resistance in attitudes of various ILs and a lack of external pressure, funding, or other support (McDermott, 2008).

Notice a distinction between involvement and engagement can be made. This distinction is supported by current research that suggests schools would benefit from focusing on parent engagement. That is, when parents are unable, for whatever reason, to become fully involved with schools, there is another avenue in which they can assist their child's educational development: school engagement. Parental engagement focuses not just on what parents do but who they are and the quality relationships they form within schools and communities (McDermott, 2008).

Therefore, it seems ILs and parents would benefit from appropriate training that helps clarify how both groups share mutual goals and can collaborate to enhance the learning experience for all students. A resource that might assist in this regard is the Family Involvement Network of Educators. This network is led by Harvard Graduate School of Education and can be accessed online.

TRUSTING TEAM CULTURE

These three words, trusting team culture, pull at the core of who we really are as human beings. Along with a safe and caring environment, they provide the foundation for the Pyramid Approach. While we should think of these terms collectively and how they will advance the instructional mission of the campus, for the purposes of this book we will discuss them individually.

What Does Trust Mean?

Trust means confidence. "Fish discover water last." This French proverb explains that fish enjoy the benefits of water without fully appreciating its essential qualities until it is tainted with pollutants. Similarly, humans behave in essentially the same way with regard to trust. Many take it for granted until it is breached (Covey, 2008). Instructional leaders who board the bus to begin their journey toward achieving academic excellence for all without first inviting trust aboard will travel on a path heading for tragedy. For too often, classroom and campus instructional leaders have lamented the following:

- I cannot follow his leadership.
- I cannot depend on them.
- He says one thing and does another.
- She has cliques on this campus.
- I will not be the fall guy.
- They just take credit for my work.
- In team meetings, they say one thing. In the parking lot, they say another.
- If she criticizes you to me, she will criticize me to you.

Campuses experiencing these kinds of distrust and lack of confidence by personnel in each other are at best just pretending to share a common organizational vision; at worst they are crippling the future of their students. Everything they attempt will be undermined by the absence of genuine trust. Genuine trust does not mean blind trust; it is what Covey (2008) calls "smart trust." "Smart trust" means one analyzes the situation and uses judgment before extending trust.

Well-thought-out strategies and plans within an organization are unlikely to bring much success without the trust of its members. On the other hand, if the organization has effective strategies and execution and a high level of trust among its members, the net result will be greater than the sum of its parts. Trust will not resolve poor strategies, but distrust will surely implode even good ones (Covey, 2008).

One of the best ways to improve trust within any organization is to understand that trust is reciprocal. The more you give, the more you receive. For example, when a receiver drops the ball in a professional football game, coaches and quarterbacks who understand the powerful impact trust plays in the success of their collective mission will immediately throw the ball to that same receiver again. What's the message? We trust you. Just imagine how hard that receiver will play after that type of experience. What will he think about their giving him another opportunity to demonstrate his ability?

Instructional leaders know the value of applying this same principle on campuses. If someone drops the ball at school, she is not singled out as the fall guy. She is immediately given the proper support and given another opportunity to succeed. Michael Irvin, in his 2007 Hall of Fame enshrinement speech, mentioned the three Super Bowl rings he and Troy Aikman won while playing professional sports, but he particularly noted the 1994 NFC Championship game that they lost.

He briefly discussed some of the challenges in the game. "That game is one of my most memorable games for all those reasons, but it had a little something extra for me. We were down 21. Troy came to that huddle with those big blue eyes and he looked up and he said, 'Hey, I'm coming to you no matter what.' Whew, let me tell you. As a wide receiver, that's all I ever wanted to hear. Just come to me no matter what. And he did, he did. He came to me no matter what." That is the kind of reciprocal trust instructional leaders should seek to cultivate with each other.

What Holds the Team Together

A team is a group linked in a common purpose. It is this common purpose that energizes its members. Without a common goal, mission, or vision, the team ceases to exist; at this point, its members are merely a social group. Vision creation is so important that if it misses the mark, everything else becomes a perfunctory exercise. This is true in all walks of life. How many times have we observed athletes who revered their coaches and teammates, yet after winning the championship say, "I just wanted to win the Super Bowl! I wanted to win the World Series! I wanted to win a gold medal!"

Maybe at this point, the coach or leader is not even mentioned. At this serial moment, these extraordinary performers reveal, unknowingly perhaps, the real leader, the real driving force behind their success, their vision. This collective vision that was hatched many months or even years ago was finally achieved. Sergiovanni labels this kind of leadership, "idea-based leadership" (1996). In other words, members of a group are not following an individual but a noble, worthy, and achievable vision. As indicated, this collective vision cannot just be any vision. It has to be a vision that galvanizes its members. George Bernard Shaw in *Back to Methuselah* wrote, "You see things; and you say 'Why?' But I dream things that never were; and I say 'Why not?'" (1921) This is the kind of vision instructional leaders must create and follow.

This quote hangs in my office to remind everyone who enters that we are here to make a difference, not maintain the status quo. I recall a superintendent who once commented, "Good followers make good leaders." Over the years, I have found this to be true. We all need to, and can, improve our "followership" skills. Again, this idea-based ability to follow is about following the organizational vision, not an individual. There are approximately two hundred countries that participated in the Olympics. All of the athletes from each country compete with the vision of winning a gold medal. Likewise, effective instructional leaders help to create visions that seek to earn the "gold medal" of teaching—students that learn and achieve at high levels.

There is a specific process for vision creation and implementation that I have observed to be effective. A great deal of research supports this process. The majority of research studies indicate that it takes approximately five years to fully implement change initiatives (Kotter, 1996; Fullan, 2001).

While five years is a reasonable timeframe to solidify deep and systemic professional instructional practice that leads to all students achieving at high levels, many campus instructional leaders do not even complete five consecutive years at one school. Based on a 2008 study conducted by the University Council for Educational Administration (UCEA) entitled "The Revolving Door of the Principalship," the following was reported:

- More than 50 percent turnover of principals occurred in Texas within a three-year period (2004–2007).
- More than 70 percent turnover of principals occurred in Texas within a five-year period (2001–2006).
- Likewise, the American Association of School Administrators reported the mean tenure for superintendents is five and a half years and median tenure is near six years. This finding is significant be-

cause superintendents' tenure is positively correlated with student achievement. Since these figures represent averages, many superintendents' mobility rates reflect two or three years in the same district.

This trend of high mobility for principals, especially in secondary schools, holds true nationally as well. The RAND Corporation found similar results in a two year study (2007–2009) of urban campus ILs mobility rate. According to the study approximately 20 percent of ILs leave their campus within two years.

In light of instability for campus and district instructional leaders, we should plan accordingly. Since the clock is ticking, we can and must implement the campus instructional vision more expeditiously. In fact, the high rate of turnover among campus instructional leaders is not always because of their lack of success; it often is, indeed, because of it. Often they are promoted to other campuses.

Extraordinary or stagnated student academic success leads to the same result for many instructional leaders—a change of address within five years. Given these facts, how should prudent campus instructional leaders proceed? As previously indicated, time is a factor and should be factored in during planning for and implementing team vision creation. I recommend the following process for implementing an effective team vision. It includes the following six steps.

Vision Creation Process

Step One: Who are the connectors, the natural captains?

Most sports teams have captains. Usually in corporate America, and in education, these people are formally selected, not elected. In corporate America, these people probably are division directors and supervisors. In education, they might be assistant principals or chairpersons. These persons have position, power, and authority because management assigned it to them. Conversely, in sports, the coach often has the members of the team elect their captains. Later, she may appoint subsequent captains, but why doesn't she appoint all of the captains? Coaches understand captains already exist on every team, even if they are not formally appointed by the coach.

In vision creation, instructional leaders will do well to remember this aspect of team dynamics. When selecting key members to participate in the creation of the organizational vision, there is nothing more important to consider. Gladwell refers to these persons as "connectors" (2002). Fullan labels them the "guiding coalition" (2009), and Collins simply identifies them as the "right people" (2001). In the vision creation and implementation process, they are indeed the right people. These captains also exist on every campus. The campus instructional leader's challenge is to identify them as soon as possible.

The mistake instructional leaders too often make is to assume position power and the power to innovate and persuade reside with the same individuals; many times, they do not. I have observed one of the best methods to identify the right people is to individually approach as many members on campus as possible and ask one question. For example, "We are forming a brainstorming team to discuss the status of our campus, who do you recommend might join us?" The names you hear most often are generally the "right people." Team members, at large, often want the "right people" on the inside so that they can seek their opinions.

Astute campus instructional leaders will compare the list of recommendations with what their feet and eyes have observed. By this, I mean effective campus ILs are rarely in their office. They constantly walk, looking to observe effective professional practices. Some ILs, wearing a pedometer, have reported they walk several miles a day.

The key point to remember in vision creation is "who" questions come before "what" questions (Collins, 2001). "Who" affects the quality of "what" and everything that follows. Now that we have identified captains, it is time to pull the cover back and analyze the status of the campus.

Step Two: Where are we? Or what are the "bare facts"?

It is impossible to discuss the status of any organization candidly without the presence of trust. In group settings, most people say what they think the leader wants to hear or what they think is politically correct. Remember, the foundation of the Pyramid is first to establish a safe, caring, and trusting team culture. In the absence of trust, team members will be apprehensive about speaking candidly.

As a result, fact-finding will be severely muted. We have already discussed how to establish team trust and how to sustain it. In addition to the trust factor, the structure of the fact-finding meetings is crucial. The campus instructional leader should communicate that there is no hierarchy in these meetings and that she will perform the role of facilitator. Recall, trust is nothing but confidence (Covey, 2008). The first time the instructional leader hears unfavorable comments is the time to build confidence by withholding judgment.

Subsequent meetings should reveal additional information regarding the state of the organization. I refer to this kind of information as the "bare facts." While collecting the bare facts, the campus instructional leader is asking questions and asking for clarification of comments discussed. Asking the "right questions" and employing quality listening skills are the focus of fact-finding.

For example, what is the source of the problem? What challenges will be involved in solving this problem? Are there other ways we can approach this issue? What has worked in the past? Ask someone to explain: What is the real problem? Clarify by asking: Did I understand you to say . . . ? The process essentially involves asking questions and listening. The bare facts should then be used to galvanize immediate action (Kotter, 1996).

Step Three: Where do we want to go, or what hill will we take?

Now that we have the bare facts, it is time to mobilize the team. In other words, what hill will we take? This is the type of question military leaders ask in combat. The IL utilizes the bare facts to create enthusiasm and a sense of urgency within the team (Senge, 1994; Kotter, 1996). This is also the time to establish that the team's vision is noble and worthy of pursuit. Personalizing the worthiness of the vision is essential. This can be done by sharing stories of students, ILs, or parents that include challenges that ultimately ended in success.

Too often in meetings, terms such as "those students" and "those parents" are used. These phrases tend to desensitize the speaker and listeners, thereby minimizing the mobilization efforts. Using real success stories that begin with very little hope and end with success appeal to the emotions of the members in the meeting (Patterson et al., 2008).

The theme of the stories should be: Now that we have the facts, are they acceptable to team members? If not, where do we go from here? Don't forget George Bernard Shaw: "You see things; and you say 'Why?' But I dream things that never were; and I say 'Why not?'" Robert Kennedy frequently paraphrased this theme. Here is another quote that resonates with groups who are pondering action: "If not us, who? If not now, when?"

ILs cannot fake their way through these meetings and processes. If they are not a believer in the team vision, the other ILs will immediately know it. These types of meetings are more meetings of hearts than they are meetings of minds. In other words, as Ron Edmonds might ask, if we already know more than we need to know, why haven't we implemented it? This is not a sympathy question, it is a moral question. There is no book that can assist ILs at this critical juncture. Either they can communicate and transmit to others the urgency of such a noble mission that will give children, our most precious resource, a step into a brighter future, or they can settle for the status quo. Why settle for bronze? Go for the gold!

Step Four: What is the best route, or how do we take that hill?

The quality of the team's plan to accomplish its vision will never exceed the quality of information acquired. Hence, the process of acquiring accurate information never ends. Team meetings become an integral part of the campus culture. Instructional leaders recognize the value of walking and observing.

High visibility of campus ILs may be frowned upon initially but over time it builds trust. Classroom ILs will come to understand that visits are designed to assist and support, not to play "I got you" games. This sincere professional growth approach to classroom visits eventually leads to classroom ILs embracing them. It should be noted these daily walks should be highly focused.

The campus IL is walking for two reasons: first, to observe a safe, caring, and trusting campus culture; and second, to observe high quality lessons that are rigorous and engaging, where students are exhibiting their maximum learning effort. Successful campuses have ILs and students who emphatically believe the mission of the campus is achievable. Effective effort will not exist without a sense of efficacy (Marzano, 2003).

No hill worth taking has ever been conquered without the willingness to apply sufficient individual and team effort. One of the best ways to increase effort is to develop challenging yet achievable benchmarks leading to the achievement of the organizational goal or vision, coupled with moments of recognition and celebration. These benchmarks cannot be perfunctory exercises; they must be aligned with the curriculum and results taken apart and analyzed. High quality results are dependent upon the quality of these data analyses.

Additionally, student feedback, reinforcement, and vocabulary development have been shown to significantly increase student academic achievement (Marzano, 2003). However, research confirms the things that most impact students' learning are the skills the classroom IL possesses and is able to demonstrate effectively (Wong and Wong, 2009). In short, the hill can be conquered with a sound and ambitious plan, based on the quality of acquired data, and the degree to which ILs truly believe the plan is achievable. The beliefs held by staff cast a very long shadow over school practices (Danielson, 2002).

Step Five: How do we communicate our vision, or how do we make it stick?

An old story about a faraway kingdom that was devastated by drought illustrates the significance of effectively communicating the organizational vision. In this kingdom, the crops were drying up and the hard ground was cracking. So the king rounded up his best digging crew and directed them to work hard digging for water. With their picks and shovels, they began digging. Six feet, eight feet, ten feet the workers kept digging. Finally, they stopped, put their picks and shovels down. They began to complain: "It is just too hot out here, nothing to drink and we will never find water. No one else has found any! We are not miracle workers."

When their behavior was reported to the king, he threw all of them in prison. Realizing this was not a feasible solution, the king's wisest advisor asked if he could speak to the men. The king granted his wish. The advisor got the men out of jail and put them in a wagon. He then took them on a tour of the kingdom. They saw the dried up fields, dying cattle, children with dust in the mouths and mothers with a stare of hopelessness in their eyes.

After the completed tour, the wise advisor took the men back to the digging site. He explained, "You are not just digging for water, you are digging to bringing life back to a kingdom." The men immediately grabbed their picks and shovels and began digging. This time there was not any complaining. They became a committed team. They dug all day, skipped breaks and dug all night until they hit water.

When the king heard about what had happened, he sent for the men so that he could shower them with gifts. After the celebration, the king could not resist asking: "I sent you men out the first time to dig and you all quit, but when you returned the second time you dug and found water; what made the difference?" They explained, "Once we understood why we were digging, we knew nothing would stop us until we had finished the job." The point is, how the vision is framed is essential. Make sure all team members know why they are digging.

Moreover, if the organizational vision is to be realized, there can be absolutely no equivocation regarding what challenges need to be addressed and how they will be resolved. A comprehensive strategy designed to accomplish this is imperative. The overriding purpose of the vision communication strategy should be to help create effective practitioners who believe they will be able to help their students learn better. In other words, the purpose of the vision is to create a learning epidemic, where a tipping point in beliefs and practices is manifested. A tipping point in this instance could be no more than a few key people spreading the message communicated in the campus vision statement.

Gladwell identifies three agents that contribute to tipping points. These come into play on every campus. First, the "law of the few" he espouses is the recognition that a few key people can cause ideas and beliefs to permeate an organization. Second, the "stickiness factor" is the skill to develop a campus vision that sticks. The central question ILs should ask when formulating a vision statement is, "Is it memorable?"

Generally, if the vision statement is meaningful it should not be difficult to internalize. In this regard, telling effective stories help to solidify the organization's vision. These stories work because they go beyond merely sharing data and reciting platitudes that many times do not resonate with the majority. They appeal to the emotions of the team and help to shape the campus culture. These stories reinforce the vision and communicate that it is noble and achievable. More will be discussed about storytelling in subsequent chapters.

The instructional leaders formulating the vision statement should consider the culture of the campus as well as the targeted audience. The audience should include all staff, students, parents, and stakeholders. The third agent is the "power of context," which says that little things in the physical and social climate of the campus can significantly affect the degree to which the organizational vision is realized. More will be said about these concepts later.

The points to remember are that a critical mass can effectively transmit the campus mission; the vision statement should be memorable; and the physical and social climate of the campus influences the level of acceptance of the organizational vision. When writing a vision statement, it should be noted that too many organizational vision statements are so verbose that they lose their desired effect.

Make them concise and alive. Storytelling and disseminating a memorable motto that encapsulates the vision of the campus can be effective. Everyone should be able to recite and internalize it. DuFour reminds us that the process of developing the vision statement is ultimately more important than the product itself (DuFour and Eaker, 1998). This vision process seeks to involve all organizational stakeholders. ILs will do well to remember this point. If the campus members do not own the vision, their attempts to live up to it will be perfunctory.

Step Six: How can professional development support the vision, or who needs assistance?

Professional development will be discussed in a subsequent chap-ter. It should be noted here, however, that for the purposes of supporting the campus vision, professional development is vital. It should be aligned with the organizational vision. Many ILs have failed to embrace the campus vision completely, not because of indifference but because of the semester approach to professional development.

That is, professional development efforts are not sustained over time; they seem to change with each new semester. Others fail to embrace the campus vision because, as students sometimes do, they would prefer to be labeled recalcitrant than be seen to not be as efficient or capable as other colleagues. Effective professional development minimizes this type of resistance.

Professional development is a continuous process of trying to get better. It includes needs assessments, mentors, an induction program, lesson study (which will be discussed in a subsequent chapter), instructional coaches, and most of all, alignment of the vision of the campus with needs of staff and students. Additionally, vision alignment includes the allocation of budgeted funds, time, and resources. Kotter's vision characteristics are fully incorporated within these six vision creation steps. As

ILs engage in the vision creation process, they should remain cognizant of Kotter's characteristics of effective visions:

Imaginable	Conveys a picture of what the future will look like
Desirable	Appeals to the long-term interests of employees, customers, stockholders, and others who have a stake in the enterprise
Feasible	Comprises realistic, attainable goals
Focused	Is clear enough to provide guidance in decision making
Flexible	Is general enough to allow individual initiative and alternative responses in light of changing conditions
Communicable	Is easy to communicate; can be successfully explained within five minutes

Table 1.3. Kotter's Characteristics of Effective Visions

Only those who are committed to the team concept and who are willing to fashion a vision and do the hard work in the trenches to carry out that vision will achieve success. Even those who embrace a trusting team culture and enthusiastically endorse a shared vision may have setbacks. But those who stand on the sidelines and look for excuses for failure have no chance of benefiting from the Pyramid Approach. Theodore Roosevelt's words apply precisely.

> It is not the critic who counts: not the man who points out how the strong man stumbles or where the doer of deeds could have done better. The credit belongs to the man who is actually in the arena, whose face is marred by dust and sweat and blood, who strives valiantly, who errs and comes up short again and again, because there is no effort without error or shortcoming, but who knows the great enthusiasms, the great devotions, who spends himself for a worthy cause; who, at the best, knows, in the end, the triumph of high achievement, and who, at the worst, if he fails, at least he fails while daring greatly, so that his place shall never be with those cold and timid souls who knew neither victory nor defeat. —Theodore Roosevelt, "Citizenship in a Republic" Speech at the Sorbonne, Paris, April 23, 1910

CULTURE IS THE ORGANIZATION'S PERSONALITY

Culture is a set of shared attitudes, values, and practices of a group. Hence, the success of any organization not only rests with having capable people in the right positions, but also, and equally important, is the quality of the relationships that exist among them. It is actually the relationships that make the difference within any organization.

How many times have we observed organizations, sports teams, or even families implode? From the outside, it appeared they had the talent, skills, and experience to be successful. Yet they, at best, achieved mediocrity. The importance of effective social skills should not be underestimated by instructional leaders. Organizational culture is really about relationships within the group, how they think and behave.

I recall working as a campus IL and overhearing a group of classroom ILs talking. This was my first year on that campus. Later that day, I asked one of the ILs what they were discussing. She said she and other classroom ILs were assisting a colleague who was also new to the campus. She ended by saying, "Dr. Woodrow, on this campus you improve or you move!" I got the impression no one was excluded from her statement, including me. That was the culture on that campus. This is the type of culture needed on every campus. ILs learn best from other ILs.

Every school employee knows there are two learning team meetings. One is posted on the school's calendar and meets at least once weekly. The second is not posted and meets in the lounge and in the parking lot. Many times the second meeting undermines the first. These second meetings are not written about in books and are rarely denounced by ILs. Interestingly, people who talk about others behind their backs seem to think this type of conduct will nurture trust and endear them with the listener. But the exact opposite occurs (Covey, 2008). Instructional leaders hold the future of students in their hands and should insist all employees be sincere and authentic in their professional practice.

Their belief system and effective practices should be apparent for everyone to observe. Until this happens, some ILs will continue to play school in lieu of having school. Colvin explains culture is "the norms and expectations that are simply in the air" (2008, p. 172). The Pyramid Approach is built on the foundational principles of a safe, caring environment, and trusting team culture. The absence of either one of these basic principles renders the organization handicapped.

Trust vs. Absolute Power

It should be noted here that leadership styles of the IL influence the degree to which trust is exhibited within the organization. Genuine trust and absolute power cannot reside within the same organization. One will either seek to gain individual and collective trust or absolute power. You cannot have both, they are incompatible. The research is replete with organizational leadership styles. And all credible sources denounce authoritarianism—in others words, my-way-or-the-highway type leadership.

Exceptions are in the event of extreme circumstances. If there is a fire in the building or some other threat to the safety of individuals, obviously this would not be a time for collaboration. If the research is clear regarding authoritarianism, why are we discussing it? We discuss it because the acquisition of knowledge does not ensure its implementation.

Over the years as a campus instructional leader and a university professor, and one who has monitored the performance of other campus instructional leaders, I have observed an amazing phenomenon. Some of the very classroom ILs who lamented that the campus ILs were dictatorial, insensitive, and could not be trusted employed many of the same leadership styles when they became campus ILs. It seems that when they initially become a campus IL, or for that matter a chairperson, they acquire amnesia and immediately forget the feelings of classroom ILs or colleagues who feel their talents and expertise are not being fully utilized.

The acquisition of a position of power poses a real challenge for some. We all remember Machiavelli, the Italian author who wrote one of the great works of all times, *The Prince*. His work is still studied and debated in most colleges and universities. *The Prince* translated means "The Leader." Machiavelli asserts that it is human nature to want and maintain power, and more is better than less. I can only speculate that if Machiavelli walked among us today, he would mock all this talk about character and trust. He would probably advise the following:

> It appears to me more appropriate to follow up the real truth of a matter than the imagination of it; for many have pictured republics and principalities which in fact have never been known or seen, because how one lives is so far distant from how one ought to live, that he who neglects what is done for what ought to be done, sooner effects his ruin than his preservation; for a man who wishes to act entirely up to his professions of virtue soon meets with what destroys him among so much that is evil. Hence it is necessary for a prince wishing to hold his own to know how to do wrong, and to make use of it or not according to necessity.

Machiavelli encourages leaders to be prepared to swim with the sharks. Steven Sample addresses this character and trust issue when he writes, "Most people confuse good leadership with effective leadership, but the contrarian leader knows that there is an enormous difference between the two" (2002, p. 107).

He asserts Hitler was an effective leader but most would not consider him a good leader. He continues by recounting his first driving lesson where his dad informed him that if an animal darted in front of the car he should run over it like a man. His dad was explaining to him that the lives of humans were more important than animals.

The point is, successful instructional leaders must know what hill to die on (Sample, 2002). The means are equally as important as the ends. Instructional leaders must continually ask, "Am I doing the right thing for the right reason in the right way?" The goal of successful instructional leaders is not to acquire and exert authoritarian power, but to advance a noble organizational mission that helps students acquire an education that will serve them well in life.

In this regard, would you prefer following someone whose mission you disagreed with but you personally liked, or someone you disliked but with whom you shared a common vision? This is an interesting question worthy of the consideration of ILs. I have observed ILs gravitate to the extreme ends of the leadership spectrum. On the one hand, some develop a dominating style that can be characterized as dictatorial or authoritarian. On the other hand, others can be characterized as laissez-faire. The dictatorial leader wants everyone to know who is in charge. And the laissez-faire leader is preoccupied with being popular. Leadership misses the mark when it is distracted from the team's mission for self-aggrandizement or petty reasons.

Research has identified many leadership paradigms: participative, bureaucratic, transformational, as well as the previously mentioned ones and others. However, they all generally fall into one of three broad categories: authoritarian, participative, or laissez-faire (Lewin et al., 1939). While research often singles out transformational leadership, at times it is wise to select the style that effectively suits the situation. This is called situational leadership. I mentioned leadership density in the introduction. Leadership density does not mean the leader abdicates her responsibilities as the organizational leader. It refers to leaders who acknowledge that no one person can effectively provide all the leadership required for an organization to operate successfully.

Some leaders, however, reason that leadership is a finite quantity, 100 percent; that is, the more they share the less they will have for themselves. Their reasoning is that if the leader shares 30 percent then there must only be 70 percent left. An interesting fact about leadership density concepts is that rather than leadership decreasing because of being shared, it actually increases. Thus, if the leader shares 30 percent, leadership expands to 130 percent of what it was (Sergiovanni, 1996).

Recall the classroom IL who stated, "On this campus you improve or you move." She was communicating that leadership is shared by everyone. This was the culture of that campus.

Some of the sayings of Lao-tzu, the Chinese philosopher, underscore leadership density principles. He said, to paraphrase him: The poor leader is he who the people despise. The good leader is one the people praise. And the great leader is one who causes the people to say, "We did it ourselves." Hence, when ILs consider leadership styles, empowering others should always be an integral part of leadership. It nurtures trust.

Tyranny of the Majority

Alexis de Tocqueville in *Democracy in America* illustrates a salient point that is important for instructional leaders to keep in mind as they work and solve problems collaboratively. He declares the majority is not always right. As we collaborate to advance the organization's mission, remember some of the best ideas are generated by the minority. Wisdom is not a permanent ally of the majority or the minority. Fullan and Hargreaves (1996) concur:

> Our schools need the growth and learning that comes from individual diversity and creativity from within and outside our own school boards. We must experiment and discover better ways of working together that mobilize the power of the group while at the same time enhance individual development. We must use collegiality not to level people down, but to bring together strength and creativity. So we must fight for collegiality, but not naively. We must protect and promote the individual too. (p. 9)

Many times we learn more from people who disagree with us than we do from people who share our views. However, too often we listen and are drawn to people who agree with us, and we prefer to avoid and under listen to those who don't (Fullan, 2001). The overriding perspective ILs should maintain is that the goal of collegiality is not to be right but to do the right thing. Focus on the quality of ideas and to what degree those ideas are congruent with the organizational vision.

REFLECTIVE THOUGHTS

What are your thoughts and beliefs regarding the following statements, and how are they manifest in your daily practice?

- Are you a good listener?
- Do you really want parents engaged on campus?
- What does trust mean to you? What are the positives and negatives of parking lot meetings?
- Why is it important to apply campus guidelines and procedures equally?
- Do you give team members credit for their ideas and work?
- Do all team members know why they are digging?
- Do you admit your mistakes?
- Trust others and they will trust you. Do you concur?
- Do the right thing while you do things right. What does this mean to you?
- Does position power adversely affect one's personality?
- How do character and competence impact trust in the workplace?
- Can you articulate what you stand for?

BARE FACTS

- There is a degree of Machiavelli in all of us.
- Ineffective instructional leaders can be found in their offices.
- Trust matters.

- Instructional leadership that advances the teaching and learning enterprise does not just focus on data collection and teaching strategies.
- This is why we, in education, are not "Waiting for Superman" or for Wonder Woman. We are waiting for effective teams.
- The mistake too many educators make is not devoting sufficient attention to first establishing a safe, caring, and trusting team culture.
- Tough times can produce tough and determined personalities. Yet, within the culture of education, too often this fact is not fully appreciated.
- The heart and soul of school culture is what people believe.
- It is only through reculturing that we begin to see dramatic progress in achieving the mission of learning communities.
- It is the second meetings (parking lot meetings) that are not written about in books and are rarely denounced by ILs.
- Collective instructional leadership should be the goal of every campus.

REFERENCES

Administration for Children and Families, Children's Bureau. (2004). Child Maltreatment 2004. http://www.acf.hhs.gov/programs/cb/resource/child-maltreatment-2004.

Baker, K. (Oct. 2007). Are international test worth anything. *Phi Delta Kappa, 89*(2), 101–4.

Bald, E. (2014). Utah incident receives debate on handling unpaid lunch debts. *Education Week*. www.edweek.org.

Barbour, C., Barbour, N. H., and Scully, P. A. (2005). *Families, schools, and communities*. Columbus, OH: Prentice Hall.

Bjork, R. A. (2013). Desirable difficulties perspective on learning. In H. Pashler (Ed.), *Encyclopedia of the mind*. Thousand Oaks, CA: Sage Reference.

Bureau of Labor Statistics. Retrieved February 18, 2014 from http://www.bls.gov/.

Burkhauser, S., et al. (2012). First-Year Principals in Urban School Districts http://www.rand.org/content/dam/rand/pubs/technical_reports/2012/RAND_TR1191.pdf.

Carey, B. (2013). Language gap between rich and poor kids begins in infancy. Stanford Report. http://medicalxpress.com/news/2013-09-language-gap-rich-poor-kids.html. Retrieved February 7, 2013.

Center for Disease Control. (2012). About teen pregnancy. Retrieved June, 20, 2014 from http://www.cdc.gov/teenpregnancy/aboutteenpreg.htm.

Chua, A. and Rubenfeld, J. (2014). *The triple package*. New York: The Penguin Press.

Coleman, James S. (1966). Equality of Educational Opportunity Study EEOS. Retrieved July 22, 2014 from http://doi.org/10.3886/ICPSR06389.v3.

Coleman-Jensen, A., Nord, M., Andrews, M., and Carlson, S. (2010). "Household Food Security in the United States in 2010." Retrieved May 11, 2014 from http://www.ers.usda.gov/Publications/err125/.

Collins, J. (2001). *Good to great*. New York: HarperCollins Publishers.

Covey, S. M. R. (2008). *The speed of trust*. New York: Free Press.

Centers for Disease Control and Prevention (CDC). (2008). www.sdc.gov.

Compton, R. (2007). *Two million minutes*. Documentary film.

Danielson, C. (2002). *Enhancing student achievement*. Alexandria, VA:ASCD.

DuBrin, A. (1984). *Human relations: A job oriented approach*. Reston, VA: Prentice-Hall Company.

DuFour, R., and Eaker, R. (1998). *Professional learning communities at work*. Bloomington, IN: National Educational Service.

Dufour, R., et al. (2006). *Learning by doing*. Bloomington, IN: Solution Tree.

Educational Leadership Policy Standards. (2008). Retrieved May 9, 2014 from http://www.ccsso.org/Documents/2008/Educational_Leadership_Policy_Standards_2008.pdf

Education Week Research Center. (2014). Equity in achievement, funding are hurdles states amid progress. Retrieved March 1, 2014 from http://www.edweek.org/ew/articles/2014/01/09/16sos.h33.html?qs=equity+in+achievement,+funding.

Epstein, J., Sanders, M.G., Simon, B., Salina, K., Jansorn, N., and Van Voorhis, F. (2002). *Schools, family and community partnerships: Your handbook for action* (2nd ed.). Thousand Oaks, CA: Corwin Press.

Fullan, M. (2001). *Leading in a culture of change*. San Francisco, CA: Jossey-Bass, Inc.

Fullan, M. (2009). *Change wars*. Bloomington, IN: Solution Tree.

Fullan, M. and Hargreaves, A. (1996). *What's worth fighting for in your school?* New York: Teachers College Press.

Gladwell, M. (2002). *The tipping point*. New York: Little, Brown and Company.

Glass, T., and Franceschini, L. (2007). *The state of the American school superintendency: A mid-decade study*. Arlington, VA: American Association of School Administrators.

Glazerman, S., Protik, A., Teh, B., Bruch, J., and Seftor, N. (2012). *Moving high-performing teachers: Implementation of transfer incentives in seven districts: Executive summary* (NCEE 2012-4052). Washington, DC: National Center for Education Evaluation and Regional Assistance, Institute of Education Sciences, U.S. Department of Education.

Glazerman, S., Protik, A., Teh, B., Bruch, J., and Max, J. (2013). *Transfer incentives for high-performing teachers: Final results from a multisite experiment* (NCEE 2014-4003). Washington, DC: National Center for Education Evaluation and Regional Assistance, Institute of Education Sciences, U.S. Department of Education.

Hanushek, E. (2014). Why the U.S. Results on PISA Matter. *Education Week, 33*(15), 20–21, 24.

Hart, B., and Risley, T. R. (2004) The early catastrophe. *Education Review, 77*(1), 100–118.

Health Behavior in School-aged Children. (1998). Heal the Behavior in School-aged Children. Retrieved July 20, 2014 from http://www.icpsr.umich.edu/icpsrweb/SAMHDA/studies/3522.

Health Behavior in School-aged Children. (2010). Retrieved May 14, 2014 from http://www.euro.who.int/__data/assets/pdf_file/0003/163857/Social-determinants-of-health-and-well-being-among-young-people.pdf?ua=1.

Heckman, J. J. (2013). *Giving kids a fair chance*. Cambridge, MA: Boston Review.

Kirchner, G. L., and Setchfield, M. S. (Fall, 2005). School counselors' and school principals' perceptions of the school counselor's role. *Education Week*.

Kohn, A. (1998). *What to look for in a classroom*. San Francisco, CA: Jossey-Bass, Inc.

Kotter P. (1996). *Leading change*. Cambridge, MA: Harvard Business School Press.

Lewin, K, Lippitt, R., and White, R. K. (1939). Patterns of aggressive behavior in experimentally created social climates. *Journal of Social Psychology*, 10, 271–301.

Lindwall, J. J., and Coleman, H. (2008). The elementary school counselor's role in fostering caring school communities. *Professional School Counseling*.

Lloyd, S. C., and Swanson, C. B. (2014). Equity in achievement, funding a hurdle for states amid progress. *Education Week, 33*(16), 35.

Machiavelli, N. *The Prince*. Marriott, W.K. (1908 translation). http://www.constitution.org/mac/prince00.htm.

Marzano, R. J. (2003). *What works in schools: Translating research into action*. Alexandria, VA: ASCD.

Maslow, A. H. (1970). *Motivation and personality* (Rev. ed.). New York: Norton.

McDermott, D. (2008). *Developing caring relationships among parents, children, schools, and communities.* Thousand Oaks, CA: Sage Publications, Inc.

Michael Irvin Hall of Fame enshrinement speech. (2007). Retrieved August 6, 2007 from http://sports.espn.go.com/nfl/halloffame07/news/story?id=2961687.

Muir, W. M., Wade, M. J., Bjima, P., and Ester, E. D. (2010). Group selection and social evolution in domesticated chickens. *Evolutionary Applications, 3,* 453–65.

National Association of School Nurses. (2009). School health nursing services role in health care; Role of the school nurse. National Association of School Nurses. Issue Brief. Retrieved January 8, 2010 from http://www.nasn.org/.

National Center for Children in Poverty. (2014). Retrieved July 22, 2014 from http://nccp.org/publications/pub_1073.html.

National Center for Education Statistics. (2009). PISA Results http://nces.ed.gov/surveys/international/tables/B_1_71.asp.

National Center for Education Statistics. (2012). Retrieved June 2, 2014 from http://nces.ed.gov/fastfacts/display.asp?id=16.

National Center for Education Statistics. (2014). Retrieved December 14, 2014, from http://nces.ed.gov/timss/results11.asp.

National Child Abuse Statistics. (2013). http://www.childhelp.org/pages/ statistics/.

National Commission of Excellence in Education. (1983). *A nation at risk: The imperative for educational reform.* Washington, DC: U.S. Government Printing Office.

National School Lunch Program. (2013). Retrieved July 7, 2014 from http://www.fns.usda.gov/sites/default/files/pd/01slfypart.pdf.

Patterson, K., Grenny, J., Maxfield, D., McMillan, R., and Switzler, A. (2008). *Influencer.* New York: McGraw-Hill.

Pedrotti, J. T., Edwards, L. M., and Lopez, S. J. (2008). Promoting hope: Suggestions for school counselors. *Professional School Counseling,12,* 100-107.

Poplin, M. et al. (2011). The madness of teacher evaluation framework. *Phi Delta Kappa, 92*(5), 39–43.

Ravitch, D. (2013). *Reign of error.* New York: Random House.

Reimer, M., and Smink, J. (compilers). (2005). Information about the school dropout issue selected facts & statistics. A publication of the National Dropout Prevention Center/Network.

Revolving door of the principalship. (2008). Austin, TX: University Council for Educational Administration (UCEA).

Sample, S. (2002). *Contrarian's guide to leadership.* San Francisco, CA: Jossey-Bass.

School health nursing services role in health care; Role of the school nurse. (2009). National Association of School Nurses. Issue Brief.

Senge, P. (1994). *The fifth discipline.* New York: Currency Paperback.

Sergiovanni, T. (1996). *Leadership for the schoolhouse.* San Francisco, CA: Jossey-Bass.

Sergiovanni, T. (2000). *The lifeworld of leadership.* San Francisco, CA: Jossey-Bass.

Shaw G. (1921). *Back to Methuselah,* part 1, act 1.

Singh, S., Darroch, J. E. (2000). Adolescent pregnancy and childbearing: Levels and trends in developed countries. *Fam Plann Perspect, 32*(1):14–23.

Stigler, W. J., and Hiebert, J. (2009). *The teaching gap.* New York: Free Press.

Swenson, W., Arendt, J., and Wilson, D. S. (2000). Artificial selection of microbial ecosystems for 3-chloroaniline biodegradation. *Environ. Mirobiol., 2,* 9365.

Tocqueville, A., and Bender, T. (1981). *Democracy in America.* New York: Modern Library.

University Council for Educational Administration (UCEA). Revolving door of the principalship. (2008). Austin, TX: University Council for Educational Administration (UCEA).

U.S. Department of Education, National Center for Education Statistics. (2014). *The Condition of Education 2014* (NCES 2014-083).

U.S. Department of Health and Human Services, Administration for Children and Families, Children's Bureau. (2004). Child maltreatment. (2002). Washington, DC.

Walberg, Herbert. (1984). Data from "Improving the Productivity of America's Schools." *Educational Leadership, 41*(8), 24.

Whitehead, A. N. (1957). *The aims of education.* New York: The Macmillan Company.

Wong, H., and Wong, R. (2009). *First days of school.* Mountain View, CA: Harry K. Wong Publications.

World Health Organization. Health Behavior in School-Aged Children. (1997–1998) Retrieved April 3,2014 from http://doi.org/10.3886/ICPSR03522.v4.

REFLECTIVE THOUGHTS

_____
_____
_____
_____
_____
_____
_____
_____
_____
_____
_____
_____
_____
_____
_____

TWO

School-Wide Instructional Strategies

A rising tide lifts all boats. —John F. Kennedy

DEVELOPING SCHOOL-WIDE INSTRUCTIONAL STRATEGIES

The quote "a rising tide lifts all boats" was a favorite of President John F. Kennedy, who used it to suggest that a rising tide of economic growth would benefit all participants in the economy. It has been used in many contexts. When applied to education, it underscores the central purpose of developing, implementing, and sustaining research-based, school-wide strategies.

When instructional leaders are able to install a core set of instructional strategies and methods that permeate the entire campus, not only will exceptional ILs demonstrate a higher level of proficiency, but all other classroom ILs will also. Over the years, I have come to recognize that every classroom IL does not possess the same level of competence; however, even the less capable, when introduced to a classroom setting equipped with effective instructional tools, strategies, and support, performs exceptionally well. Peter Senge, in *The Fifth Discipline*, concurs. He writes, "When placed in the same system, people, however different, tend to produce similar results" (1990, p. 42).

School-wide instructional strategies seek to alter the campus system by identifying what methods work most effectively and to ensure these same methods are utilized by everyone so that student learning is maximized. The term everyone implies school-wide instructional strategies are to be utilized with appropriate students at the most effective moment. They do not seek to minimize the creativity and individuality of ILs. Marzano reviewed the effects classroom ILs and schools have on the achievement level of students. He identified the worst and best learning environments. I list his results in descending order from worst to best (2003, p. 74).

- Least effective school and least effective teacher
- Most effective school and least effective teacher
- Average school and average teacher
- Least effective school and most effective teacher
- Most effective school and average teacher
- Most effective school and most effective teacher

Instructional leaders are not surprised to see that most effective schools and the most effective teachers have the greatest significant impact on student proficiency. However, what stands out for many are the first two categories. Regardless of the quality level of campuses, ineffective classroom ILs cannot hide. Students will not achieve well in classrooms where pedagogical malpractice is allowed to exist.

While these data do not address the skill level of students, the research is overwhelming. At-risk students assigned to at-risk classroom ILs is analogous to exposing Superman to kryptonite. This situation must be preempted. I underscore the deleterious effects of such a combination because this practice still occurs; that is, assigning the least prepared IL with the least prepared students.

Notwithstanding pressures from experienced team members to only instruct particular students, courageous leadership does not allow this combination to exist. Coaching, care, induction programs, mentoring, and ongoing professional growth experiences are strategies and tools campus ILs employ to redress ineffective professional practices. Also, as mentioned previously, school-wide instructional strategies provide research-based methods that should assist developing classroom ILs to improve their professional practice.

In many situations, campus ILs are forced to repair the train while it runs on the tracks. For instance, with shrinking budgets and ever increasing diverse student populations juxtaposed with the pressures of the standards era only serve to compound the problems of overcoming ineffective schooling. I have found one of the best ways to accomplish these types of repairs is to utilize school-wide strategies effectively. At first glance, this seems simple enough to accomplish on any campus. But not so fast—getting from here to there is the focus of this chapter.

Identifying Campus Learning Disabilities

In the educational ecosystem, no one takes responsibility for poor performance of students. Peter Senge describes seven mental archetypes in organizations that impede accomplishing the organizational vision. These attitudes and mental images he labels "organizational learning disabilities." His central point is that learning disabilities in children are exacerbated when they go undetected and unchecked, and that this same phenomenon devastates companies when their organizational learning disabilities are not confronted head on and redressed. I have modified these organizational learning disabilities for schools by omitting some, giving them different names, and adding others: the "black hole," the "big stick," as well as "I don't believe it."

Some of these campus learning disabilities exist on most campuses. I have listed six. I am confident there are others. The mission of each campus should be to identify them and immediately begin to eradicate them. Senge postulates that companies fail to respond in the face of overwhelming evidence that something is wrong and needs to be redressed. He points out most companies are poor learners. These learning disabilities prevent even the best companies from realizing their full potential (1990).

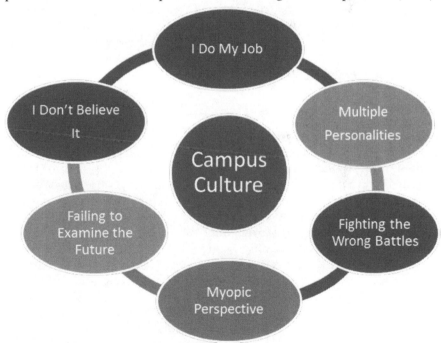

Figure 2.1. Six Campus Learning Disabilities

I Do My Job

We too often limit the perception of our campus responsibility to our specific job, not the vision of the campus or district. When ILs focus only on their individual responsibilities and not the overall mission, they assume little responsibility for the failure or success of the campus mission. Their thinking is, "I did my job." The goal of ILs is not to do their job but to get the job done. One who holds the former view may believe he needs to position himself to declare, "I did what I was supposed to do," so someone else apparently dropped the ball. The latter perspective suggests the issue is not who dropped the ball but what needs to be done to accomplish the mission.

This is just one illustration of why it is so important for ILs to have choices and input from the very beginning stages of developing school-wide efforts. This level of participation moves people from independence to interdependence. And interdependence fosters systems thinking. In addition, language can assist with developing group participation.

For instance, using the name of the campus or metaphors such as team, family, and group reinforces joint efforts. "I am an IL," can be a symptom of a deeper problem. "I don't trust you." In other words, some classroom ILs remain compartmentalized because they are attempting to avoid sniping from others. "If I just stay in my room, when something goes wrong I won't be the fall guy." In terms of trust building, many times actions speak louder than rhetoric. School-wide instructional strategies depend on team support.

Fighting the Wrong Battles

Psychologists would perhaps label this type of campus disability a defense mechanism. Defense mechanisms enable us to feel good; that is, whatever the problem, we are not responsible. Some external force is the culprit. This type of mindset leads to some ILs offering various excuses to ignore school-wide strategies. For example: "The parents are not parenting the way they did when I was growing up, so the school-wide strategy targeting increased parent participation will not be successful. . . . The teachers before me just socially promoted these students, so I am not convinced campus-wide strategies are what we need. . . . The climate on this campus is not conducive to teaching and learning and until it is, school-wide efforts are a waste of time."

Comments similar to these may possess degrees of truth but becoming preoccupied with them prevents ILs from turning attention to possible solutions. As long as ILs are fighting the wrong battles, they will never "take that hill." Anxiety is minimized when individuals feel in control. Suppose a fourth grade IL lamented that the third grade IL did not adequately prepare her students. She might recommend that vertical teaming become a school-wide strategy the following year. In a learning team meeting, she might recommend a review of research that will possibly yield methods and materials that might address her concerns. Demonstrating a positive and optimistic attitude will always yield more productive results. Fighting the wrong battles creates a perception of hopelessness. Asking, "What can I do?" or "How can I make a more significant contribution," generally leads to positive action. Establishing a more proactive approach could very well begin the process of altering the current situation.

When ILs begin the planning process to develop school-wide strategies, they should be prepared to resist fighting the wrong battles and stay focused on what will make a difference in student academic achievement. A famous statement by the cartoonist Walt Kelly highlights the first battle some ILs must win if they are going to ensure all students achieve at high levels: "We have met the enemy and he is us."

Myopic Perspective

School-wide instructional strategies are based on the premise that there are academic needs that have not been met. When ILs fail to recognize the causes of minimal student academic achievement, these same impediments to learning go unattended. Sometimes impediments to learning are so gradual that what has become abnormal appears to be normal. Those persons who have been a part of this gradual deterioration within the campus learning environment are the ones who are least likely to recognize a need for an action plan. Gradualism can dull one's perception.

To illustrate this point, imagine a frog is placed in boiling water; obviously it will immediately jump out. However, if it is placed in room temperature water, it will remain immersed in its environment, apparently happy. When the water is gradually heated until it eventually becomes extremely hot, the frog will remain in the water without attempting to get out while at the same time behaving as it did when the water was comfortable. Why did the frog behave the same way in two drastically different environments? The frog can only recognize drastic temperature changes (Senge, 1990).

There are times ILs may need to view the campus environment with a new set of eyeglasses. The changes to the learning environment may have been so gradual they went unrecognized. In the midst of this type of complacent campus environment, needed instructional strategies will go undeveloped because a critical mass of ILs may not see the need for their development. Collins underscores this point when he says, "Good is the enemy of great" (2001, p. 1). Not only can ILs overlook a gradually deteriorating instructional environment, they can become preoccupied with daily campus events at the expense of a debilitating campus culture that impedes learning.

The primary threat to the learning environment is not events but established customs and behaviors. One goal of school-wide instructional strategies is to contribute to the reculturing process of the campus. We have to move beyond the management of day-to-day events and focus on critical issues within the school that have long-term significance. Thus, we see the forest and the trees.

Effective ILs engage in continuous reflection. Reflection is the practice of reviewing, analyzing, and drawing conclusions about one's previous actions. When done effectively, it improves professional practice. The reflection process should enable ILs to give attention to rapidly changing events as well as those that change over time.

Failing to Examine the Future

It is espoused we learn best from our experiences. Nevertheless, many times we do not have the pleasure of observing the consequences of our decisions. We all have a "learning horizon." It is the ability to see the connections and impact of our decisions into the future (Senge, 1990). To evaluate instructional strategies and their impact on student learning, ILs must strive to create ways to broaden their "learning horizon."

We could label the lack of interest in this area as "I am my school." In other words, when students leave elementary schools, these same ILs may not be interested in the impact their elementary instructional strategies had on their former students' ability to learn in middle school, high school, and college. Middle and high school ILs may have a similar lack of interest in the future success of their students. One reason this is so is because it is difficult to accurately measure the impact instructional strategies introduced two or three years earlier have on current student performance.

Nevertheless, insightful ILs look beyond their classrooms and their campuses. They understand the quality of education students receive is the sum total of all their school experience. Vertical teaming and planning is one method to begin assessing the long-term impact of instructional strategies. Obviously, ILs use formative and summative assessments to evaluate school-wide instructional strategies. When campuses are receiving or sending students to another campus, it helps to establish a rich dialogue that leads to joint collaboration. I have observed this process work exceptionally well. This type of insight and commitment can lead to campuses sharing school-wide instructional strategies. Just think how effective a set of feeder pattern instructional strategies connected to a common set of students would be.

States are beginning to develop a set of K–16 objectives, understanding the benefits of articulation among and within all levels of the educational system, including colleges and universities. To the degree that ILs consider the experiences of students on other campuses, their own students' transition from campus to campus will improve among these schools and students' learning will be significantly enhanced.

Multiple Personalities

Developing effective school-wide instructional strategies involves data analysis, planning, and collaboration. Moreover, it requires a sincere drive and commitment to lay the bare facts on the table regarding the learning environment and explore ways to deliver more effective instruction—the kind of instruction that yields results. To accomplish this goal, the participants must be willing to explore and consider new approaches and ideas. With support and sustained assistance, they must be willing to move from their comfort zone to perhaps unexplored areas.

I have observed three types of personalities that participate in these kinds of planning sessions. The presence of multiple personalities is not intended to suggest all three behaviors reside within one individual, but that all three behaviors can be found in team meetings. The first two impede the advancement of the organizational vision. The third advances it.

The first I label the "big stick." The second is the "black hole." And the third is the "head follower" (Sergiovanni, 1996). Some people "speak softly and carry a big stick"; however, these ILs don't quite have the same objective in mind as Teddy Roosevelt. In brainstorming and planning sessions, they are quick to pull out their "big stick" and proceed to beat down many credible researched-based, time-proven instructional strategies and methodologies before they can be fully discussed and analyzed. The "big stick" person is a defender of the status quo who believes this is the way we have always done it—so why change? Some believe we "have been there, done that." Not everyone who questions the relevancy and validity of proposed initiatives is wielding a "big stick." In education, it is not uncommon to implement innovations one year only to exchange them for new ones the following year.

The problem arises when an individual only articulates what will not work while refusing to consider possible alternative methods objectively. Others attempt to camouflage their need for professional development opportunities that involve the use of innovative instructional strategies by beating them down. They attempt to shift the focus of the meeting on the wrong issues. The insightful instructional leader recognizes these persons are asking for support and need assistance. As their skills improve, so will their support for change.

The second type of personality that is present in some planning sessions is the opposite of the "big stick." These persons are generally polite and give the appearance they are on board with implementing the new instructional strategies or initiatives. In reality, however, they are engaging in passive resistance. I refer to this type of personality as the "black hole." In general relativity, a black hole is a region of space in which the gravitational field is so powerful that nothing, including light, can escape its pull. The black hole has a one-way surface called an event horizon into which objects can fall, but out of which nothing can come.

This personality type takes in all the dialogue and recommendations during planning sessions, but upon closer examination, other ILs recognize no appreciable change in that person's professional practice. In other words, "I will listen and then continue doing what I have always done." Another phenomenon ILs should monitor is the "black hole" meeting. Elaborate and detailed school-wide plans are developed in this type of meeting. However, months later, or perhaps the next semester, there is very little evidence that planning meetings occurred or that plans were agreed upon. ILs should practice developing agreed-upon benchmarks following planning sessions. These benchmarks can serve as valuable feedback for the group.

The third personality type that is present in these planning sessions is the "head follower." This person, unlike the first two types, remembers the noble team mission established by all team members and is committed to following it. Recall that Sergiovanni (1996) refers to this personality type as the "head follower." Head followers are flexible and open to innovations when they are supported by sound research. These persons are not always influential but when they are, ILs should take full advantage of their persuasive powers to diminish the impact of those with the described personality archetypes.

I Don't Believe It

Of all the campus learning disabilities, "I don't believe it" is the most debilitating and detrimental to students' learning. If all the other organizational disabilities did not exist, this one would still severely curtail teaching and learning efforts. The beliefs of ILs and how they impact student proficiency will be developed in subsequent chapters. It should, however, be noted that the Pyramid Approach considers the belief system of educators, along with the effort of students, to be the gold standard of instructional leadership and high student achievement. I will make the case that the belief system of some ILs is the elephant in the room—that indeed some ILs don't believe or fully embrace current research regarding student learning.

James Coleman is the one who, in the 1960s, declared that schools and ILs made very little impact on student achievement. Ron Edmonds, in the late 1970s, challenged Coleman's finding and concluded there were common professional practices (correlates) that indeed make a difference in the achievement level of students. Below are Edmonds' effective school correlates. Marzano highlights them (2003, p. 16). See table 2.1. Marzano updates the correlates and renames them "school-level factors." He lists these school-level factors in rank order based on their impact on student learning (2003, p. 19).

Ron Edmonds	Robert Marzano
Correlates of an Effective School	**School-Level Factors**
Strong administrative leadership	Opportunity to learn
An emphasis on basic skill acquisition	Monitoring and Pressure to Achieve
High expectation for student achievement	Parental Involvement
A safe and orderly atmosphere conducive to learning	School climate
Frequent monitoring of student progress	Leadership

Table 2.1.

I delineated these correlates and school-level factors for two reasons. First, ILs should take advantage of research on school-level factors when developing school-wide instructional strategies. Second, note that beliefs are not specifically delineated in either list. They are certainly implied, but is that sufficient? I am convinced the mental archetypes of some ILs is the learning disability least discussed, yet it can be the most debilitating to their professional practice. This type of misaligned thinking falls into the "I don't believe it" category of professional learning disabilities. This issue will be explored in detail in the next chapter.

Effective School Characteristics Defined

Safe, Caring, and Trusting Team Culture

Achieving academic success for all students begins with firmly establishing the appropriate context for schooling. Culture is essentially what members of the organization believe and the way they behave. Culture drives the organization, for good or bad. It can be altered effectively through first engaging in reculturing efforts that lead to successful restructuring; that is, ILs should strive to alter minds and behaviors as they alter organizational structures. This can be done in reverse order. However, doing so is analogous to painting a wood framed structure without first inspecting and treating it for termites. It looks good but ultimately the frame will crumble. Organizational structure is important but it is not the solution—culture trumps structure. Reculturing is another way of stating our attitudes and behaviors need to improve. These kinds of behavioral changes lead to establishing a safe, caring, and trusting team culture that provides fertile ground for growing dendrites, thus helping students to become smarter.

Opportunity to Learn Rigorous Curricula

What should all students be expected to learn, and to what extent are they given the opportunity to learn it? This question helps to keep ILs focused. Opening up students' opportunity to learn examines rigor and relevance. It also explores, as a result of frequent observations and assessments, to what extent a gap exists between stated learning objectives and students' demonstration of proficiency with these objectives.

Factors affecting opportunity include alignment of resources, availability of time, instructional methods, textbooks and materials, scope and sequence of the syllabus, school-wide instructional strategies, and professional development. The focus here should be on teaching concepts and content that have the most potential to make a significant impact on stated curricula objectives and the quality of students' future lives.

Research-Based Belief System

A research-based belief system helps instructors make a practical connection between pedagogical beliefs and student outcomes that really helps them in the classroom. The beliefs of ILs about their own professional efficacy and students' capacity to demonstrate proficiency with rigorous curricula determine the extent of students' academic success. In line with the research, this type of belief system embraces effort-based teaching and learning principles. When all students are not performing at the desired level, ILs examine collective and individual beliefs as well as behaviors of campus members. Beliefs matter.

Collective Instructional Leadership

Collective instructional leadership refers to the significant impact organizational leadership has compared to individual or small-group leadership. Collective instructional leadership seeks to lead each individual to own the organizational vision. The belief that all children can learn must be the underpinning of such an organizational vision. This type of leadership does not replace or strive to usurp the authority of the campus instructional leader; it complements and assists leadership by seeking to have "all brains in the game" and "all hands on deck."

The central premise is that everyone is following the organizational vision, not an individual vision or personality. Collective instructional leadership offers educators a twenty-first-century paradigm for improving schools. This kind of leadership encourages systems thinking and finds the campus IL asking critical questions that lead to quality decisions as well as the development of collaborative plans that ultimately produce success. It may take a village to raise children but it takes collective instructional leadership to educate them.

Parental and Community Involvement

When developing plans to connect the goals of instructors, students, and parents, the first question that needs to be answered is: Do schools really need and want parental and community involvement? When parents find it difficult to volunteer and visit campuses because of work and other conflicts, parental engagement provides another avenue to connect parents with the school and their child. Engagement focuses not just on what parents do but who they are and the quality relationships they form within schools and communities; even though they may not be physically present on campus, they remain connected.

ESSENTIAL COMPONENTS OF SCHOOL-WIDE INSTRUCTIONAL STRATEGIES

Professional Learning Communities (PLCs)

Because school-wide instructional strategies require campus-wide collaboration, they naturally complement the principles of professional learning communities. Teachers in professional learning communities recognize their obligation to work together on school-wide matters. No one person can effectively develop these school-wide efforts, nor can any one person cause these efforts to be ingrained into the campus culture. From the very outset, it should be communicated that school-wide means all hands on deck and every brain in the game.

The primary purpose of PLCs is to improve learning for all. Furthermore, PLCs are based on the premise that ILs are not only responsible for students' learning, but for their own learning as well; hence, PLC members work interdependently to achieve a common goal, learning for all (DuFour, 2006).

Participants in PLCs acquire a greater appreciation for the connectedness between their learning and students' learning. Thus, campus ILs would benefit from participating in PLCs with their colleagues. This could be accomplished easily by establishing an agreed-upon calendar of meeting locations and dates. They should apply the same process as classroom ILs. The bottom line is that after learning collaboratively, two questions should be answered: What actions did we take? And to what degree were our actions successful?

The focus of PLCs should not just be on process. It should also be on results. An ancillary goal of professional learning team meetings should be to develop a process of communication that leads to quality decision-making. I have modified such a model developed by Peter Senge (1990). The model requires discussion, dialogue, and an effective facilitator.

Discussion

The fundamental purpose of discussion is to present and defend one's views in hopes of identifying the best strategy for success. Team discussions should expose the "bare facts," and at the same time participants should avoid becoming defensive. Discussion should occur prior to making decisions.

Dialogue

Various perspectives are presented in an effort to acquire a new and collective perspective. I view this process as simply brainstorming. The team presents possible strategies that might alter the current course of action. During dialogue, the emphasis should be on listening, suspending assumptions, and withholding judgment. This allows all team members' views to be presented and equally considered. Both dialogue and discussion can result in changing course. Discussion, however, generally focuses on current actions, whereas dialogue usually focuses on possible different courses of action.

Facilitator

The facilitator is responsible for ensuring there is no hierarchy and the team meeting is authentic. That is, members suspend assumptions, distinguish between dialogue and discussion, and the facilitator keeps the meeting from stagnating or getting off course. She intervenes only when necessary. She should remind members that the purpose of team meetings is not to assign blame. Collins frames it this way: Teams should conduct autopsies without blame (2001).

The following are suggested learning team ground rules offered by Senge. These ground rules are designed not so much to render decisions as to enable the exploration of the viability of possible new school-wide instructional strategies.

- Suspension of assumptions. Typically people take a position and defend it, holding to it. Others take up opposite positions and polarization results. In this session, we would like to examine some of our assumptions underlying our direction and strategy and not seek to defend them.
- Acting as colleagues. We are asking everyone to leave his or her position at the door. There will be no particular hierarchy in this

meeting, except for the facilitator, who will, hopefully, keep us on track.

- Spirit of inquiry. We would like to have people begin to explore the thinking behind their views, the deeper assumptions they may hold, and the evidence they have that leads them to these views. So it will be fair to begin to ask other questions such as: "What leads you to say or believe this?" Or "What makes you ask about this?" (1990, p. 261)

Professional Transformation Study Groups

To reap the full benefits of instructional strategies, there must be recognition of the need in education to move beyond mere discussion and studying of information. While both are needed and beneficial, until some ILs experience a professional transformation, proficiency for a segment of students will remain stagnant. Professional learning communities provide a forum for collaboration, discussion, and invaluable professional learning. They enhance the viability of school-wide instructional strategies by increasing the efficacy of ILs.

The stated purpose of PLCs is to improve practitioners' learning in a way that leads to collaboratively solving learning challenges for all students. Conversely, the primary purpose of professional transformation study groups (PTSG) is to provide a forum for practitioners to examine their beliefs regarding capacity and effort-based principles. That is, what do ILs believe about their own capacity to teach all students, and what do they believe about all students' ability to learn challenging curricula. This is an area some educators are reticent to discuss. They also meet to examine and discuss effort-based teaching methods. If pressed for a candid response, I believe many would acknowledge that beliefs in education about practitioners' and students' capacity are major impediments to accomplishing campus proficiency goals.

Professional transformation study groups begin with the premise that beliefs about efficacy matter. Ignoring this issue only exacerbates it. PLCs and PTSGs are the same yet they are different. They are the same because they seek common outcomes: all students learning at high levels. They are different in that they share common goals but their approach to them emanates from different angles. Both are needed.

Additionally, PTSGs attempt to answer the question of why the acquisition of knowledge often times is not manifested in daily practice. And it postulates that the mindset of some instructors limits their own success and the success of their students. It should be noted, though, that professional transformation cannot be directed or mandated. It begins internally. How one internalizes information shapes its impact on professional practice. Research-based inquiry drives discussion and learning. Some will immediately reject the premise of what they read. Other readers will deem the information to be interesting but not implementable, while others will objectively view what they have read and consider how it might improve their professional practice.

The ultimate goal of every campus is to move from the acquisition of knowledge to its implementation as quickly as possible. This process creates a sense of renewed energy and professional efficacy on campus as well as within the classroom. It is potentially one of the most effective professional growth activities available to instructional leaders. It is only natural that improving people should be a vital part of improving schools.

Campus ILs would benefit from participating in PTSGs with their colleagues as much as they would with participating in PLCs. This could be accomplished easily by establishing an agreed upon calendar of meeting locations and dates. They should apply the same process as classroom ILs. The significance of developing a research-based belief system on campus will be explained more fully in the next chapter. When creating professional transformation study groups consider the following.

Purpose

Professional transformation study groups facilitate the effectiveness of level three in the Pyramid Approach. The groups should establish the purpose for discussion sessions. Learning objectives should be agreed upon prior to discussion sessions. Obviously, the primary purpose is to improve student proficiency by examining and discussing research materials regarding capacity and effort-based concepts of ILs and students. Doing so naturally leads to improved professional practice and student learning due to the IL acquiring a research-based belief system. PTSGs have a slightly different focus from PLCs. They focus on practitioners' beliefs about professionals' and students' capacity as well as effort concepts ("grit").

Planning

Only high quality materials such as research-based articles, case studies, and personal success stories should be considered. If the materials are not research-based, the study sessions lose credibility. The number of participants will vary. Five to fifteen is a good number. A calendar of times and meeting dates should be agreed upon. Participants do not meet regularly all year, as do PLC participants. PTSG members organize one or two sessions a year. Each session meets three to five times.

After the first meeting, campus leadership should determine whether subsequent meetings will be voluntary or mandatory. Remember, if one's thinking is transformed, it is likely to occur during the reflection stage. PTSGs could be one component of an induction program for ILs new to the campus. PTSGs are designed to cultivate a culture that believes ILs can and should be effective. The same room should be reserved for all sessions. Consider a quiet area where the group will not be interrupted. Decide whether refreshments will be provided.

Facilitator

The facilitator keeps everyone on topic and moves the discussion forward. One facilitator may serve during all discussion sessions or the position may be rotated. After reading the material for discussion, the facilitator develops an outline that underscores critical information and attempts to connect it to the group's professional practice. Prepared questions and stories should be used to stimulate discussion.

Ground Rules

The group should establish ground rules for discussion sessions. For instance, be courteous, allow one person to speak at a time, genuinely listen, resist distractions, stay on topic, respect differences, and be patient. Such behaviors help to establish trust among members. In the absence of trust, members will hesitate to speak freely. Members should not attempt to convince others to change their views. Attempting to do so causes participants to become even more intransigent with regard to their beliefs about their own abilities and their students' capacity to learn.

The goal is to share research, case studies, and testimonials (stories) that will naturally lead to a transformation in one's thinking about human capacity to learn. We are more likely to facilitate this process with our questions and genuinely listening, not with assertions and convincing.

Reflections

Reflection is considered the centerpiece of professional transformational study sessions. Each member must commit to maintaining an open mind while engaging in discussions. Subsequently, members continue reflecting, weighing the pros and cons of the information discussed.

Reflection improves professional practice. It is at this stage that educators will begin to realize the ability to foster the student academic success they desire or be forced to accept the status quo. Be patient. Reflection does not necessarily cause an epiphany; professional transformation is incremental. It is a process. And the process is different for each individual member.

Evaluation

Student outcomes provide the best assessment of PTSGs' efforts. However, this process takes time, patience, trust, and perseverance. Members should be aware that they may not observe a direct cause-and-effect benefit as a result of their efforts. When I think of evaluating the effectiveness of PTSGs, I think of a duck in a pond. Above water, it may be difficult to discern the benefits PTSGs make on the belief system of ILs, while below water PLCs are working feverishly to augment the daily practice of ILs. They complement each other. As I indicated earlier, this process can be very effective in transforming how one thinks about capacity and effort concepts. During the evaluation stage, members should ask: What's the next step? Will there be follow-up sessions?

Transformation

The best evaluation will ultimately be personal, one's self-evaluation. Questions that should be asked by participants are: Did I maintain an open mind during the session? What questions do I still have? How has my professional practice been affected by our discussions and what I read? How will I use this information to improve student proficiency? Finally, did student proficiency improve because of my participation in professional transformation study groups?

Professional Transformation Study Group (PTSG)

Purpose:

_____

_____

_____

_____

Participants:

_____

_____

_____

_____

Planning:

_____

_____

_____

_____

Facilitator(s):

_____

_____

_____

_____

Ground Rules:

_____

_____

_____

Evaluation:

_____

_____

_____

_____

Consensus and Alignment

Consensus building is paramount to implementing school-wide efforts successfully. These efforts should be aligned with the campus vision. The campus vision can be used effectively as a catalyst to generate buy-in for the support of campus-wide strategies, to help build a consensus around them. I underscore that supporting school-wide efforts is an indication of the degree to which one embraces the campus vision.

When school-wide efforts are aligned with the campus vision, the vision and school-wide strategies will be in harmony. It is essential for daily professional practice to support the campus vision. In this process of consensus building, campus ILs should remember to identify the connectors on campuses and work to gain their support.

Data Analysis

Any school-wide plan developed with flawed or incomplete data is itself a flawed or incomplete plan. Hence, prudent ILs devote sufficient attention to analyzing all relevant campus, staff, parents, and student data. The analysis process should focus on two broad categories: one is a targeted approach, the other is generic. Targeted analysis is done to gain insights into specific areas ILs want to address. For example, the mathematics performance of the entire campus might be targeted.

Generic focus on data analysis attempts to review current research looking for pedagogical and structural methods that when applied school-wide will support and complement other strategies. For instance, requiring students to maintain portfolios might support more targeted instructional strategies in all classrooms. It should be noted that data analysis is not limited to student data.

It includes the entire operation of the campus. The library may need more books and technology. Parent meetings may need to be relocated to feeder campuses so they become more accessible to parents. The campus schedule may need to be modified to facilitate maximum learning. Anything that will improve the opportunity for all students learning at high levels should be on the table for consideration.

IMPLEMENTING AND MONITORING SCHOOL-WIDE
INSTRUCTIONAL STRATEGIES

Monitor Implementation

As with other outstanding organizations, successful campuses have a monitoring system in place. Monitoring, however, is a double-edged sword. That is, while it is essential to the implementation and maintenance of authentic performance, if applied inappropriately it can, and too often has, deleterious effects. It is human nature to seek a certain degree of independence. And when independence is minimized, buy-in decreases. The insightful campus IL strives to replace professional practice that relies solely on independence for professional practice that is supported by interdependence. By doing so, classroom ILs more fully embrace school-wide plans, because not only do they feel a sense of independence, they also recognize the interconnectedness with their colleagues.

This type of interconnectedness has a powerful and lasting impact on the performance of all ILs. They understand that other ILs expect and trust that every team member is supporting the vision of the campus. Interdependence naturally leads to individual and team monitoring. Once this level of commitment occurs, implementation of school-wide instructional strategies takes on a life of its own.

I have observed classroom ILs at this point engage in reflective practice as they begin to self-correct their own professional methods. They begin to discuss and share more, all the time understanding reciprocal benefits of team trust. DuFour and Eaker recommend four critical questions team members should consider (1998, p. 28):

- What is our fundamental purpose?
- What do we hope to achieve?
- What strategies are available for becoming better?
- What criteria will we use to assess our improvement efforts?

Low-Achieving School-Wide Strategies

Certain strategies are guaranteed to thwart efforts to establish effective school-wide instructional strategies. The following attitudes will limit success:

- Convincing yourself and others that whatever we do will be an "exercise in futility."
- Utilizing curriculum materials and methods that are not aligned with current learning objectives.
- If your students are not mastering the curriculum, blame the parents and the previous instructors.

- You are not the reading teacher; therefore, it is not your responsibility to teach reading comprehension skills and writing to students with deficient literacy skills.
- You do not assign home assignments because students will not complete them.
- You do not work well within a team because you know what you are going to do and someone may take credit for your ideas.
- You are a new employee at "Want To Be Great School" or you are transferring to another campus next year; hence, students' academic proficiency is not a priority for you.
- While you would not publicly admit it, you know the students at "Want To Be Great School" do not possess the intellectual capacity to demonstrate proficiency with rigorous curricula.

Improve Students' Thinking

Research supports the need to teach thinking at all levels in schools. There is a high correlation between quality thinking and quality learning. One will not exist without the other. Thinking can be taught and effectively monitored. Following are research-based methods and strategies that foster improved critical thinking.

Metacognition

ILs can significantly improve students' thinking by deliberately teaching the process of quality thinking. In too many classrooms, some ILs behave as though the quality of thinking is constant, that you either have the ability to engage in quality analyses or you don't. Research does not support this belief. Richard Paul defines metacognition as thinking about thinking while you're thinking in order to make your thinking better (2005).

Costa says students learn to metacogitate when teachers ask them to describe and discuss the plans and processes they use to solve problems (2001). One can only imagine how much the quality of students' thinking would improve if they were asked to do this on a daily basis. There are times when teaching methods stifle quality thinking. For example, when students are given the "one best" method to think or when students are:

- not allowed to share their thinking process in class;
- assigned to classroom ILs who believe waiting for students to discover solutions is an ineffective use of class time;
- assigned classroom ILs who do not give students partial credit for having the wrong answer even though they employed credible methods;
- assigned classroom ILs who do not model their thinking out loud for students to observe.

Thinking Questions—Socratic Method

When students uncover, discover, find, investigate, and conclude for themselves, the end result is richer and has a deep, lasting impact on their learning. Questions that engender little or no thinking should not be asked.

These types of questions are pervasive in too many classrooms. Costa offers an example of the type of question that limits thinking: "Who can tell me . . . ?" This type of question suggests not everyone can contribute, while questions like, "What do we know about . . . ?" send a signal the IL expects everyone to reflect and be ready to respond (2001). This simple example can be used to initiate a serious dialogue in grade-level and departmental team meetings to begin discussing the quality of questions classroom ILs ask every day. I cannot think of a better place to start when planning school-wide instructional strategies than improving the quality of questions students encounter in classrooms. A questioning classroom is a thinking and learning classroom.

Instructional leaders understand that well planned questions often are as important as the responses they generate. Recall I indicated in the introduction, the wrong answer to the right question is more important than the right answer to the wrong question. Effective classroom ILs strive to get the questions right. They utilize wait time and encourage students' questions. Many times the questions asked by students themselves are more helpful than the ones asked by classroom ILs. Carl Smith (1992) reinforces the value of student-generated questions.

The powerful impact questions have on students' learning is not a new phenomenon. Over two thousand years ago, the ancient Greeks such as Aristotle, Plato, and Socrates understood their impact on knowledge acquisition and exploited it. I am convinced answering questions with questions, while offering cues and prompts that ultimately lead students to quality solutions, engender real learning. Some have labeled this style of instruction the Socratic Method.

The more opportunities students are given to practice their thinking, the better they become at it (Costa, 2001). Richard Paul (1993) delineates certain thinking questions worthy of consideration. He espouses that one should employ thinking that identifies elements of thought that are present in all analyses about any problem. One then attempts to make logical connections between those elements and the problem under consideration. That is, one should identify commonalities in quality thinking that can be applied to any given problem. To foster this kind of thinking, he postulates the thinker will regularly ask similar kinds of questions as these:

- What is the purpose of my thinking?
- What precise question am I trying to answer?

- Within what point of view am I thinking?
- What information am I using?
- How am I interpreting that information?
- What concepts or ideas are central to my thinking?
- What conclusions am I coming to?
- What am I taking for granted? What assumptions am I making?
- If I accept the conclusions, what are the implications?
- What would the consequences be if I put my thoughts into action? (p. 22)

Benjamin Bloom, a psychologist, developed a hierarchy of questions that are familiar to educators. Notice his hierarchy has been slightly revised by one of his former student, Lorin Anderson, and a group of researchers. They changed his six major categories from noun to verb forms. Synthesis is now at the very top of the hierarchy in their version and renamed — creating. In addition, evaluating is below creating. However, the core premise of Bloom's hierarchy remains the same.

Reflecting upon its relevance and utilizing it appropriately supports a "thinking questions" learning environment. Bloom theorizes six levels of the cognitive domain ranging from the lowest level (knowledge) to the highest and most complex (evaluation). (See Table 2.2.)

Appropriately designed thinking questions lead readers, writers, and learners in general to utilize the following thinking skills effectively: predicting, classifying, comparing, and sequencing (Commission on Reading, 1985). In addition, highlighted are other types of thinking skills that support quality learning: decision making, problem solving, drawing conclusions, recognizing cause and effect, and distinguishing fact from opinion (Costa, 2001).

Original Version (Nouns)	Revised Version (Verbs)	Possible terms for framing questions
1. Knowledge	**Remembering:** Recognizing or recalling knowledge from memory. Remembering is when memory is used to produce definitions, facts, or lists, or recite or retrieve material.	name, define, list, memorize, recall, repeat,
2. Comprehension	**Understanding:** Constructing meaning from different types of functions be they written or graphic messages activities like interpreting, exemplifying, classifying, summarizing, inferring, comparing, and explaining.	restate, paraphrase, classify, describe, discuss, explain, express, identify, locate, recognize, report, review, select, translate,
3. Application	**Applying:** Carrying out or using a procedure through executing, or implementing. Applying related and refers to situations where learned material is used through products like models, presentations, interviews, or simulations.	apply, choose, demonstrate, dramatize, employ, illustrate, interpret, operate, practice, schedule, sketch, solve, use, write
4. Analysis	**Analyzing:** Breaking material or concepts into parts, determining how the parts relate or interrelate to one another or to an overall structure or purpose. Mental actions included in this function are differentiating, organizing, and attributing, as well as being able to distinguish between the components or parts. When one is analyzing he/she can illustrate this mental function by creating spreadsheets, surveys, charts, or diagrams, or graphic representations.	appraise, compare, contrast, criticize, differentiate, distinguish, examine, experiment, question
5. Syntheses	**Evaluating:** Making judgments based on criteria and standards through checking and critiquing. Critiques, recommendations, and reports are some of the products that can be created to demonstrate the processes of evaluation. In the newer taxonomy evaluation comes before creating as it is often a necessary part of the precursory behavior before creating something.	arrange, compose, assemble, construct, create, design, develop, formulate write
6. Evaluation	**Creating:** Putting elements together to form a coherent or functional whole; reorganizing elements into a new pattern or structure through generating, planning, or producing. Creating requires users to put parts together in a new way or synthesize parts into something new and different a new form or product. This process is the most difficult mental function in the new taxonomy.	arrange, compose, assemble, construct, create, design, develop, formulate write

Table 2.2. Blooms Hierarchy of Questions and Anderson's Revisions

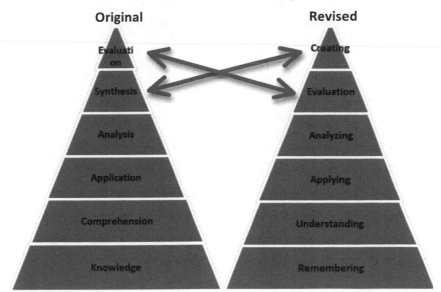

Figure 2.2.

When discussing the development of students' analytical growth, ILs should identify the specific skills students will be expected to master. Costa and Kallick offer sixteen such analytical skills they label "habits of mind" (2008). They say these habits of mind transcend all subject matters commonly taught in school. They are the characteristics high performers possess. "A Habit of Mind is a pattern of intellectual behaviors that lead to productive actions" (Costa and Kallick, 2008, p. 16). Costa and Kallick are quick to point out these sixteen characteristics are not intended to suggest that there are no other worthy intellectual behaviors, but that these sixteen are indeed significant.

Habits of Mind

Employing habits of mind requires drawing forth certain patterns of intellectual behavior that produce powerful results. They are a composite of many skills, attitudes, and proclivities including the following:

- Value: Choosing to employ one pattern of intellectual behavior rather than another less productive pattern.
- Inclination: Feeling the tendency toward employing a pattern of intellectual behavior.
- Sensitivity: Perceiving opportunities for, and appropriateness of, employing the pattern of behavior.
- Capability: Possessing the basic skills and capacities to carry through with the behaviors in the pattern.

- Commitment: Constantly striving to reflect on and improve performance of the pattern of intellectual behavior.

The sixteen habits of mind identified by Costa and Kallick include the following:

- Persisting
- Thinking and communicating with clarity and precision
- Managing impulsivity
- Gathering data through all senses
- Listening with understanding and empathy
- Creating, imagining, innovating
- Thinking flexibly
- Responding with wonderment and awe
- Thinking about thinking (metacognition)
- Taking responsible risks
- Striving for accuracy
- Finding humor
- Questioning and posing problems
- Thinking interdependently
- Applying past knowledge to new situations
- Remaining open to continuous learning

The habits of mind encourage and support "thinking questions." Costa recommends the best method to teach the habits of mind is for teachers to model them in class (2009). As ILs improve the quality of questions in the classroom, increased students' proficiency will naturally follow. Students should be challenged to think by asking them how, why, and what they are thinking. Barell declares the best question ILs can ask students is, "How do you know?" (2003, p. 129).

This question is powerful and thought-provoking. ILs will do well to ensure it and similar questions permeate the entire campus. Implementing school-wide strategies provides a systematic way of infusing "thinking questions" into every classroom. Barell (2003) offers a list of different types of "thinking questions" for consideration:

- Elaborating on your thinking

  - Will you please tell us more? We're interested in your thoughts; will you share them?

- Clarifying, explaining

  - Can you explain or expand on your thinking?

- Seeking relationships

  - How can you relate this to what Jennifer has said or to other concepts?

- Sharing feelings
  - How does this make you feel?
- Seeking reasons for conclusions
  - How do you know? What led you to that conclusion?
- Encouraging students to develop metacognitive awareness
  - Can you tell us how you figured that out? (2003, p. 53)

Research and practice have identified two basic teaching methods: direct instruction and constructivist teaching. When used appropriately, both enhance students' learning and promote the use of "thinking questions." Direct instruction is teacher centered while constructivist teaching is student centered. The two methods can complement each other by utilizing direct instruction to present essential concepts followed by using constructivist teaching methods to promote higher-level analysis. Constructivist teaching will be discussed first, followed by an outline of direct instruction methods.

Constructivist Strategies

One of the best methods to incorporate critical analysis in every lesson is for ILs to first use the principles of constructivist teaching. According to Thomas Sergiovanni, constructivism embraces five broad purposes of schooling: "helping students to communicate effectively, to know, to think, to be good, and to commit to something by learning to do it well" (1996, p. 129).

This type of teaching supports the maintenance of learning communities. Constructivist methods strive to travel beyond simple recall knowledge. They lead students to acquire knowledge in order to build new knowledge. It is essential that students integrate their new knowledge with existing knowledge and for students to monitor their learning and problem solving. Knowledge and process should be blended in a way that leads to students acquiring important content while enhancing their analytical skills.

In others words, ILs should teach in a way that promotes students' ability to master content and apply that information efficiently in the real world. This type of teaching and learning supports the notion that students learn best by doing. Sergiovanni identified nine principles of constructivist research (1996, pp. 133–34). I have summarized them as follows:

- Not all subject-matter content is equal in teaching for understanding. The most powerful subject matter generates thinking about real-life issues, and such generative subject matter should dominate the curriculum.

- Less is more. It is better to cover less subject matter but cover it well.
- Combining process with substance is unbeatable. The most powerful learning opportunities exist when challenging and interesting subject matter is taught in a context that helps students learn how to think.
- Project planning and teaching is better than lesson planning and teaching. It involves students in an in-depth investigation of disciplinary and interdisciplinary problems.
- Students are more producers of knowledge than they are consumers of it. What students learn does not automatically follow from what they are taught.
- Teaching and learning must be personalized. By doing so, teachers are able to help students construct their own knowledge.
- The best indicator of what a student knows is in the work itself. The work of students is important, and should comprise a record to be revisited by classroom ILs and students for further teaching and assessment.
- An important aspect of teaching understanding is setting up social norms that promote respect for other people's ideas. It encourages the sharing of ideas.
- The aim of teaching is to provide the conditions for learning. Simply delivering concepts, facts, and ideas to students is secondary.

Direct Instruction Models

Studies have consistently shown that direct instruction can be effective in promoting students' high academic achievement. Direct instruction stresses following a defined sequence of presenting the lesson. Madeline Hunter, Robert Marzano, and Gordon Cawelti offer three direct instruction models. All three models embrace five fundamental components of direct instruction: focus, modeling, guided practice, independent practice, and closure. Madeline Hunter's lesson design and direct teaching methods have been prominent among educational leaders for decades.

Table 2.3 is a summary of her eight-step lesson plan format (1984, pp. 169–92), followed by table 2.4 with Robert Marzano's seven elements of lesson design (2001, p. 84). Gordon Cawelti (1999, p. 14) delineated a six-phased process for direct instruction model, which is provided in table 2.5.

1. Anticipatory Set (focus)	The student's attention is drawn to what will be learned.
2. Purpose (objective)	The central purpose of the lesson is specifically stated and how students will benefit from it.
3. Input	Input outlines what students need to know to successfully master the lesson.
4. Modeling (show)	Classroom ILs demonstrate what students will be expected to do.
5. Guided Practice	Classroom ILs monitor students' progress as they practice.
6. Check Understanding	Classroom ILs answer students' questions to be sure students understand the lesson.
7. Independent Practice	Students practice what they have learned in groups.
8. Closure	Students demonstrate what they have learned.

Table 2.3. Madeline Hunter's Lesson Plan Format

1. Anticipatory Set	This is a mental set that causes students to focus on what they are expected to learn.
2. Objective and purpose	Students are apprised of the importance and purpose of the lesson.
3. Input	Students are apprised of what skills and knowledge are necessary to complete the lesson successfully.
4. Modeling	Classroom ILs model several options students might adopt to demonstrate mastery of the lesson.
5. Checking and Understanding	Before students are expected to perform a task, classroom ILs check for understanding.
6. Guided Practice	Students are given an opportunity to practice their newly acquired knowledge under direct classroom ILs' supervision.
7. Independent Practice	Students are allowed to practice only after they have demonstrated a level of competence acceptable to classroom ILs.

Table 2.4. Robert Marzano's Seven Elements of Lesson Design

1. Daily review, homework check, and, if necessary, re-teaching.
2. Presentation of new content and skills in small steps.
3. Guided student practice with close teacher monitoring.
4. Corrective feedback and instructional reinforcement.
5. Independent practice in seatwork and homework with a high (more than 90%) success rate.
6. Weekly and monthly reviews.

Table 2.5. Gordon Cawelti's Six-Phased Process for Children

There has to be a recommitment to teaching differently if students are going to improve the quality of their thinking. As mentioned earlier, I have observed classroom ILs successfully marry direct instruction and constructivist methods. For example, salient content and concepts might be introduced through direct instruction, followed by the utilization of constructivist methods that allow individual or group opportunities for students to apply this newly acquired knowledge by engaging in activities that facilitate analysis, synthesis, and evaluation.

Obviously, the reverse could be just as effective. The lesson might open with a problem. Then students would be given ample time to explore possible solutions. This process would be followed with the IL using direct instruction to fill in the missing pieces. There does not have to be an either/or solution.

In addition, ILs are unlearning the old three "Rs" (reading, writing, and arithmetic) and embracing the new ones: rigor, relevance, and relationships. Obviously, literacy, written composition, and mathematics are as critical as they have ever been; however, without ensuring that the new three "Rs" are completely infused into lessons school-wide, students will not realize the gains ILs seek. ILs, in learning-team meetings, should agree upon definitions of these terms.

Everyone should know and agree how they look and apply to effective teaching and learning. I say this because research studies have revealed the primary distinction in teaching mathematics between higher achieving countries and the United States is that U.S. educators focus more on process while higher achieving countries focus more on concepts (Stigler and Hiebert, 2009). Increasing the number of problems that focus on procedures is not rigor. Highlighted below are definitions of the new three "Rs" by Boggess (2007):

- Rigor: It is shifting focus from quantity to quality. More of the same is far from rigor. When rigor is instilled in the classroom, students will regularly work above average on Bloom's taxonomy, and engage in analysis, synthesis, and evaluation.

- Relevance: It complements rigor. Regardless of how rigorous learning becomes, if it is not relevant, learning is misaligned. Students may be knowledgeable but unable to apply their knowledge in the real world.
- Relationships: As stated earlier, students do not care what ILs know until they know that they care. Students are more motivated to learn in the atmosphere of a safe, caring classroom.
- When school-wide strategies seem to produce mediocre results, prudent ILs revisit the implementation of these new three "Rs."

Processing Information

Students sometimes need help with processing information that is needed to understand more difficult concepts (Marzano, 2009). Marzano delineates five simple strategies that can assist students and ILs.

- Chunking: During a lesson, ILs should consider progressing from the piece to the whole. That is, divide information into easily learnable pieces. Pause during the lesson to give students an opportunity to interact and process information.
- Scaffolding: The lesson should have a clean and logical sequence to it. Students should be able to connect the first, second, and third parts of the lesson to make sense of their learning.
- Interacting: The key point here is to ascertain how effectively students are processing new information. They might be grouped to discuss and summarize what they just learned, while the IL observes and asks questions to see how much they comprehend.
- Pacing: ILs adjust the speed at which learning progresses.
  - Naturally, students' comprehension influences pacing. Effective ILs realize they are teaching the students, not the material.
- Monitoring: Effective ILs teach a little and check a little all the time, monitoring the mastery level of students.

Once students demonstrate comprehension, I believe ILs should utilize school-wide instructional strategies to provide opportunities for students to apply, analyze, synthesize, and evaluate their newly acquired knowledge or concepts.

Re-teach and Reassess

When ILs take responsibility for students' learning, achievement improves. It follows then that re-teaching and reassessing instructional strategies should be incorporated into the teaching cycle in all class-rooms. When student assessments reveal less than acceptable results, ILs should not only ask what mistakes students made but what mistakes they themselves made.

Some strategies that embrace re-teaching and reassessing are tutoring, homework, and designing lessons that continuously revisit and reinforce concepts and knowledge previously introduced. ILs who teach in this way know they are more effective, and they firmly believe students have the capacity to learn. And it is this belief that leads to their perseverance in motivating their students and tapping into their individual learning styles. To claim "I taught it but they didn't learn it" is to engage in "fighting the wrong battle."

Learning-styles models are built on the assumptions that learners differ significantly in their styles of learning, that those styles can be assessed, and that knowledge of which styles work for which students can help both teachers and learners (Glatthorn, Boschee, and Whitehead, 2009). The following are well established learning styles: auditory, visual, kinesthetic, global, and analytic.

A cautionary note regarding learning styles; not everyone is convinced of their veracity in education. Riener and Willingham (2010) reported the data supporting this approaching to teaching is essentially hyperbole. Still, while one style of learning may or may not prove superior for particular individuals, we all benefit from exposure to multiple methods of instructional delivery. Hence, effective instructional leaders should ensure students have frequent opportunities to hear, see, and become physically engaged with their schoolwork. Doing it this way minimizes the need for re-teaching and reassessing students.

Feedback

Feedback can be formative or summative. Summative is generally a cumulative assessment at the end of a lesson or unit. Formative, on the other hand, is continuous, ongoing, and used to guide instruction. It should be specific and closely related to students' performance. Some have described this process as "teach a little, check a little." Praise should be relevant, meaningful, and not overused. ILs should recognize they are not teaching content but rather students who possess different skill levels. And many of these students process information differently; hence, feedback is imperative for deep and lasting mastery to occur.

Another reason feedback is so powerful is that it enables ILs to correct students' performance and thinking processes immediately. On top of this, teaching students metacognition skills allows them to provide feedback to themselves as they engage in the lesson. They are able to think about their own thinking and performance and apply this information to self-correct. Specific individual feedback preempts having to re-teach.

Further, Paul Black and Dylan William (1998) concluded effective feedback can add an equivalent of two grade levels to students' achievement. Specifically, when feedback is utilized properly, students are able to answer three questions regarding learning objectives (Hattie, 2012):

- What is the goal?
- How am I going there?
- What is the next step?

ILs should communicate the goals of the lesson. These goals must be challenging but not so challenging that they discourage effective effort. ILs and students should monitor progress toward achieving these goals. At this point, students should be informed of a plan or process designed to move them from a starting point to a level of mastery.

In other words, answer the question: How am I going to get there? Students should be informed concisely in descriptive terms what they are doing well and what they need to work on—strategies. Ideally, students begin to anticipate the answer to the third question: What is the next step? The focus should be upon comparing students to established criteria, not a comparison among students. As a result, students' motivation increases at each succeeding step. The primary purpose of feedback is to ensure continuous student academic progress occurs.

Moreover, ILs should benefit from regular discussions regarding the effective use of feedback. For example, they might discuss when and how to provide descriptive feedback to individual students, small groups, and the whole class. How frequently should it be given? What is too little or too much feedback?

To illustrate the importance of effective feedback, I am reminded of a story by an unnamed author. A mother wishing to encourage her young son's piano performance took him to hear a famous concert pianist. While briefly visiting with a friend sitting behind them, the little boy walked behind the stage and gazes at a door that said, "No Admittance."

Suddenly, the lights dimmed and as the mother turned around, she noticed her son was no longer sitting next to her. The curtains opened and he was sitting at the piano attempting to play the tune she had been teaching him.

At that moment, the great master piano player walked on stage, sat next to the little boy and whispered in his ear, "You can do this. You are on the right track." He quickly placed his left hand next to the boys left and played the correct tune for him. Next, he placed his right arm around the child and continued to play as he stated, "Here is the next step."

To everyone's amazement, the artist gradually stopped playing and the boy continued to play on his own. Together, the master teacher and student transformed an unsettling and challenging event into a wonderful learning experience. Mom and the audience were mesmerized. This is the power of effective feedback.

The next time your students set out to accomplish great feats, I hope they listen carefully; and then hear your voice whispering in their ear, "You can do this. You are on the right track. Here is the next step."

In summary, here are some specific components for effective use of feedback:

- Set challenging goals.
- Explain to students that with hard work, they have the ability to achieve established goals.
- Number and letter grades are not effective feedback.
- Offer descriptive information about what was done well and what needs to improve.
- Praise students' effort.
- Do not confuse praise with feedback.
- Feedback should be given frequently.
- Teach students to use a problem solving model that facilitates self-assessing their own learning—metacognition.
- Information that focuses on process yields greater gains than focusing on absolute performance.
- Promote the belief that failure is a part of learning.

Retention Reduction

The research is mixed regarding the negative impact or benefits that retention has on students (Jimerson, 1999). However, Sagor declares that "most retained students experience far more damage than benefits from this practice" (2000, p. 40). He continues by also asserting that only about a fourth of students profit from retention. Yet, other researchers are not so optimistic that a fourth of retained students benefit from grade retention. These researchers concluded that few if any students benefit from being retained in school.

They studied students who were similar in academic performance. Some were retained and some were promoted. A year later, the promoted group demonstrated better academic performance, healthier social skills, and had a more positive perception of school (Berliner & Glass, 2014; Jimerson & Renshaw, 2012). Still, supporters of retention argue that retention reinforces high standards. And opponents express that it lowers students' self-image. Wherever the truth lies, I am convinced that the vast majority who recommend retention do not request a second year to accelerate the learning of those same students. Another point worth noting is that some high performing countries like Finland and Korea rarely permit students to be retained (Berliner & Glass, 2014).

I recall as a kindergarten student there were several distinct rows of students. The IL seemed to have different assignments for each row. Sometimes she would intermingle assignments across rows. Later in the school year, I understood that there were three different grade levels in one classroom and that when appropriate she assigned what was deemed second grade work to first graders and first grade work to kindergarteners.

Today we would refer to this type of teaching as differentiated instruction. Also in this class there were times the older students assisted the younger ones. This was a small private school so I am sure students were arranged in this manner for economic reasons. I wonder if the arrangement of that classroom offers another way to think about retention. I am not suggesting multiage groups. Given that neither seems to work well, do campuses have to choose between retention and social promotion? Is there middle ground?

Retention implies students who fail to demonstrate academic proficiency would benefit from having additional time to learn. Repeating the same grade is one way to provide extra time. There are, however, other effective ways to increase students' opportunity to learn during the regular school year other than retention. Research has demonstrated the benefits of the following: tutoring, mentoring, emphasis on learning styles, after-school programs, and summer school programs specifically designed to redress students' academic deficiencies. Take Korea for example. It is a world leader in education and seven out of ten students participate in tutoring classes. In the United States, less than two in ten students take tutoring after school (Ripley, 2013). Further, ILs should recognize the benefits of summer school on student achievement.

Karl Alexander and his colleagues have accumulated more than twenty years of research in this area and assert that summer learning rooted in family and community influences widens the achievement gap across social lines, while schooling offsets those same types family and community influences (2007). They stress that students of low socioeconomic backgrounds, compared to students of high socioeconomic backgrounds, perform less well academically because of the stark disparity between the quality of their summer experiences. They conclude that summer school neutralizes many of these background experiences. Additionally, vertical team articulation among grade levels can be used as an alternative to retention.

I have observed athletes stepping on and off a weight scale several times before accepting the results. They were behaving as though they thought repeating what they had just done would alter the previous results. I believe achievement will improve when more ILs begin thinking differently about retention. More of the same is not what is needed. Some retention factors are universal; however, some are campus specific and require uniquely tailored approaches filled with sufficient amounts of care and research-based school-wide strategies. The dropout rate alone should be motivation enough to engender a reassessment of retention practices. Retention is one of the primary indicators of future dropouts.

And further, everything done in the name of high standards is not always best for students (Kohn, 2000).

Not only should ILs consider the impact retention has on the individual students being held back, but they should also weigh the pros and cons retention might have on students who are promoted. One research study, headed by Clara Muschkin at Duke University, discovered that retaining students may negatively impact the overall climate of the campus. Specifically, they discovered if 20 percent of students were older than their pears, the chances that other students would commit an infraction or be suspended increased by 200 percent (Stancill, 2014).

Portfolios

Student portfolios complement school-wide instructional strategies by providing feedback. They provide effective means of helping teachers and parents reflect on student growth over time. Over time, they can become a bridge that connects ILs, parents, and students. Progress of students is conveniently catalogued and monitored. For example, students can log summaries of books they are reading.

This is an excellent strategy to get students hooked on reading and writing. They can be used to teach note-taking and study skills. Parents can be encouraged to sign students' work and return it to school. Students are able to track and monitor their own academic progress. Many begin to take pride in their visible improvement. In most instances, the portfolio is more authentic and representative of students' skill level than grades on report cards. They also indicate the level of rigor employed within each classroom. Robert Marzano (2003, pp. 39–46) recommends three action steps to implement challenging goals and effective feedback:

- Implement an assessment system that provides timely feedback on specific knowledge and skills for specific students.
- Establish specific challenging achievement goals for the school as a whole.
- Establish specific goals for individual students.

The effective utilization of student portfolios can undergird these three action steps. These action steps also highlight strategies previously discussed: rigor and feedback.

Curriculum Alignment—Opportunity to Learn

More than 130 research studies underscore the relationship between opportunity to learn and students' academic achievement level (Cawelti, 1999). Curriculum alignment between subjects is a central key to ensuring students have an adequate opportunity to learn. Curriculum alignment has several components: recommended, written, supported, taught, tested, and learned.

The recommended curriculum is the suggested curriculum by experts and scholars. The written curriculum is a detailed cataloging of the recommended. The supported curriculum focuses on time allocation and resources. The taught curriculum is what classroom ILs actually deliver in class. The tested curriculum is the curriculum that is assessed.

Finally, the learned curriculum is all that students have learned because of being on campus, particularly what is learned in class (Glatthorn, Boschee, and Whitehead, 2009). ILs should be keenly aware of the significance of curriculum alignment. That is, there has to be a good fit among various curricula. The most sophisticated school-wide instructional plans will not advance all students' learning unless they are broadly applied. Otherwise, the opportunity for students to learn will be compromised.

Curriculum alignment, time, resource allocation, classroom management, and school climate all affect opportunity to learn. Hence, alignment is essential for maximum learning. In fact, the highest level of math studied in 9-12 schools is the strongest predictor in post-secondary school (Jeannie et al., 2000).

Further, textbooks often do not cover the breadth and depth required for student mastery. Ultimately the classroom IL must ensure students have an appropriate opportunity to learn. Obviously, the quality of students' learning is impacted by the knowledge level of classroom ILs. Developing strategies to address these issues is not a simple matter. There is not enough time in the current system to address all the content in states required curriculum. So what can ILs do? Below Marzano offers five recommended action steps to improve opportunity to learn.

- Identify and communicate the content considered essential for all students versus that considered supplemental or necessary only for those seeking postsecondary education.
- Ensure that the essential content can be addressed in the amount of time available for instruction.
- Sequence and organize the essential content in such a way that students have ample opportunity to learn it.
- Ensure teachers address the essential content.
- Protect the instructional time that is available.

In future chapters, I make the point that beliefs matter and that students can be taught to be effective in their efforts. Therefore, it follows that essential elements of curriculum alignment and opportunity to learn include a research-based belief system held by ILs, and students learning that as their effort increases so does their proficiency. If ILs are going to realize the level of students' achievement they espouse, they will first have to have candid, ongoing dialogue with their colleagues regarding these issues—beliefs and effort. Further, this kind of dialogue must generate effective action.

Vocabulary Development—Background Knowledge

Researchers consistently point out that high achieving students possess a more comprehensive vocabulary than their lower-achieving classmates. This fact alone should be used as a catalyst for ILs to consider implementing school-wide vocabulary development strategies. While there is great agreement regarding the benefits of teaching vocabulary development, again there is debate about what is the best way to teach it.

For example, direct instruction versus constructivist teaching has been debated for decades. Moreover, the answer does not completely rest with either one but with both. Some believe there is just not enough time to teach vocabulary development independently (Stahl and Fairbanks, 1986). While others such as Marzano espouse that direct teaching of vocabulary is more productive, he also acknowledges the benefits of comprehensive reading strategies. I highlight three instructional strategies he offers: 1) expose students to a variety of quality life experiences; 2) engage students in reading programs that focus on vocabulary development; and 3) introduce vocabulary terms and phrases that are specific to the content being taught (Marzano, 2003).

Additionally, studies have shown vocabulary acquisition and high achievement are positively correlated with the number of books students have access to. On some campuses, students are not allowed to take textbooks home. Only one book at a time may be checked out of the library. In many instances, students' access to the campus library is limited; often it closes when the last bell rings. Libraries have become media centers filled with computers. This is great, but computers should not be substituted for books; we need both. Students in some communities have limited access to books and technology at home and would benefit from being exposed to as many books as possible at school (Coyle, 2009).

Establishing diverse, high-interest, libraries in every classroom would improve students' vocabulary development. I recall on one campus, we purchased high-interest paperback books. We explained to students that they would not be graded for reading these materials. After advertising the many titles and genres available to students, we invited them to select as many books as they desired. We also explained there was no one available to record who selected which titles; hence, there was only one rule: the books must be returned to school. As you might imagine, many of the paperbacks were never returned.

There are two interesting aspects to this experience. First, we didn't particularly want the books returned. Our goal was to improve reading and vocabulary by increasing access to and interest for reading books. And second, we observed students whispering about who had a copy of a title they wanted and wondering whether someone would trade books. The paperbacks were being discussed between classes, during lunch, and before and after school. Following are vocabulary-acquisition strategies ILs should implement as appropriate:

- High-interest classroom libraries
- Silent reading
- Teach root words
- Use portfolios to catalogue vocabulary words
- Combine reading and writing activities
- Quality field trips that support vocabulary acquisition
- Compare and contrast key terms
- Display key terminology in classroom
- Reinforce the use of new words

Classroom Management

Classroom management is a prerequisite to effective teaching and learning. The most effective teachers in this area are those who take responsibility for the climate in their classroom. Years ago, I attended an educational conference in Cincinnati, Ohio. While there, I toured a demonstration campus. William Glasser, the psychiatrist and classroom management theorist, was presenting a lesson to a group of students in attendance at that campus. I was observing from the hall when he stepped in the doorway for a brief moment.

I recall asking him what I could say to teachers that might assist with classroom management. He responded simply, "They have to be believable to their students." I am convinced his response is correct. While classroom management strategies are important, they are not as important as the person who implements them. Students have a sixth sense that enables them to identify ILs who are apprehensive. To new or experienced classroom ILs, I offer the same recommendations:

- Know yourself.
- Rehearse a believable three-to-five-minute speech designed to set the tone for the year. Deliver it on the first day and the very second all students are seated.
- Know your subject matter.
- Communicate in various ways that you care about your students.
- The first time contacting parents should be to offer positive reports.
- Develop and consistently maintain a few routines and procedures.
- Correct the class, not individual students, when possible.
- Effective instructional delivery preempts many potential classroom management issues.
- Always be calm and professional. Sarcasm does not work, and indeed causes much damage.

- Listen to your students and connect with them.

In addition, think about classrooms that create a caring environment and compare them to classrooms where you might here the following: "You all act like you don't have any home training! Now that was stupid." It is not surprising that ILs who make similar statements generally have more student discipline problems than those who cultivate positive relationships with their students. Even when these types of comments are framed as irony or "just kidding," they create problems. Learning is diminished in an environment where students feel devalued.

Secret to Classroom Management

Over the years, I have asked teachers with effective classroom management skills what their secret was. They generally said something like, "I love all of them." "I am fair." "I have just a few rules." "I am consistent" but above all, one teacher's answer struck me as being the real key to successful classroom management. She said, "I give them what they want most." Before I share her answer, I would like to tell you a story about John Lister.

John had a friend, Joe Davis. Really, he was more like family—an uncle or stepdad. It had been a while since John had seen him, the elderly man. He had been very busy jumping hurdles in his own life: his job and just life itself were nonstop. He was chasing his dream. In fact, he had very little time for his own family.

One day his mom called to tell him his mentor, Mr. Joe Davis had died. The funeral was soon and Mr. Davis had been like a stepdad to John after John's dad died. Because John was so busy, he thought Mr. Davis had died long ago. John's mom reminded him of the many fun times he and Mr. Davis had when John was a boy. He always talked about you John, his mom said. He loved recalling all of the things he taught you: carpentry, being a good boy and helping others. John told his mom that he owed most of his success to Mr. Davis. "I will take the time to attend his funeral mom."

After the funeral, John asked his mom where was the little box Mr. Davis kept on a stand in his home. His mom had no idea where it was. John asked him many times what was in that box. His response was always the same, "The thing I value the most." John commented, "I will never know what was so valuable to him."

Approximately a week after John returned home, he received a package from the post office. Inside the package was the little box John had asked about. He ripped open the package and immediately recognized the unique handwriting of Mr. Davis on the package. "Upon my death, please forward this box and its contents to John Lister. It's the thing I valued most in my life."

Tears in his eyes, John opened the box. Inside he found an attractive antique gold pocket watch. And inside its casing, he found these words engraved: "John thanks for your time, Joe Davis." The thing he valued most was my time. John cleared his calendar and vowed beginning this day he would give more of his time to others.

Returning to the secret of classroom management—respect and time. This is the answer I was given for creating an effective learning environment in the classroom. "I give them respect and my time," the IL said. Some students are a joy while others are more challenging. Both groups want to be respected and recognized by educators. Students connect with ILs who listen to them and show mutual respect. They just want educators to take a brief moment to get to know them—to care. Sometimes a few moments can make all the difference in the world to a student.

They want to talk about the topic of the day, their pet, lost supplies, upset friends and relatives, their job, school activities and occasionally, some of what is heard can be alarming. Pre-K–12, they all want the same thing, your validation of them and your time.

Showing respect means students should never be intentionally embarrassed. Shaming students can result in having a very quiet, even fearful group or anarchy. Either environment is unacceptable because students in these types of classrooms do not feel safe enough to study and learn effectively. The goal of appropriate classroom management is to maximize learning.

So give students respect and your time then watch them reciprocate by responding positively to your caring personality. Remember, they won't care about what you know until they know you care about them. This does not mean one has to exchange care for rigor. Both can coexist and should. Further, it is important that students feel that their classroom ILs want them to learn—not just so they can perform well on standardized tests, but for their overall long-term growth as well.

Homework

Homework should be meaningful. It should be graded in a timely fashion and used as feedback to guide students' academic growth. It should not be time consuming and overwhelming. Research has revealed homework is more effective in middle and high school than in elementary school. Also, designing homework assignments that focus on improving specific skills has shown to be extremely beneficial for students' academic development (Marzano, Pickering, and Pollock, 2001).

Differentiated Instruction

Differentiated instruction is another tool available to ILs. It essentially places emphasis on students producing the majority of the thinking and

work. The teacher considers content, process, and product when planning lessons. Content is focused on what knowledge or skill students will
acquire. Process provides the opportunity for students to internalize the
information to be learned (Tomlinson, 1999).

The classroom IL attempts to match the students' level of readiness
with the lesson. The product is an opportunity for students to utilize
learned content to produce an original piece of work or extend on the
knowledge gained. Students might be given an opportunity to develop a
project. In a differentiated classroom, students are given choices. There
are many instructional arrangements and various materials are provided.
The differentiated IL is in tune with the emotions of individual students,
not just the class as a whole. The IL frequently utilizes flexible groupings
of students. Assessment is ongoing. Differentiated instruction does not
mean differentiated achievement targets.

Reciprocal Teaching—Peer Tutoring

Research has long documented the beneficial effects of reciprocal
teaching. Reciprocal teaching methods allow the teacher of new information or skills to learn at the same time as the recipients of this new knowledge learn (Brandt, 2000). Students learn not only from ILs but from their
peers too. ILs should take full advantage of the rich learning opportunities peer tutoring offers. Students and teachers will benefit from this
type of experience.

WHAT WORKS BEST

We have discussed the importance of developing and implementing a
comprehensive school-wide instructional plan that works, one that has
the input and support of all ILs on campus. Possible strategies have been
outlined as well as a cautionary note regarding the pitfalls of "campus
learning disabilities." Each campus is unique and would benefit from the
design of strategies that embrace their unique needs. Notwithstanding
the uniqueness of campuses, most would like to know if some strategies
carry more punch than others.

John Hattie, a professor of education at the University of Auckland,
attempts to provide an answer. He is credited with conducting the most
comprehensive study regarding factors that affect students' learning. He
has compiled more than 800 meta-analyses of 50,000 research articles,
about 150,000 effect sizes, and about 240 million students (Hattie, 2012, p.
1). Table 2.6 highlights some of his findings regarding the strongest influences on students' achievement. These achievement influences should be
effectively incorporated into school-wide instructional strategies.

Influence	Effect Size	Percentile Gain
Feedback	1.13	40
Students' prior cognitive ability	1.04	34
Instructional quality	1.00	34
Direct instruction	.82	29
Remediation/feedback	.65	24
Students' disposition to learn	.61	23
Class environment	.56	21
Challenge of goals	.52	20
Peer tutoring	.52	19
Mastery learning	.50	19
Television	-12	-39
Retention	-15	-43

Table 2.6. John Hattie's Influences on Student Achievement

I have provided the equivalent percentile score for each effect size score. An explanation of effect size is provided with the table. For our purposes, we want to know which factors are most significant. They are listed in rank order. Because IL are the primary ones who provide feedback to students, notice no influence on students' learning is greater than that of educators. This is no surprise. Research has overwhelmingly documented that it is what the classroom IL knows and can demonstrate that makes the most dramatic impact on students' achievement (Wong, 2009; Hattie, 2003; Marzano, 2001). It follows that instructional strategies are effective but only to a point. The skill level of ILs determines whether the full benefit of strategies is realized.

Now note the first and last influences on student achievement—feedback and retention, respectively. It is imperative students receive immediate corrective feedback as needed. According to Hattie, retention may not be an effective instructional strategy. ILs should consider utilizing as many high-yield strategies as deemed appropriate to maximize achievement and minimize retention. Marzano, Pickering, and Pollock (table 2.7) also delineate instructional strategies that are highly correlated with student achievement (2001). Reflecting on these lists of research-based instructional strategies, I am reminded of Ron Edmonds. "We can, whenever and wherever we choose, successfully educate children whose schooling is of interest to us, and we already know more than we need to know to do that; and whether or not we do it must finally depend on how we feel about the fact that we haven't so far."

John Hattie explains that effect size, rather than other statistical measures; more accurately reflects what factors have the greatest impact on students' learning. For example, the effect size expresses how many standard deviations the average score of students engaged in peer tutoring (the experimental group) is above the average score for students (the control group) who did not engage in peer tutoring.

This means the peer tutoring group scored .50 standard deviations above the score of the average student who was not exposed to peer tutoring. In addition, an effect size of .50 is equivalent to a 19 percentile improvement for those students in peer tutoring compared to students not in peer tutoring. This is assuming all other factors are equal. For our purposes, however, we should note that the higher the effect size, the higher the percentile gain will be also. In addition, negative effect size scores indicate a negative influence on students' learning.

Marzano, like Hattie, developed a list of categories for instructional strategies and their impact on students' learning. They are listed in descending order beginning with the ones that impact learning most.

Category	Ave. Effect Size (ES)	Percentile Gain
Identifying similarities and differences	1.61	45
Summarizing and note-taking	1.00	34
Reinforcing effort and providing recognition	.80	29
Homework and practice	.77	28
Nonlinguistic representations	.75	27
Cooperative learning	.73	27
Setting objectives and providing feedback	.61	23
Generating and testing hypotheses	.61	23
Questions, cues, and advance organizers	.59	22

Table 2.7. Categories of Instructional Strategies That Affect Student Achievement. *Source:* **Marzano, Pickering, & Pollock, 2001.**

The predominant reason some schools do not develop high-performing students is because of the belief system held by a critical mass of ILs. Regardless of how sound school-wide strategies are, they will produce minimal success in this type of campus culture. The next chapter will offer recommendations for altering this type of misaligned thinking that significantly impedes learning for both ILs and students.

REFLECTIVE THOUGHTS

What are your thoughts and beliefs regarding the following statements, and how are they manifested in your daily practice?

- How can campus learning disabilities be overcome, and what are some you are aware of that have not been mentioned?
- What are your thoughts regarding opportunity to learn?
- What classroom management strategies work for you?
- What are your thoughts regarding retention?
- What are your ideas on "thinking questions"?

BARE FACTS

- Indeed, some instructional leaders don't believe, nor fully embrace, current research regarding student learning.
- Retention is one of the primary indicators of future dropouts.
- Give students respect and your time: then watch them reciprocate by responding positively to your caring personality.
- Everything done in the name of high standards is not always best for students.
- Effective classroom management is a prerequisite to successful teaching and learning.
- When placed in the same system, people, however different, tend to produce similar results.
- Regardless of the quality level of campuses, ineffective classroom ILs cannot hide.
- Assigning at-risk students to at-risk classroom ILs is detrimental to both groups.
- ILs should benefit from regular discussions regarding the effective use of feedback.
- Campus learning disabilities exist and must be overcome.
- When ILs are able to install a core set of instructional strategies and methods that permeate the entire campus, not only will successful ILs excel even higher, but all other classroom ILs will also.

REFERENCES

Alexander, K. L., Entwisle, D. R., Olson, L. S. (2007). Lasting consequences of the summer learning gap. *American Sociological Review, 72*, 167–80. http://www.nayre.org/Summer%20Learning%20Gap.pdf.

Anderson, L. W., and Krathwohl, D. R., et al (eds.). (2001). *A taxonomy for learning, teaching, and assessing: A revision of Bloom's taxonomy of educational objectives*. Boston, MA: Allyn & Bacon (Pearson Education Group).

Barell, J. (2003). *Developing more curious minds*. Alexandria, VA: ASCD.

Berliner, D., and Glass, F. (2014). *Myths and lies that threaten American public schools.* New York: Teachers College Press.

Black, P., and William, D. (1998). Assessment and classroom learning. *Assessment in Education: Principles, Policy, and Practice, 5*(1), 7–74.

Bloom's Hierarchy. New version: http://www.odu.edu/educ/roverbau/ Bloom/ bloom-staxonomy.htm.

Brandt, R. (2000). *Education in a new era.* Alexandria, VA: ASCD.

Boggess, J. (2007). Techniques. http://www.thefreelibrary.com/The+three+Rs+ redefined+for+a+flat+world.-a0163705846.

Cawelti, G. (1999). *Handbook of research on improving student achievement.* Arlington, VA: Educational Research Service.

Commission on Reading. (1985). *Becoming a nation of readers.* Washington, DC: National Institute of Education.

Costa, A.L., (2001). *Developing minds: A resource book for teaching thinking.* Alexandria, VA: ASCD.

Costa, A. L., and Kallick, B. (2008). *Learning and leading with 16 habits of mind.* Alexandria, VA: ASCD.

Costa, L., and Kallick, B. (2009). *Habits of mind across the curriculum.* Alexandria, VA: ASCD.

Coyle, D. (2009). *The talent code*: New York: Random House.

Danielson, C. (2002). *Enhancing student achievement.* Alexandria, VA: ASCD.

DuFour, R., and Eaker, R. (1998). *Professional learning communities at work.* Bloomington, IN: National Educational Services.

Edmonds, R. (1979). Effective schools for the urban poor. *Educational Leadership, 37*(15–18): 20–22.

Everett, R. M. (1971). *Communications of innovations.* New York: The Free Press.

Glatthorn, A., Boschee, F., and Whitehead, B. (2009). *Curriculum leadership: Strategies of development and implementation.* Thousand Oaks, CA: Sage Inc.

Hattie, J. (2003). *Teachers make a difference: What is the research evidence?* University of Auckland: Australian Council for Educational Research.

Hattie, J. (2012). *Visible learning for teachers: Maximum impact on learning.* New York: Routledge.

Hunter, M. (1984). Knowing, teaching, and supervising. In P. Hosfrod (Ed.), *Using what we know about teaching.* Alexandria, VA: ASCD.

Jeannie, O., et al. (2000). Coursetaking and achievement in mathematics and science. Retrieved from http://archive.wceruw.org/nise/News_Activities/Forums/ Oakespaper.htm.

Jimerson, S. R. (1999). On the failure of failure: Examining the association of early grade retention and late adolescent education and employment outcomes. *Journal of School Psychology, 37*, 243–72.

Jimerson, S., and Renshaw, T. (2012). Retention and social promotion. *Principal Leadership, 13*(1), 12–16.

Kohn, A. (Sept. 27, 2000). Standardized testing and its victims. *Education Week.*

Marzano, R. (2003). *What works in schools: Translating research into action.* Alexandria, VA: ASCD.

Marzano, R. (2009). Helping students process information. *Educational Leadership, 67*(2), 86–87.

Marzano, R., Pickering, D., and Pollock, J. (2001). *Classroom instruction that works: Research-based strategies for increasing student achievement.* Alexandria, VA: ASCD.

Paul, R. (1993). *Critical thinking: What every person needs to survive in a rapidly changing world.* Santa Rosa, CA: Foundation for Critical Thinking.

Paul, R. (2005). *Critical thinking: Tools for taking charge of your learning and your life.* Upper Saddle River, NJ: Prentice Hall.

Riener, C., and Willingham, D. T. (2010). The myth of learning styles. *Change, 42*, 32–35.

Ripley, A. (2013). *The smartest kids in the world.* New York: Simon and Schuster.

Sagor, R. (2000). *Guiding school improvement with action research*. Alexandria, VA: ASCD.

Sample, S. (2003). *The contrarians: Guide to leadership*. San Francisco, CA: Jossey-Bass.

Senge, P. M. (1990). *The fifth discipline: The art and practice of the learning organization*. New York: Currency Doubleday.

Sergiovanni, T. (1996). *Leadership for the schoolhouse*. San Francisco, CA: Jossey-Bass.

Smith, C. (1992). *A commitment to critical thinking*. Bloomington, IN: Grayson Bernard Publishers.

Stahl, S., and Fairbanks, M. (1986). The effects of vocabulary instruction: A model-based meta-analysis. *Review of Educational Research, 56*(1) 72–110.

Stancill, J. (2014). Discipline problems increase when students repeat a grade. ASCD SmartBrief February 28. Retrieved March 3, 2014.

Stigler, W. J., and Hiebert, J. *The teaching gap*. New York: Free Press.

Tolstoy, Leo. (1894). *The Kingdom of God is Within You*. Chapter III. http://www.kingdomnow.org/winyou03.html%20 (e-transcribed in 2002).

Tomlinson, C. (1999). *The differentiated classroom: Responding to the needs of all learners*. Alexandria, VA: ASCD.

Walberg, Herbert. (1984). Improving the productivity of America's schools. *Educational Leadership, 41*(8), 24.

Williams, B. (2003). *Closing the achievement gap: A vision for changing beliefs and practices*. Alexandria, VA: ASCD.

Willingham, D. T. (2012). *When can you trust the experts*. San Francisco, CA: Jossey-Bass

Wong, H., and Wong, R. (2009). *First days of school*. Mountain View, CA: Harry K. Wong Publications.

REFLECTIVE THOUGHTS

THREE

Select Believers and Develop a Research-Based Belief System

The illiterate of the twenty-first century will not be those who cannot read and write, but those who cannot learn, unlearn and relearn. — Alvin Toffler

BELIEFS MATTER! RHETORIC DOESN'T

When suspects in detective movies are brought to trial, three interesting questions are generally asked by the bailiff. "Will you tell the truth, the whole truth, and nothing but the truth?" With regard to the impact beliefs have on students' achievement, this chapter will answer these three questions forthrightly at its outset. The truth is, notwithstanding economic and political challenges, beliefs about all students' capacity to learn rigorous curricula are the number one impediment to realizing this very noble goal. The whole truth is that both innate ability and environment impact students' learning. Nothing but the truth is that students are smart enough to demonstrate proficiency with rigorous college preparatory curricula.

Bill Russell's teenage days underscore this point. When he was in high school, he tried out for the football and cheerleading teams. He did not make either team. He then tried out for the junior varsity basketball team. After completing tryouts, the coach passed out uniforms to fifteen players. That was the exact number of uniforms the school owned. Bill Russell was the sixteenth player. Based on his performance, he should have been released; however, he was allowed to join the team. "Bill candidly notes that he was clearly the worst of the sixteen that were left" (Nelson, 2005, p. 16). He and another player alternated suiting up for games.

Bill's basketball coach saw something the other two coaches apparently did not see. He perhaps saw something even Bill Russell did not see in himself. Bill developed into a fine basketball player. Actually, some consider him the best ever to play the game. Bill played on two NCAA championship teams, won an Olympic gold medal, and earned eleven NBA championship rings (Nelson, 2005).

Effective instructional leaders possess the same kind of insight as Bill's high school coach. They understand that while students enter the classroom at different levels of readiness, those same students possess approximately one hundred billion neurons of intellectual potential. This is significantly more intellectual capacity than is required to master rigorous curricula. These kinds of statements separate the believers and the nonbelievers. No, I am not referring to religion but to education. The believers and nonbelievers I am referencing are those ILs who believe (believers) emphatically that they possess the knowledge, skills, and teaching methods to cause students to become significantly smarter.

On the other hand, those nonbelievers believe students are born with innate abilities, and that it is those innate abilities that are the determining factors in their academic achievement. To be sure, innate ability does exist. Debating whether it exists or not misses the point. The central question for ILs is, "Do my students possess, or are they able to develop, the intellectual capacity to learn rigorous curricula?"

When discussing the research of psychologists regarding innate ability, Gladwell (2008) asserts achievement is a combination of talent and preparation and that the closer psychologists study this issue, "the smaller the role innate talent seems to play and the bigger the role preparation seems to play" (p. 38). The significance of preparation will be developed in the following chapter. Intelligence quotient (IQ) is not a topic generally discussed on campuses and, for that matter, it is not confronted head-on in many of the books written about education issues.

Some books address the beliefs of educators indirectly at best while others ignore it altogether. James Comer, a renowned Yale professor, also recognizes this belief issue as a concern. In 2008, he posted an open letter to the President of the United States on his website in which he stated, "It must be reconceptualized because traditional education is based on a wrong notion: a belief that academic-learning capacities are almost exclusively an outcome of genetically determined intelligence."

The Pyramid Approach makes the case that we cannot progress significantly from our current position in education until our belief system is aligned with our stated goal: "All children are educable." I define educable as demonstrating proficiency with rigorous college preparatory curricula. And I define "all" as all students except those who have been properly identified as having a congenital mental malady, or a student, who through injury, has an equivalent condition.

As you will see, this exception is a very small percentage of the total student population. And given recent research in the field of neuroplasticity, there are promising signs for many of these students as well. In this regard, Doidge (2007) writes, "I met people whose learning disorders were cured and whose IQs were raised" (p. xix). To illustrate how realistic and achievable "all" is, Arthur Jensen, a professor of educational psychology indicates:

> The four socially and personally most important threshold regions on the IQ scale are those that differentiate with high probability between persons who, because of their level of general mental ability, can or cannot attend a regular school (about IQ 50), can or cannot master the traditional subject matter of elementary school (about IQ 75), can or cannot succeed in the academic or college preparatory curriculum through high school (about 105), can or cannot graduate from an accredited four-year college with grades that would qualify for admission to a professional or graduate school (about 115). Beyond this, the IQ level becomes relatively unimportant in terms of ordinary occupational aspirations and criteria of success. (1980, p. 113)

Most would not consider Arthur Jensen's IQ threshold numbers to be written in stone. That is, there is variability within each threshold relative to students' motivation, effort, and other factors. However, I make the case that IQ altogether is unimportant for the purposes of ILs beyond providing assistance and programs for students who have been, using multiple measures, properly identified as needing those types of specialized services. Colvin (2008) agrees, saying, "The research tells us that intelligence as we usually think of it—a high IQ—is not a prerequisite to extraordinary achievement" (p. 45). IQ is rarely used by educators unless in a clinical context; to some it is a pejorative term.

However, euphemisms are too often used. For example, "They are doing as well as expected"; "my off-grade level babies," "my challenged students," "my slow group," or other pet names are expressed. "IQ teaching" or what I call "bell-curve teaching" adversely affects professional practice.

"Bell curve teaching" reminds me of a story about a master archer who wanted to become even better. So one day he decided to search the land for one who possessed even more expert skills. He traveled through the hills, small villages, and towns. No one demonstrated superior archery skills. Walking in the forest one morning, he spotted an arrow in a tree stuck in the dead center of a painted target. He was curious, so he scoured the area. To his amazement, he saw arrow after arrow in the bull's eye of painted targets throughout the forest. He knew he had finally located his mentor. Right outside the forest was another small town. He began inquiring about the expert archer who must live nearby. He was directed to a small house and barn filled with perfect arrow shots. He immediately saw a man walking awkwardly out of the barn. He asked the man if he was the one responsible for the perfect arrow shots. "I am," replied the gentleman. "Will you share some of your secrets?" the man asked. "It is easy," he said. "You just shoot the arrow and then paint the target around it" (Simmons, 2007).

"Bell curve teaching" or "IQ teaching" embraces this kind of thinking. After observations, objective and subjective assessments are formed. Stratified targets are painted for students. These targets are partially supported by a well-established research concept—the bell curve. ILs are familiar with it. It is a symmetrical bell-shaped curve that represents the distribution of values for a set of data. The bell curve or normal distribution has many appropriate applications. Serving as the foundation for ILs' teaching philosophy is not one of them. Effective ILs set one lofty and rigorous target for all students, and then methodically drive them toward that target. They reject "bell curve" teaching.

IQ generally describes a score on a test that rates the individual's cognitive ability as compared to the general population. IQ tests use a standardized scale with 100 as the median score. On most tests, a score between 90 and 110, or the median plus or minus 10, indicates average intelligence. A score above 130 indicates exceptional intelligence, and a score below 70 may indicate one needing specialized services. Approximately 98 percent of the student population has an IQ at or above 70. Approximately 90 percent of the student population possesses an IQ at or above 80. Furthermore, "There is not all that much agreement among experts as to what intelligence is, much less how to measure it" (McConnell, 1983, p. 521).

As indicated earlier, innate ability does exist. The central question, however, is to what degree does it affect learning in the classroom. Eric Jensen, author of *Teaching with the Brain in Mind*, addresses this question. "Today, consensus tells us that heredity provides about 30 to 60 percent of our brain's wiring, and 40 to 70 percent is environment impact" (1998, p. 30). He continues, "You can't make a 70 IQ person into a 150 IQ person, but you can change their IQ measure in different ways, perhaps as much as 20 points up or down, based on the environment" (p. 31).

Sebastian Seung (2012), a professor of computational neuroscience and physics at MIT explains there is groundbreaking research currently underway to further examine to what degree environment and other factors impact the wiring and the efficient operation of the human brain. Neuroscientists have established that each individual has approximately 100 billion neurons (brain cells) and approximately 150 trillion synapses (brain connections). By using new imaging techniques, scientist have observed dendrites (branch like structures in the brain) changing over the course of just two weeks.

What does all this mean for ILs? It means that finally, researchers may be able to more clearly establish where nature meets nurture. Scientists have successfully mapped the entire sequencing of the human genes. The end result of this process is referred to as our genome. We are born with our genome. It is the hand we are dealt. However, the genome is only part of who we are. There is a second and equally important part of humans that makes us unique. It is referred to as our connectome. The connectome is the mapping of all connections in our brain. Our connectome is developed after birth. There are scientists around the world participating in this exciting effort. They have named their work the Human Connectome Project; emphasizing the significance of the project, Seung argues, "One of the most important ideas of our time is connectionism, the doctrine that emphasizes the importance of connections for mental function. According to this notion, changing our brains is really about changing our connectomes" (p. 274).

These studies and data alone debunk the misguided notion by whatever label applied that IQ teaching should ever intrude the classroom setting and that "all is achievable, making allowances for those students requiring specialized services. Michael Fullan and Andy Hargreaves (1996) recognize the flawed thinking of some educators. They suggest the changes needed in schooling are "new mind sets, knowledge-base, and day to-day dispositions" (p. x).

Malcolm Gladwell (2008) shares a basketball analogy that reinforces Fullan's and Hargreaves' declaration. He says Michael Jordan is six-foot-six. And he is considered the best of his era. Other basketball players are taller than he is but are not considered better players. Why? It is because after one reaches a certain height other factors matter more than height. One probably needs to be approximately six feet, just tall enough. At this point, jumping, agility, and shooting the ball become more important than height. Gladwell (2008) declares the same is true in regard to IQ; one just has to be "smart enough" (p. 80). At this point, opportunity to learn, beliefs, motivation, and effort become key determining factors in students' academic success. To accomplish the academic goals of pre-K–12 campuses, the students are indeed smart enough.

Smart Enough and Getting Smarter

General ability is all we really need to perform extraordinarily well (Colvin, 2008, p. 45). Acquiring general ability and raising students' IQs is achievable. Postulating that IQ can be raised is testable. James Flynn has studied trends in IQ scores and concluded that scores are rising at an approximate average of three percentage points each decade.

This phenomenon is referred to as the Flynn effect. This is another example of the ability to become smarter. Sandra Scarr and Richard Weinberg, in a research study, reinforce the principle of getting smarter. They placed adopted children in homes of college graduates and those with professional jobs. They then reasoned that, based on the adopted children's genetic backgrounds, the children might have been expected to end up with IQs well below the national average (McConnell, 1983).

In fact, they scored far above average with scores almost equaling children who were born in similar home environments. They became smarter. "The single best way to grow a better brain is through challenging problem solving. This creates new dendritic connections that allow us to make even more connections," according to Jensen (1998, p. 35).

Here is another example of students getting smarter. Rick Heber and colleagues identified forty infants in an area in Milwaukee where 3 percent of the population lived but 33 percent of the children residing in that area were classified as "educable mentally retarded." The mothers of the infants studied had IQs below 75, and the fathers were absent from the home. Twenty infants were randomly selected to receive almost daily educational enrichment from thirty months old to age six. The other twenty children received no special educational intervention. When all forty were administered IQ tests, the experimental group consistently scored 20 points above the control group (McConnell, 1983). These studies should not be considered anomalies. They have been replicated consistently and the results showed a significant gain in IQ; sometimes as much as 20 percentage points (Jensen, 2006).

The following study reveals why some do and some do not perform well on tests (McConnell, 1983). Benjamin Bloom and Lois Border examined how college students with high or lower scoring IQs respond to mental challenges. They noticed the high scoring IQ students tended to carefully read instructions and eliminate obviously incorrect answers while the lower scoring IQ students rushed through reading instructions and were impatient when working and seeking solutions. They did not develop a logical step-by-step process to arrive at a solution. Bloom and Border decided to teach their students how to improve their critical thinking skills.

First, the lower scoring students who had not performed well were asked to read the instructions aloud. According to them, this forced the students to pay attention to the instructions. Next, they were required to discuss their solutions aloud. Bloom then discussed their solutions with them, providing feedback. The correct solution was then read to the students. The students were asked to explain where they went wrong. The students initially struggled with this step; however, the instructors showed a lot of patience as these critical thinking skills were being developed. "But once the students began to recognize that they actually could learn how to reason, they did so with increasing frequency" (McConnell, 1983, p. 520).

McConnell connects the finding of Arthur Whimbey, a psychologist, with those of Bloom. One of Whimbey's proficiencies is assisting people in raising their IQs. He recommends the best way to teach reasoning is to use immediate positive feedback and practice. Jensen (1998) offers two more recommendations from the field of brain research and enrichment. "One is to eliminate threat, and the other is to enrich like crazy" (p. 40). Effective ILs already know how to apply these two basic teaching and learning techniques judiciously. However, ineffective professional practice encourages "bell curve" teaching. I have read hundreds of mission and vision statements. All have stated in some form "all students will achieve academic success."

Likewise, I have interviewed hundreds of educators and again, without exception, I have heard some form of "all children are educable." Yet upon closer examination, the behaviors and methods of some were not congruent with their rhetoric. As stated earlier, the nonbelievers engage in "bell-curve" teaching. This is the belief that intelligence, and hence ability, are distributed or proportioned within a normal distribution. Generally speaking, this type of thinking postulates that at birth a few children are fortunate enough to receive super neurons while an equal number are unfortunate in that they received much weaker neurons, and the majority received an average set.

The problem with "bell-curve thinking" is that it encourages ILs to expect some students to exceed class standards, some to demonstrate an average performance, and others to perform poorly in class. At this point, the task of the nonbeliever is to determine which group received which set of neurons. Jeff Howard, a Harvard professor and founder of the Efficacy Institute, says these types of ILs are attempting to identify which students have the "right stuff."

In regard to the "right stuff," Michael Merzenich recalls that his cousin was the teacher of the year for all of America. After a ceremony in the White House, she visited Merzenich and his mom. Merzenich's mom asked, "What are your most important principles in teaching?" The response was, "Well, you test them when they come into school, and you figure out whether they are worthwhile. And if they are worthwhile, you really pay attention to them. And you don't waste time on the ones that aren't" (Doidge, 2007, p. 68).

Merzenich goes on to lament how this type of educational belief system debilitates the performance of ILs and students. He says, "It's just so destructive to imagine that your neurological resources are permanent and enduring and cannot be substantially improved and altered" (Doidge, 2007, p. 69). ILs should replace the "bell curve" with the "J-curve." The "bell curve" reinforces students' academic failure—some are projected to fail.

Conversely, the "J-curve" reinforces students' academic success—all are projected to realize academic success. It postulates that given the opportunity to learn along with teachers' efficacy and students' effort, academic mastery is achievable for all. See figure 3.1, the "J-curve" paradigm supports the ubiquitous mantra "all children can learn." Moreover, a high failure rate does not indicate rigor. These types of issues are under discussed on many campuses.

Perhaps one reason this belief issue in education is not a popular topic of discussion is because it can be uncomfortable to think about and discuss. Why would it be an uncomfortable topic? Because research is revealing daily that what we once believed is no longer accurate. Some research makes the case that specifically targeted innate abilities are simply fiction (Colvin, 2008).

There is not a reading gene, a math gene, a science gene, or a literature gene. All that can really be stated is that no specific genes identifying particular talents have been found (Colvin, 2008). Ericsson reports, "Early accounts commonly attribute these individuals' outstanding performance to divine interventions, such as the influence of the stars" (Ericsson et al., 1993, p. 363).

He continues by explaining that there are still those who "assert that the characteristics responsible for exceptional performance are innate and are genetically transmitted" (1993, p. 363). He concludes, however, "The search for stable heritable characteristics that could predict or at least

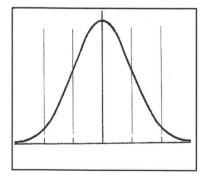 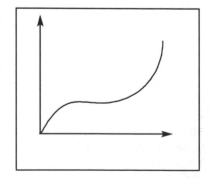

Figure 3.1. Bell curve and J curve

account for the superior performance of eminent individuals has been surprisingly unsuccessful" (1993, p. 365).

Notwithstanding, changing our beliefs in this area generally creates some anxiety. This happens because our beliefs are a part of who we are, and exchanging them for new ones is generally a process, not an event. James Coleman informed us decades ago that if we knew the zip codes of our students, we would then essentially know their intellectual capacity. Since the early 1970s, Ron Edmonds, Larry Lazotte, Jeff Howard, Robert Marzano, and many others have made a convincing argument that ILs can indeed make a difference in the academic achievement level of students.

Ron Edmonds was the first to identify school correlates that he asserted were behaviors, procedures, and professional practices that aligned with high student academic achievement. Master basic skills, high expectations, frequent monitoring, a safe and orderly campus, and strong administrative leadership were the correlates he identified (Marzano, 2003) Since Edmonds published his "effective school correlates," high expectations have been the mantra of educators.

This phrase, "high expectations," has out served its usefulness and has become anachronistic. In many instances, it has become an impediment to achieving proficiency because it masks what it really is supposed to represent—beliefs. The term has lost its punch.

Many consider the two terms "expectations" and "beliefs" to be synonymous. In most contexts they are indeed the same. However, for the purposes of educators, I make a distinction between them. The Wikipedia Encyclopedia defines "expectations," in part, as follows: "In the case of uncertainty, expectation is what is considered the most likely to happen." And it defines beliefs as "The psychological state in which an individual holds a proposition or premise to be true." Notice the distinction between the two. The former underscores what is considered likely and the latter highlights what is considered to be true. The second definition leaves no ambiguity. You either believe "all" students have the capacity to learn challenging curricula or you do not. The point is, even though the two terms are synonymous, we are more invested in our beliefs than we are in our expectations.

Some researchers have retreated from using the phrase "high expectations" altogether and have replaced it with even less definitive terms; for example, "appropriate monitoring and "challenging goals." High expectations are not high enough to take us from our current circumstances to where we need to go. The "bare facts" are that in education one's belief system trumps expectations. Instructional leaders should progress from expectations to beliefs. This is a minor distinction but a major transformation. Beliefs matter. They form our perception, and perceptions guide profession practice. Bandura concurs when he explains, "Perceived collective efficacy will influence what people choose to do as a group, how much effort they put into it, and their staying power when group efforts fail to produce results" (1986, p. 449). In the next team meeting, have members read this belief statement without clearing their throat.

Instructional Leader's Belief Statement

INSTRUCTIONAL LEADER'S BELIEF STATEMENT

I possess the knowledge and skills, supported by a **research-based belief system** and **effort-based teaching methods** that will cause **virtually all** students enrolled in my class the entire school year **to literally become smarter** to the point that they are able to demonstrate **proficiency with rigorous curricula** or at the very **least demonstrate the potential to do so**.

Notice I mentioned the term proficiency in the Instructional Leader's Belief Statement. Achievement is used many times in similar contexts. For example, the achievement gap highlights academic assessment differences among various demographic groups. This type of analysis may not support researched-based thinking. That is, continuing to think in this way presupposes that the highest group's academic assessment level is the appropriate standard of comparison.

But suppose the highest performing demographic group's performance in a given instance is average. Then average becomes the standard. The term proficiency may more accurately embrace the belief that all students possess the capacity to learn. Hence proficiency gap, according to Jeff Howard, is a more appropriate term when making academic assessment comparisons among groups. This type of comparison is potentially powerful because it suggests all students are expected to attain the same rigorous standard. Just because some students' achievement level is higher than others does not mean they are excluded from improving. Thus, different demographic groups (in this instance) are compared against a proficiency standard. not each other. ILs should transition from achievement gap to proficiency gap when appropriate. It promotes a shift in our thinking and the thinking of others. The National Assessment of Educational Progress (NAEP) and similar assessments could be used for this purpose. In addition, it is helpful to set rigorous proficiency benchmarks within each classroom and measure all students' performance against them. This kind of thinking is not intended to push students farther from the target but to illustrate what ILs truly believe—all students can become smarter.

Pygmalion Effects in the Classroom

The effect of perceived ability was demonstrated by Rosenthal and Jacobson with their Pygmalion experiment conducted in 1968. They borrowed the name Pygmalion from George Bernard Shaw's play. The plot of the play centered on Professor Henry Higgins' assertion that he could transform Eliza Doolittle, a flower girl, into a duchess. Eliza explains to Higgins' friend Pickering that how she is treated will have a more significant impact on whether she becomes a duchess than what she does herself.

In the play, Eliza says, "You see, really and truly, apart from the things anyone can pick up (the dressing and the proper way of speaking and so on), the difference between a lady and a flower girl is not how she behaves but how she's treated. I shall always be a flower girl to Professor Higgins, because he always treats me as a flower girl, and always will, but I know I can be a lady to you because you always treat me as a lady, and always will" (Garner, 2005).

Rosenthal (1968) sets the stage to test his hypothesis that students could become smarter. In other words, do the beliefs of ILs matter regarding students' proficiency? He picked eighteen classrooms in an elementary school, three at each grade level. All classrooms had students who were considered to have below, average, and above average ability. All students were given an intelligence test, "The Harvard Test of Inflected Acquisition."

So far, this sounds like any other school in America. Classroom ILs were informed this test was designed to identify intellectually "blooming" students. In fact, the test was a deception to enable the researchers to test their hypothesis. Approximately 20 percent of the students in each classroom were randomly selected to form the experimental group. The classroom ILs were apprised that based on "The Harvard Test of Inflected Acquisition," these identified students possessed the ability to demonstrate extraordinary academic gain during the next eight months.

Rosenthal had successfully isolated the "beliefs" of the ILs; the only difference between the control and experimental groups was the "beliefs" of the ILs. When the school year ended, all students were retested with the same intelligence instrument. The students in the experimental group outperformed the control group. Rosenthal and Jacobson had convincingly demonstrated the Pygmalion effect is real. Instructional leaders should note that the Pygmalion effect is a double-edged sword. Nominal beliefs about human capacity can also produce low performance. Beliefs matter!

Two people can employ essentially the same strategies under similar circumstances, and experience significantly different results. Why? Because beliefs are the first steps to achieving a self-fulfilling prophecy. Remember the words of Eliza in George Bernard Shaw's play that "the difference between a lady and a flower girl is not how she behaves but how she's treated."

Pasi Sahlberg (2010), the author of *Finnish Lessons*, underscores the fact that Finland has one of the highest educated citizenry in the world. And the Finns too recognize the importance of educators' beliefs about students' capacity to learn high-level twenty-first-century curricula. To transform their average educational system of 1980s into its celebrated status of today, Finland began by examining what educators believe regarding students' academic capabilities.

Sahlberg writes,

> A fundamental belief related to the old structure was that everyone cannot learn everything; in other words, that talent in society is not evenly distributed in terms of one's ability to be educated. In Finland, there were echoes of the Coleman Report, favoring the view that a young person's basic disposition and characteristics were determined in the home, and could not be substantially influenced by schooling. It was important the new schools shed these beliefs and thus help to build a more socially just society with higher education levels for all. (p. 21)

Notwithstanding the fact Finland is a small homogenous country, its success in schooling cannot be ignored. I will demonstrate, in the following chapter, Finland is not alone in embracing this notion that beliefs about learning and who has the potential to perform well in school is in fact a key driving force behind their success and the success of other top tier performing countries. This is why I encourage ILs to advance the notion that: You can *change your results by changing your mind*.

HOW TO TRANSFORM ONE'S BELIEF SYSTEM

To acquire a research-based belief system, we first start by examining what we read. We are a product of what we read (Sample, 2003). Steven Sample, the tenth president of the University of Southern California, recommends reading the supertexts. He postulates that reading rapidly changing current events will not provide the in-depth knowledge required to become successful leaders. Remember, I consider all campus and classroom ILs to possess leadership capacity. ILs are leading students, colleagues, parents, and communities. They should strive to become "lead followers" of the campus vision.

Here is a partial list of the main books he, Sample, recommends: the five great religious books (The Bible, Koran, Bhagavad Gita, The Teachings of Buddha, and The Teachings of Confucius), Plato's *The Republic*, Aristotle's *Politics*, Machiavelli's *The Prince*, and Shakespeare's most famous plays. Additionally, ILs should consider reading articles and books that discuss the relationship between neurological research and teaching.

For example, Michael Merzenich, considered to be one of the leading researchers in brain plasticity, asserts that when proper teaching occurs, one learns with enhanced precision, speed, and retention (Doidge, 2007). Norman Doidge explains that all normal human brains have approximately one hundred billion neurons. The brain has the capacity to make connections between neurons. These connections are "tree-like branches" referred to as dendrites. They receive input from other neurons. Without getting too deeply into discussing the synapse, axons, and other structural parts of the brain, the central point is that a simulating, rich learning environment grows dendrites. The brain has the capacity to change and improve its efficiency through neuroplasticity (Doidge, 2007). This means students can literally get smarter.

In addition, reading educational classics by Jean Piaget, John Dewey, Albert Bandura, Alfred North Whitehead, and similar authors; participating in professional book clubs; reading professional journals and original sources on the Internet should prove enlightening. For instance, who do you think uttered this statement?

> Intelligence is susceptible to development; with practice and training and especially with appropriate methods of teaching, we can augment a child's attention, his memory, his judgment, helping him literally to become more intelligent than he was before.

How ironic that Alfred Binet himself stated in a translated version from one of his major books, *Modern Ideas About Children*, that intelligence is susceptible to development, yet there are those who continue to believe more than one hundred years later it is a trait fixed at birth (Dweck, 2006, p. 5).

Binet, the person who developed the first IQ test in 1908 is confirming, in this statement, what all successful ILs already know: with effective teaching methods aligned with a research-based belief system and grounded in effort-based principles, students will become significantly more intelligent. Most children already possess more intellectual capacity than is required to learn rigorous curricula, and those who do not can develop more.

Some who read this quote by Alfred Binet will immediately think of Howard Gardner. He is the Hobbs Professor of Cognition and Education at the Harvard Graduate School of Education. He is an author of over twenty books translated into twenty-seven languages. Gardner developed the multiple intelligence theory. He originally identified seven intelligences.

Surely he believes intelligence is fixed at birth. In his book, *Multiple Intelligences Around the World*, he addresses this issue of fixed intelligence by declaring:

> "People are not born with a given amount of intelligence, which serves as some kind of limit. We each have potentials across the intellectual

spectrum; the extent to which these potentials are realized depends on
motivation, skill of teaching, resources available, and so forth." (Gardner, 2009, p. 7)

So it appears that he too is convinced the human brain is malleable and
has the capacity to grow and strengthen itself after birth.

Neuroplasticity is not a newly discovered phenomenon. William
James is credited with first developing the concept of neuroplasticity in
1890. His idea was largely ignored for about fifty years. Then in the 1940s,
Donald Hebb began neuroplasticity research. In the 1990s Michael
Merzenich led research that confirms what neuroplasticity scientists have
believed all along: the brain has the capacity to improve its efficiency
(Begley, 2007). Merzenich helped pioneer brain research by using microelectrodes to analyze how the brain learns. Microelectrodes are small
enough to be inserted inside a single neuron. After studying Merzenich's
research, Doidge asserts, "The brain is not an inanimate vessel that we
fill; rather it is more like a living creature with an appetite, one that can
grow and change itself with proper nourishment and exercise" (Doidge,
2007, p. 47).

Beyond reading materials, ILs might consider embracing the use of
different metaphors for schooling. Nehring, discussing the origin of industrial language in schools, remarks, "The record shows that pre-indus-
trial language tended to be agrarian. Learning was 'cultivated.' Children
were 'nurtured' and 'shepherded.' The teacher 'tilled the soil'" (Nehring,
2007). Not only does language give insight into how educators think and
teach, but also it highlights their belief system regarding how students
learn. This belief system shapes teaching practices. It is impossible to
separate one's beliefs from routine professional practices.

I submit that in the twenty-first century, "growing dendrites" is a
more appropriate metaphor. This is what effective ILs do. They create a
rich and challenging learning environment that engenders dendrites to
flourish. What we say and how we say it impacts the professional practice of ILs as well as students' learning. Beyond recommending reading
the right books and the use of language containing positive, appropriate
metaphors, what else can leaders on campuses do to inspire their colleagues to fully embrace and implement research-based belief methods
into daily practice? Kerry Patterson and colleagues (2008) have explored
some interesting possibilities.

Vicarious Experiences

Dr. Albert Bandura, a professor and researcher at Stanford University,
wanted to change the beliefs of people who were terribly afraid of snakes.
The persons who participated in this study were truly living with a pho-
bia of large snakes. Bandura understood the participants were not likely
to change their minds and drape a six- foot boa constrictor around their

necks through just trying to convince them to do so. Sometimes persuasion fails because it is perceived as an attack or criticism. The person being persuaded begins to look for inconsistencies in a persuasive argument.

He also acknowledged the obvious: If the phobics were able to overcome their fears by themselves, they would have already done it. Not being able to convince them to change their beliefs, and knowing they were unable to change their thinking all by themselves, he sought to find middle ground.

Here is what he decided to do. When the participants arrived for the research study, they were told to observe Bandura's assistant from a window in a room opposite the researcher. Bandura had some participants pretend they were afraid of snakes. The persons who had phobias about snakes were informed that the participants were pretending to be afraid of the snakes. After observing several times, the actors nervously touched the snakes. Then they put the snake on their shoulder. All the while, the persons who were fearful of snakes observed. Now it was their turn. Within three hours, they had placed the snake on their shoulder also.

The incredible part of this experiment was that the results lasted for a lifetime. Bandura has posted a portion of this experiment on the Internet. What happened to the persons with phobias about snakes is referred to as a vicarious experience. A vicarious experience is essentially learning by observing. Many times when we observe, we step out of ourselves and temporarily become the participants. Have you ever observed a close relative perform in fine arts or in a sporting event and when it ended, you felt exhausted? You had a vicarious experience. It really works.

Ms. Allison Shows the Way

When recalling Bandura's experiment, I immediately thought about an IL who is now retired. We will refer to her as Ms. Allison. I was the campus IL and she was the talented and gifted classroom IL. Talented and gifted was a pullout program during that time. Today, most campus-enrichment programs are incorporated into the regular class or they are made available to all students in another format. At that time, it was a pullout program for third through sixth grades. She rotated meeting with different grade levels since she pulled students from all four grade levels.

One day in the fifth grade team meeting the three classroom ILs, who were outstanding instructors, lamented that each had a few students who were below grade level. They explained despite their best effort, these students were destined to fail the state's examination given in the spring. Ms. Allison solicited more information. They responded, "These students can hardly pronounce words when reading and their comprehension skills are nonexistent!" They continued describing the deficient skill level of their lowest performing students. When they finished, Ms. Allison looked at me and stated, "I will take them." I responded, "What do you mean you will take them?" "If you will allow me to modify my schedule so that I am able to teach all of my regular students but designate a time that will enable me to work with the students they identify as hopeless," she explained, "I will take them."

We immediately made the minor schedule adjustments to accommodate her request. Over time, the regular teachers began to notice improvement in their designated students' class performance. And just as Bandura explained, the regular teachers began making arrangements to visit Ms. Allison's classroom. They wanted to see for themselves what was responsible for their students' improvement. One hundred percent of these "hopeless" students were successful on the state assessment. Again, as Bandura would have anticipated, those outstanding classroom ILs became even more outstanding the following year. After that, if I ever inquired about a pullout plan to provide assistance for their students, the response was always the same, "Thank you but I can teach all of my students."

There are Ms. Allisons on every campus and there are colleagues who would benefit if they were given opportunities to observe what makes them so successful. Observing outstanding teaching on other campuses and viewing videos modeling effective teaching methods are also effective. It should be noted however, I am not equating quality instruction with successful students' performance on standardized assessments. To paraphrase Alfie Kohn again, not everything done under the banner of the standardized era is beneficial for students. I am merely underscoring Alfred Binet's comments and the overwhelming research that has revealed that with proper stimulation and instruction, students can become smarter. I am convinced that all of the Mr. and Ms. Allisons on campuses are growing their students' dendrites. Now, what are the basic steps for modeling to be effective? Bandura's steps required for successful modeling are briefly summarized below:

Modeling Procedure

- Attention: The observer cannot be distracted. He must remain keenly focused during the presentation. If the observer considers the modeler to be prestigious or holds her in high esteem, the modeling experience is more likely to be successful.
- Retention: The observer must retain the salient components of what he observed.
- Reproduction: The observer must be able at least to reproduce the basic attributes of what has been observed and consistently practice them.

- Motivation: The new skill will be reinforced if the observer receives positive reinforcement and support.

Lesson Study

Another form of modeling instruction that deserves the attention of ILs is lesson study. It is a common practice in Japan. Lesson study is built on the premise that ILs' learning drives students' learning. This type of learning does not descend from Mount Olympus, and is not delivered by an "expert." In most instances it is presented by the ILs on campus—the Ms. Allisons, for example. Other key components of lesson study include having small groups of ILs engaged in learning tied to the curriculum they teach.

In addition, they research how to improve lessons, demonstrate the lessons, evaluate and reflect, and then repeat the process. I like to frame the benefits of lesson study as follows: The art of teaching may be difficult to teach. However, lesson studies provide opportunities where it is easier to learn. This is how we learn to teach and continue to improve our methods and techniques—collective instructional leadership.

Improving the campus culture for teaching and learning carries inherent challenges. Stigler and Hiebert (2009) report that because teaching activities and ILs' learning opportunities are grounded in cultural norms, change in both areas are difficult to achieve.

They reached this conclusion from analyzing 1999 videos of classroom ILs teaching. The participants were from the United States and six other higher achieving countries (Japan, Hong Kong, Australia, the Czech Republic, the Netherlands, and Switzerland). The videos were a part of the 1999 Trends in International Mathematics and Science Study (TIMSS). ILs in these countries agreed to be videoed as they taught their students. Stigler and Hiebert also concluded that the methods observed in the U.S. videos were similar to those employed in American classrooms for the last century. It was revealed that ILs in higher achieving countries extend more opportunities for students studying mathematics to become engaged in struggling with core concepts rather than practicing procedures and recalling information. Thus students in America, compared to students in higher achieving countries, had starkly fewer opportunities to learn mathematical concepts.

Let's digress from lesson study and analyze some important aspects of what it takes to effectively teach and learn math, since this has become a conundrum on many campuses. According to Daniel Willingham (2010), a professor at the University of Virginia, there are three pillars required to demonstrate proficiency with math: factual, procedural, and conceptual knowledge.

Factual knowledge is needed because it is positively associated with increased performance on more complex math tasks. Students can focus on more complex aspects of a problem rather than giving attention to basic computation. This is why memorizing basic math facts and having the ability to recall them as needed improves performance. Procedural knowledge is a sequence of steps that is commonly used to solve particular types of problems.

Willingham explains "conceptual knowledge refers to an understanding of meaning; knowing that multiplying two negative numbers yields a positive result is not the same thing as understanding why it is true" (2010, p. 17).

While there seems to be consensus that all three pillars (factual, procedural and conceptual knowledge) are essential to learning math, there appears, however, to be disagreement about what order these knowledge concepts should be taught. For example, should concepts be taught before or after procedures? The predominant thinking today is that procedures and concepts should be taught in concert—one supports the other (Willingham, 2010). Notwithstanding, in Japan concepts generally precede procedures (Sigler and Hiebert 2009).

As indicated, American students need to improve their proficiency with conceptual knowledge. Willingham shares two examples that illustrate this point. One college student at a prestigious university argued that 0.015 was a larger number than 0.05 because 15 is more than 5. And as few as 25 percent of American sixth graders possess a deep understanding of the equal sign (=). They do not understand it refers to equality or mathematical equivalence. "Students often think it signifies put the answer here" (2010, p. 17). This is why conceptual knowledge is so critical. Students who think the equal sign means put the answer here will be confused when they encounter equations with terms on both sides of the equal sign. Using students' background knowledge to build relevant examples has proven effective when introducing new concepts.

Hence, the learning of new conceptual knowledge is related to previously learned concepts. At this point students either grasp concepts or simply memorize algorithms and apply them without understanding (Willingham, 2010). So when modeling in lesson study sessions or when teaching math, ILs should teach all three: factual, procedural, and conceptual knowledge while using examples and analogies to explain important concepts.

In fact, the teaching of these three pillars of learning should be employed regularly in all disciplines, not just mathematics. They help develop the fourth pillar of learning—wisdom. Wisdom is the effective utilization of factual, procedural, and conceptual knowledge. Recall, merely possessing knowledge, does not make one wise. Thus students benefit from having many novel opportunities to analyze all types of knowledge. Wisdom cannot be taught; it can only be learned. That's why effective ILs create a learning environment that stimulates and guides its growth.

Returning to math specifically, in 2008, twenty-four expert panelists, including a number of leading mathematicians, cognitive psychologists, and mathematics educators (The National Mathematics Advisory Panel), reviewed more than 16,000 research studies before preparing a final report containing policy advice on how to improve mathematics proficiency for all students in the United States. The panel's recommendations for mathematics instruction are:

- Critical Foundations. Proficiency with whole numbers, fractions, and certain aspects of geometry and measurement are the critical foundations of algebra.
- Fractions. Knowledge of fractions is the most important foundational skill not currently developed among American students.
- Conceptual understanding, computational and procedural fluency, and problem-solving skills are equally important and mutually reinforce each other. Debates regarding the relative importance of each of these components of mathematics are misguided.
- Automaticity. Students should develop immediate recall of arithmetic facts to free the "working memory" for solving more complex problems.
- Major topics of school algebra include symbols and expressions; linear equations; quadratic equations; functions; algebra of polynomials; and combinatorics and finite probability. More students should be prepared for and offered an authentic algebra course in grade eight.
- Effort matters. A focus on the importance of effort will improve outcomes. If children believe that their efforts to learn make them "smarter," they show greater persistence in mathematics learning and their performance improves.
- Most children develop considerable knowledge of mathematics before they begin kindergarten. Children from families with low incomes and low levels of parental education and those of single parents often have less mathematical knowledge when they begin school than do children from more advantaged backgrounds. This tends to hinder their learning for years to come. There are promising interventions to improve the mathematical knowledge of these young children before they enter kindergarten.
- Teachers' mathematical knowledge is important for students' achievement. The preparation of elementary and middle school teachers in mathematics should be strengthened. Teachers cannot be expected to teach what they do not know.

Stories Work, Lectures Don't

Stories are another method of engaging in a vicarious experience. They are ten times more memorable than speeches. People may not remember all the elements of your stories but they will, however, remember their message. It is this powerful message that over time transforms beliefs, and beliefs shape professional practice.

Effective stories have the potential to be more powerful than the sum of their individual details. These can be stories you read or personal ones. The key is to make sure they connect the goals of the listeners with the goals of the organization. They can be effectively communicated in a large staff meeting or small setting such as a learning team meeting. A classroom IL can demonstrate the inner workings of her class procedures and teaching methods by delivering an effective story. Can you tell a good story? What should be included in an effective story?

Effective stories use language that is comprehensible and easily understood by the targeted audience. Vivid details work better than summaries. The listeners should be able to imagine they are actually participants in the story. The story should be believable, touching, and authentic. Emotions (humor, tragedy, hope) are what make the story memorable. Intertwining emotions connects the storyteller and the listener. These emotions and common connections cause people to reflect and act. They help to paint a coherent picture of cause and effect that alters peoples' perceptions of the consequences of their actions or beliefs (Patterson et al., 2008).

In short, effective storytelling requires preparation and practice. A story about a wise man in an ancient village illustrates this point. He, this wise man who on occasions acted foolishly, was invited to speak to the villagers on three consecutive weeks. Notwithstanding all his knowledge and wisdom, this wise man neglected to prepare for his remarks. Knowing he was wise, he decided to "wing" all three appearances. During his first appearance, he stood proudly in front of the villagers. He then asked, "My dear villagers, who among you knows of which I speak?" The villagers looking stunned replied, "We are common villagers. We do not know of which you speak." He then put his robe on and declared, "Well then, there is no need for my presence," and walked out of the building.

Because the villagers were curious, even more people assembled for the second presentation. Being no more prepared than the first occasion, the wise man again asked "My dear villagers, who among you knows of which I speak?" The villagers were prepared. This time they stood and shouted, "We do! We know of which you speak!" Without hesitation, the wise man stated, "Well then, there is no need for my presence." He then put his robe on and walked out of the building.

On the third and final gathering, the wise man, still no more prepared than the previous times, again stated his question, "My dear villagers, who among you knows of which I speak?" To his amazement, the villagers had a plan. Half stated, "We do not know of which you speak." And the other half stated, "We know of which you speak!" The wise man paused for a moment and replied, "Then if those of you who know would tell those who don't there is no need of my presence." With that, he put on his robe and walked out of the building (Simmons, 2007).

Instructional leaders should devote thoughtful preparation and practice to the art of storytelling. Our audience will know when we are attempting to "wing it" no matter how wise we attempt to appear. As a result, our stories will lose their desired impact. So choose stories that resonate and be prepared to deliver them well.

Still, for some, a story may not be effective for two reasons: lack of trust and skepticism regarding the motives of the speaker dilute the impact of stories (Patterson, 2008). Annette Simmons (2007) presents six types of stories that I have briefly summarized for our purposes. When they are practiced and perfected, ILs should be able to utilize them to facilitate the proliferation of a research-based belief system.

All six are important; however, I think the first two expand the ILs opportunity to utilize the remaining four effectively. They emphasize trust. If there are those who do not trust us it does not matter what we say or what stories we share. Trust will not resolve poor strategies but distrust will surely cripple even good ones (Covey, 2008).

Hence, the goal of all ILs should be to develop genuine professional relationships that foster effective teamwork. By nurturing positive collegial relationships, the stories of ILs are more likely to have the desired effect. The first two types of stories give ILs an opportunity to build positive relationships. I am not recommending that ILs strive to be deceptive or duplicitous as Machiavelli recommended. I am simply stating the obvious: all ILs have stories to tell that could benefit the teaching practices of their colleagues. I am recommending that these stories be told in a powerful and coherent manner.

In addition, when we tell effective stories, it should be noted that some words are more effective than others—"power words." For example, the most powerful word we can use when telling stories is the name of the individual or group we are addressing. We all appreciate hearing our name. It follows that the word "you" would also fall in this category. It can be used interchangeably referring to one person or a group. Now may be the second most powerful word ILs can deploy when telling effective stories. That is because the culture of organizations too often seeks to preserve the status quo. Following are other power words to consider: absolutely, stop, choice, important, results, naturally, and easily. Incorporate them in stories as appropriate.

Here is a framework for telling an effective story:

- It should not be too long-winded or too rushed. Five to ten minutes is about right, but that will depend on the content.
- Build up to your main point. Don't deliver the punch line until right near the end.
- Include a part of the story that will appeal to their emotions. I think this is a key to powerful storytelling.
- Conclude on a positive note (Patterson, 2008).

Also, adding an element of surprise, when appropriate, enhances the story—the truth is often stranger than fiction. Paint a picture of a brighter day. The listening audience will have two essential questions: "Will it be worth it?" and "Can I do it?" These two questions must be answered convincingly by the way you tell your story (Patterson, 2008). I have already shared the story about a coach who never discussed winning. The members of the team knew he did not expect his players to win.

What type of IL do you aspire to become? Recall William Glaser's suggestion to me when I asked him what I could say to classroom ILs regarding effective classroom management. He said they have to be believable. Will you behave like the coach I just described or will you model what Glaser recommends? Will it be worth it? Is there a nobler mission than developing the lives of the next generation? Most would declare there is none. Can I do it? Let's be earnest; this question is the elephant in the room. Some ILs possess a low sense of their own effectiveness, but we can help them to begin overcoming that with inspiring stories about effective teaching.

The research is clear that this low sense of efficacy creates a downward spiraling effect on one's professional practice and students' effort. On the other hand, those ILs with a strong belief in their effectiveness know they possess the knowledge, skills, and methods to ensure the academic success of all their students, which increases students' effort.

Simply put, it is the difference in beliefs regarding research-based knowledge and effort-based principles that distinguishes these two groups of ILs from each other. It is important to communicate through powerful stories that all ILs have the ability to acquire this same effectiveness. The astute ILs will be prepared to select and deliver effective stories. They should practice their delivery techniques, lowering and elevating their voice at the appropriate time, while all the time monitoring the body language of their audience. Motivate them to act just as Demosthenes did in his day. It is reported that when Cicero spoke, the audiences said, "Great Speech!" But when Demosthenes spoke, the crowds said, "Let's March!" Give them a compelling reason to march. Here are six types of identified stories (Simmons, 2007):

Six Types of Stories

1. "Who I Am" Stories—If you tell a "Who I Am" story when you first become a member of a new team or campus, you can give a lasting insight into what really motivates you. This can break down walls and help your team realize that you're a person just like them.
2. "Why I'm Here" Stories—These are very similar to "Who I Am" stories. The goal is to replace suspicion with trust and help your team realize that you possess no hidden agendas. You want to communicate that you are authentic and that you want to work together with them to achieve a common goal.
3. Teaching Stories—Tell stories that have a message. Many times stories are more effective than giving mere instructions. This is true because stories paint a clear picture of what is expected and how to do it. Specific skills and instructions can be incorporated into stories.
4. Vision Stories—Vision stories inspire and give the team hope for a brighter day. They explain what is in it for them. This story should connect with the team. The storyteller should express genuine felling and a belief that notwithstanding real difficulties, we will prevail.
5. "Values in Action" Stories—Do what is right because it is right.
6. "I Know What You're Thinking" Stories—This story shows the speaker is aware of the objection of some in the audience, and explains why their objection does not apply in this instance.

Below I have developed brief hypothetical examples illustrating each type of story.

"Who I Am" Story

When one first becomes a member of a team, the new member might say, "I recall when I first became a campus leader (campus IL). I thought that if my staff would just listen and follow my directions we would be successful. After encountering lots of problems with this approach, though, I quickly developed an appreciation for seeking the input of others, and then things went much more smoothly.

So you should know, at the beginning, it is not my desire for the group to rubber-stamp all of my ideas, but rather for us to pursue the best possible solution. To develop this level of effectiveness will naturally require the full participation of all team members. And I welcome the participation of you all." Revealing a small flaw or mistake helps the group to realize you are authentic and sincere.

"Why I'm Here" Story

In one of the first meetings with a staff that was not familiar with her, one campus IL shared a story regarding a previous experience. She explained, "On another campus, I explained to one group of teachers that I planned to use every ethical means to determine the quality of instruction delivered in each classroom, including asking students what they had learned in randomly selected classes.

Later that same day, one of the members who was present in our meeting shared his opinion with me about soliciting students' comments regarding class activities. He said he thought such a method would undermine the credibility of classroom ILs. I explained that the purpose for asking students' opinions regarding classroom lessons was not to undermine the classroom IL, but to absolutely support and assist him and others. Occasionally, students misunderstand lesson objectives. Thus, when they return home it is possible parents are also misinformed. Establishing a dialogue with students enables me to be more proactive as opposed to being reactive.

It also gives me the opportunity to offer feedback to the classroom IL that benefits him as well. I concluded by saying, 'That's why I am here.' My job is to support and assist, not to undermine anyone." The members in the meeting got the message that the campus IL was there to help them and not to play the "I got you game" with them.

Teaching Story

The chairperson of one of the core disciplines explained in a team meeting that the department lost one of its promising new members from last year. She stated, "The person who resigned from 'Want to be Great School' stated her reason for leaving was that while she felt she really did want to teach at our school, it appeared the other department members were too busy preparing for their own classes to assist her as she became oriented to our campus. Because of her frustration, she resigned. Now this should be a teachable moment for all of us.

To achieve the goals we all seek, I think it is important that we not allow this to happen again this year with our new staff members. When we assist each other, ultimately our students are the beneficiaries. In fact, we benefit as well. Every IL's job is made more difficult when we have to fill in the gaps because of frequent faculty turnover." As opposed to admonishing someone, a teaching story might prove more effective.

Vision Story

To highlight the school's vision, a particular campus IL includes a story in his remarks written by Leo Tolstoy, a Russian writer. We'll call him Mr. Davis. He began by saying "One day it occurred to this ancient emperor that if he knew the answer to these three questions, he would become more successful. One, what is the best time to engage in each activity? Two, who are the most important people to work with? And three, what is the most important thing to do at all times?

The emperor announced to the people whoever could answer his three questions would become a very rich person. He received many suggestions for his first question. What is the best time to engage in each activity? Some responded, develop a strict schedule and then follow it without exception or pay attention to everything in order to know the best time to do each activity. Or better still, have a group of the Wise to advise the best time to do things.

To the second question, who are the most important people to work with? He, the emperor, should put his trust in monks, physicians, or warriors some recommended. In regard to the most important thing to do at all times, they suggested the pursuit of science or military skills.

The emperor was not satisfied with these responses and decided to seek the advice of a hermit who was considered the wisest person in the land. The hermit only received poor people so the emperor disguised himself as a peasant and traveled alone into the mountains. He found the enlightened man digging a garden. The emperor offered to dig so the hermit, an older man, could rest. The emperor asked his three questions several times while digging. However, the hermit never answered one of them.

Suddenly a wounded man appeared. The emperor and hermit nursed him back to health. The wounded man explained he had planned to kill the emperor but was wounded by two of the emperor's soldiers. He thanked the emperor for his kindness. At this point, the emperor turned to the hermit and asked him for the last time to answer his three questions.

The hermit indicated the questions had already been answered. The emperor looked confused. 'Yesterday, if you had not assisted me with digging my garden, you would have returned home and been attacked, possibly killed. Therefore, the most important time was when you were digging my garden and when you assisted the wounded man who urgently needed your help. The wounded man and I were the most important people because we were the only people with you at that moment. And the most important pursuit was offering your assistance to us in a time of need.'"

Mr. Davis continued, "These same three questions and answers ring true on our campus today. They are worthy of our reflection. Think about it, there is only one important time—Now. Our students expect us to seize this moment on their behalf. We can only act in the present. Procrastinating positive action serves no useful purpose. The persons we are with at the present are indeed the most important. That's why it is only natural to make your students, colleagues, and parents feel they are important to you. Learning for all thrives in such a culture. This type of rapport fosters trust, collaboration, and genuine effort. And the most important endeavor is to engage others in the pursuit of noble causes. It is what makes us happy and gives life meaning."

"Notwithstanding real challenges," Mr. Davis explained, "this is the key to succeeding in schooling or any other enterprise. There is no cause more noble and rewarding than helping to shape a positive and productive future for our students. I am certain everyone recalls one of our seniors crying on stage last year during the awards assembly as he explained that he would not have graduated if it were not for one of his classroom ILs, Ms. Bradley.

He expressed that, 'because she cared so much about our success in school, the last thing I wanted to do was disappoint her by not graduating.'" Mr. Davis closed his remarks by stating, "We have a choice regarding the type of campus we create for students. Our job is to save all of them. If we don't give up on them, they will not give up on themselves. You see Ms. Bradley and others on campus could have answered the emperors' three questions. The answers are manifested in their daily behavior."

Remember this is a heart and emotion story that envisions a brighter day.

"Values in Action" Story

There is a familiar story of a little boy walking into an ice cream parlor. He sat at a table and waited for someone to take his order. Eventually the waitress came to his table. "How much is an ice cream cone" he asked. The waitress paused and quoted the price of his order.

The little boy counted his money several times, and then asked "Ok, how much is a cup of ice cream?" The waitress again quoted the price, this time for one cup of ice cream. "That's what I'll have," he stated. He paid her when she returned with his order. After scraping his cup clean to make sure he did not leave a drop of ice cream, he left. Later, when the waitress returned to his table, she noticed the money he left. It was her tip for serving him which was the exact amount he needed to purchase an ice cream cone.

You see, this little boy could have bought an ice cream cone but refused to exchange his values for temporary gratification. The goal of this type of story is to make clear "What hill you are willing to die on?" The most important possession ILs have is their good name and it should not be traded for anything.

"I Know What You're Thinking" Story

Ms. Jacobs, an IL, was highlighting some of her goals for student academic success in one of the grade-level meetings. She noticed the looks of disbelief by some in the meeting as she made her case for improvement. She had anticipated such a reaction and immediately began sharing a convincing story that demonstrated the achievability of the stated goals, by revealing similar circumstances that produced a successful outcome in the past. She shared a story about a student that was in her class last year.

She stated, "I had a student last year. His name is Joe. He was failing my class. One day, after engaging the class in an activity, I stepped to my door with him. I quietly asked him what the problem was. Why was he not completing his assignments and giving a better effort in my class? He reluctantly explained, he wanted to do better in class but 'I just don't read well,' he explained. "Tell me what you mean when you say you don't read well," I asked. He indicated he didn't have a major problem pronouncing the words in our text but that he just did not remember much of what he read. I explained to him that effective reading skills required practice. In addition, I stressed if he came to tutoring, I would help him improve his reading comprehension as well as give him reading comprehension strategies to practice at home. He agreed. By the end of the school year, I noticed significant improvement in his class performance. The teacher he has this year said Joe works hard for him also."

Ms. Jacobs concluded by declaring, "Now just stop and think for a moment. When we all take the time to listen and attempt to connect with our students, we may discover ways to help them improve their academic performance, just like Joe. They all have potential. We just have to discover how to tap into it." Recall the "big stick" and the "black hole" personalities that surface in meetings. Many times stories work with them, where lectures don't. Stories make the truth more palatable.

One Person Can Change Beliefs

In the 1960s, Stanley Milgram, a psychologist, wanted to know why soldiers in the German army during World War II committed so many inhumane acts (Patterson, 2008). So Milgram staged an experiment where the participants were told the focus of a study was to identify the impact of negative reinforcement on learning. As participants reported to engage in the experiment, a man in a white lab jacket greeted them. Not all persons participating were outsiders. Some were actually working with the research team. Each person was asked to select a slip of paper from a container. Ostensibly, each outside person had an equal chance of receiving a slip of paper with "teacher" or "learner." But, in fact, all slips of paper had "teacher" on them. This ensured all outside participants would receive "teacher."

Next, the "teachers" and the "learners" were apprised that the teacher was to administer a 45-volt shock up to a 450-volt shock for any incorrect answers given by students. At this juncture, one participant working with the research team stated that he had a mild heart condition. He was told that while he would feel the voltage, it was not dangerous. The stage is set. Here is what happened. The teacher would read pairs of words the first time. The second time he would read only the first words of each pair and ask the "learner" to recall the second term.

When the "learner" was unable to recall a word, he received a shock. The "learner" and "teacher" were both on opposite sides of a wall and could not see each other. Before beginning the research activity, the "teacher" is given a 45-volt shock to prove that it works. However, when the teacher pulls the lever, the "learner" pretends to receive a shock but he really does not feel anything.

A sample group of psychologists were asked to predict what percent of participants would administer the maximum voltage. They predicted 1.2 percent would go all the way to the end. At first, the "teachers" laughed when hearing the "learners" moan and grunt. As they increased the voltage, they began to show signs of concern. Some asked that the purpose of the research be restated. The researcher in the white jacket would instruct the "teacher" to continue shocking the "learner" up to five times or until the "teacher " administered the 450 volts. Some "learners" stopped responding. There was utter silence on the other side of the wall.

The researcher in the white jacket would say the research required the "teacher" to continue. When the experiment concluded, 65 percent of the "teachers" had administered the maximum shock. Why did average, well-adjusted people, behave in a way contrary to their belief system? I wonder if the man in that white jacket influenced their behavior. As it turned out, he did influence the behavior of the "teachers" (Patterson, 2008). People who are respected and revered have a great deal of influence on colleagues.

In this experiment, the researchers discovered that if one of their researchers pretended to be a "teacher" and pulled the lever just before the non-researcher "teacher" in the 65 percent group, the percentage of administering the maximum voltage increased to 90 percent. Conversely, it decreased to 10 percent within that same group if the researcher pretending to be a teacher refused to administer the maximum voltage. Even though respected colleagues matter, sometimes, just because someone is courageous enough to take action first, others will follow. Think about the "wave" phenomenon that was popular years ago at sporting events. One person stands up at a football game and 70,000 other fans eventually stand up and sit down again to create a wave effect. To begin adopting a research-belief system on your campus, someone has to standup first. Will that person be you?

We all are cognizant of influential people on campuses. It was pointed out in an earlier chapter, with regard to vision creation, that the "connectors," the "guiding coalition," and the "right people" are vital. These people are essential in promoting a research-based belief system. The impact they can make on members of the organization adopting new knowledge and methods should not be underestimated.

In this regard, Christakis and Fowler (2009), in their book *Connected*, observed how interconnected humans are through social networks, and to what degree we influence each other's behavior. To do this, they first recounted yet another experiment conducted by Stanley Milgram. Milgram demonstrated that only six people separate individuals, on average, from any other given person. When we think about it, this is an incredible discovery. He labeled this phenomenon "six degrees of separation." What he means by this is: your friends are one degree from you; your friends' friends are two degrees and so on. This chain of connections continues until six degrees is reached. At this point, and to this degree, you are connected to everyone on the planet.

Milgram made this discovery by giving a letter to hundreds of people in Nebraska and instructed them to send the letter to a friend or associate that might know the targeted person who lived in Boston. Consistently, the letter traveled through the hands of six people before reaching its destination; hence, the term "six degrees of separation." This experiment was replicated by Duncan Watts and colleagues on a world-wide scale using the Internet. And again it took six steps, on average, to reach the targeted person (Christakis and Fowler, 2009).

It should be noted, however, that just because we are connected by six degrees of separation to any other given person in the world, our influence does not necessarily extend six degrees. In fact, Christakis and Fowler (2009) observed that our influence only extends half as far. They refer to this discovery as the "three degrees of influence rule." Everything we do and say tends not only to influence our friends and associates but their friends and associates as well, and one more extension before it dissipates. The three degrees of influence works both ways. That is, our friends and associates also possess the potential to influence us by three degrees.

Now, having established that we literally live in a small world and that our actions affect others directly and indirectly, what's the point of all this? The point is ILs should understand the tremendous power they possess to influence, and possibly alter the beliefs and actions of others within the organization, for good or bad. What we do and say matters greatly. Not only do we influence the beliefs and actions of those we meet with regularly in team meetings, but also our influence may very well permeate the entire campus. We have always known the aphorism "Birds of a feather flock together" was true. But now we understand our influence can extend far beyond just our inner circle on campus.

We possess the potential to influence people on our campus that we rarely engage. As indicated earlier, the campus IL has the most authority and power on campus, but he does not always possess the most influence. This fact is humbling but true. At various times, we all serve as informers or influencers. As an informer, we share information. Sometimes the information is good, other times it is bad. As an informer, we often are not concerned with how one reacts to the information we share. We reason, I have met my responsibility by sharing the information that was given to me. How others internalize the information is their decision. On the other hand, as an influencer, we are indeed concerned how others act upon the information they receive from us. I have observed influencers galvanize others to action not so much with what they say, even though they tend to say the right things at the right times. These individuals influence others with their consistent and persistent actions and positive attitudes. Their position is, "I will support and assist you but if you are not interested in advancing the cause of the organization, step aside and allow the rest of us to experience success." Their reach goes wide and far within the organization. It is difficult to measure, but those within the organization know that it exists.

Figure 3.2 illustrates how Christakis' and Fowler's three degrees of influence might apply on campuses. If three degrees of influence can theoretically spread half way around the world then one's influence is potentially even more significant on any given campus. In the diagram, the campus IL is in the middle; however this could be any other person conducting a meeting. The vertical arrows connect the first and second degrees of influence while the arrows on the perimeter connect the third degree of influence. The different shapes represent people.

The eight larger shapes encircling the campus IL could represent chairpersons who will share the results of their meeting with colleagues. The sets of four smaller shapes represent the grade levels or departments on campus. Within the total group, informers and influencers are represented. To a lesser degree, those who exert negative influence within the organization are represented as well. It would be nice to imagine that negative influencers do not exist on campuses but in reality, we know they do. The issue is not whether they exist but how do we convert or neutralize them altogether.

Earlier, we discussed possible methods of redressing this issue. Finally, study the Information Influence Diagram that follows. Do aspects of it resonate with you? How might three degrees of influence impact your campus, or any campus, given not everyone is supportive or a believer? Do you think one person can really influence several layers of colleagues—even ones he does not frequently engage?

Not everyone desires to be an influencer. Some are content to be conduits for information.

Remember, influence is a two-edged sword. For example, in the famous Hans Christian Andersen fairy tale, the emperor, who loves clothes, hires two crooks who claim they are tailors. They explain they are able to design a fabulous suit from the most beautiful cloth. They do not intend to design such an outfit. They convince the emperor that any-

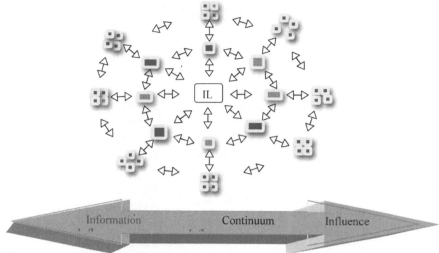

Not everyone desires to be an influencer. Some are content to be conduits for information.

Figure 3.2. Information Influence Diagram

one who cannot see this imaginary garment is not very intelligent or is not worthy of his position. Thus, his ministers pretend to see the imaginary suit for fear that they would appear unintelligent or receive retributions from the emperor. And so it is on campuses. Influential persons can use their persuasive powers to advance or torpedo the campus vision. This is why firmly establishing the vision is so crucial. Team members who have truly embraced the vision of the organization have little patience for pettiness and distractions. I have observed otherwise influential people rebuffed because the mission was too important to allow personalities, politics, and personal agendas to stifle progress.

In addition, leadership authority should not be concentrated in the hands of a few people. We should strive to disperse leadership talents throughout the school. Collective instructional leadership is what effective campuses should strive to acquire. Then, just as in the voltage experiment, this influential power can be harnessed to alter the beliefs of those who are slow to adopt a belief system that is grounded in the notion that all students can become smarter.

Innovation Adoption Curve

Everett Rogers (1995) published the most notable research in regard to the adoption of innovations. Inherently, all credible innovations call upon ILs to change their behavior and their beliefs even when one engages voluntarily (Fullan, 2001). As indicated earlier, beliefs and practices can spread through the group like an infection from one person to the next (Fullan, 2001; Ridley, 1996). Rogers published his research regarding the rate of adoption for novel information or methods in the early 1960s.

He demonstrated that a critical mass of the right group is required to reach a tipping point. As pointed out in an earlier chapter, this is vital knowledge for ILs who desire to establish a research-based culture. Bring the right people on board first and the majority will follow. Potential adopters look to early adopters for advice and information about innovations. The early adopter is considered "the man to check with" before using a new idea (Rogers, 1971, p. 184). Rogers developed the Innovation Adoption Curve. Here are the ways he identifies people in terms of adopting innovation, and the percentage of the population they represent.

- Innovators—They are very eager and willing to experiment (2.5 percent).
- Early Adopters—They carefully review the validity of new concepts and approaches before adopting them. They are held in high esteem by others (13.5 percent).
- Early Majority—They are analytical but are more willing to adopt different methods and innovations than the average (34 percent).
- Late Majority—They wait until after the debugging process and it appears the majority is on board (34 percent).
- Laggards—They are intransigent and believe that their beliefs are the only way (16 percent).

Unlearn-Relearn Is Not Easy

Elisabeth Kubler-Ross was a physician from Switzerland who, because many other doctors during the time of her practice resisted accepting terminally ill patients, began treating and studying them. As a result, she developed what is known as the "Grief Cycle." In her 1969 book *On Death and Dying*, she postulated survivors of loved ones generally experience some or all of the following experiences. It is considered normal for one to experience these identified emotions; the challenge arises when one gets bogged down in a particular stage. For instance, one may behave as though he has not lost a loved one or that a significant change in his life has not occurred.

Grief Cycle

- Denial: Finds it difficult to accept the information just received
- Anger: Asks the question, "Why did this happen to me?"
- Bargaining: If I only had more time
- Depression: Melancholy and withdrawn
- Acceptance: Finally accepts reality

Some have attempted to apply the "Grief Cycle" to circumstances that don't relate to death and dying. Below are the emotions I think some participants experienced as we listened to the Harvard presenter regarding the ability of "all" students to learn. This was discussed in the introduction. I labeled this process "unlearn-relearn cycle." The focal point here is on practitioners' beliefs, not their professional practice. However, as has been demonstrated, daily practice can be profoundly affected by one's beliefs.

Unlearn-Relearn Cycle

- Shock: What did he just say?
- Denial: I don't believe what he said.
- Objective Research and Analysis: I wonder whether his beliefs are correct and mine are incorrect.
- Acceptance: I now possess new information and knowledge.

To illustrate how common this type of thinking is, think about your own childhood experiences. Many families tell children there is a Santa Claus or a tooth fairy. Santa Claus comes down the chimney to bring children presents. If there is not a chimney, Santa finds creative ways to enter the home and leaves presents anyway.

The tooth fairy has a similar modus operandi so that the child's tooth may be replaced with money. The point is, children are eventually told there is not a Santa Claus or tooth fairy. How do they react to this new information? Generally, they are shocked. Perhaps they think the older child who just shared this very unsettling new information is the most misinformed person they have ever met.

For a period of time, they deny that their beliefs are inaccurate. At some point, a research and analysis process begins to emerge. They ask older friends and siblings for their thoughts. Eventually they come to understand that Santa and the tooth fairy live in their home.

Not all parents participate in these types of traditions; however, the point I am attempting to illustrate is that, for adults as well, receiving new information that challenges previously held beliefs does not always precipitate an epiphany. There is a process of acceptance that takes place. I am not suggesting this type of analytical thinking is inappropriate; I am just pointing out it does occur. Some are able to make the transition from unlearning to relearning more efficiently than others. Anwar Sadat seems to have possessed this unique trait. Covey recounts a conversation he had with Anwar Sadat's widow, Jehan. She reflected how willing her husband was to "relearn" what he thought he already knew (2008, p. 71). Professional or personal growth often forces us to move out of our comfort zone. A problem arises when one is hesitant to move from denial to objective research and analysis. This type of intransigence can lead to conformation bias.

Conformation Bias

Peter Watson (1971), a cognitive psychologist, was one of the first to study conformation bias. Conformation bias is a consistent way of thinking that attempts to confirm currently held beliefs while failing to consider information that may contradict those beliefs. "Research shows we tend to ignore or forget, or attempt to discredit, information that does not match our beliefs" (Doidge, 2007, p. 304). Below is one example of the types of experiments Watson conducted to demonstrate conformation bias. He posed a problem. "If a card has a vowel on one side, it must have an even number on the other side." He then placed four cards on a table and asked which two cards must be turned over to test his hypotheses.

E 4 7 K

Before reading further, ask yourself which two cards would you turn over? Remember the definition of conformation bias. Most people choose E and 4, which are incorrect. E and 4 are examples of conformation bias because they confirm the hypotheses but will never prove it to be false. According to Watson, E and 7 are correct.

Explanation:

- The "E" is correct if there is an even number on the other side and it is incorrect if an odd number is on the other side.
- The "4" is incorrect because if a vowel is on the other side, we were already given this information and if it has a consonant it does not matter because we are looking for vowels with even numbers.
- The "K" is obviously incorrect because it is not a vowel.
- The "7" must be turned over to test the hypotheses that if a card has a vowel on one side, it must have an even number on the other side. It doesn't really matter if a consonant is on the other side but if it is a vowel the hypotheses is incorrect. Most people omit turning over the "7" card because of conformation bias. That is, they are preoccupied with proving the hypothesis to be true while not considering it may be false.

Selecting E and 4 demonstrate how easy it is to limit our thinking thereby missing opportunities to grasp new insights. Instructional leaders who consistently engage in this type of analytical thinking may eventually fall in Everett Rogers' "laggard" category. They strive to preserve the status quo without embracing a willingness to consider other valid possibilities that might exist.

A more current examination of this kind of thinking was conducted by Shankar Vedantam (2010), in his book, *The Hidden Brain*. He cites studies where volunteers believed they were acting objectively, yet their actions were at odds with their intentions. They intended to do one thing but they did something else. He labels this phenomenon, "hidden mechanisms." In other words hidden mechanisms are influences of the unconscious mind that impact our memory, emotion, attention, and judgment. He asserts this phenomenon is well documented by social psychologists, psychologists, and neuroscientists. However, what is interesting is that controlled experiments and new technology are confirming previously held hypotheses.

These hidden mechanisms are subtle and most times we are unaware of them. Thus, they are potentially powerful influences on our judgment and decisions. For instance, Vedantam recalls a study that examined unconscious perceptions of hiring teams. Job applicants and hiring team members were allowed to sit in the same waiting room prior to their interview session. Some applicants sat by themselves, some by persons whose appearance was deemed undesirable, and a third group sat next to people who were of comparable appearance.

The findings in this experiment revealed the hiring team assigned a lower ranking score to the applicants who sat next to the undesirable candidates compared to the candidates who sat alone or next to persons of similar appearance. Without being aware of it, these volunteer hiring teams penalized applicants not because of their interview and skills but because of their proximity to candidates the hiring team considered unsuitable for the vacant job.

In another study, office workers were asked to purchase coffee and tea in the break room. The purchases of the beverages were on an honor system. Workers put their money in a container near the drinks. The quantity of the drinks was secretly measured and the total amount of money was counted each day. On alternating days, the total amount of money was significantly more. Sometimes it was as much as seven times higher. What caused the discrepancy?

The researchers alternated signs each day highlighting the price for the drinks. However, above the price of the drinks, the researchers posted flowers on one day and a set of watching eyes the next. On the days flowers were posted, the total amount of money plummeted and on the days the eyes were posted money collected skyrocketed. When this simple experiment was revealed to the workers, they were amazed. No one had noticed that flowers and a pair of eyes were posted every other day. This is plausible, given they were possibly in a hurry to drink their beverages and return to work; or perhaps they were engaged in conversations with each other and not consciously focusing on the signs.

Now what can ILs learn from being aware of conformation bias and hidden cognitive mechanisms? One, we are influenced by things that never register in our conscious mind. Two, assuming human behavior is just a product of expert knowledge and conscious intentions is flawed. And three, to alter professional practice and beliefs, ILs indeed need knowledge as well as coaching, stories, lesson studies, professional transformation study groups, influencers, reflection, patience, and persistence as well as an understanding that real transformation is a process. It is the preponderance of these efforts that will yield the best results.

I should note that hidden cognitive mechanisms and conformation bias are not gender, ethnicity, or age issues. That is to say, this type of thinking can and often does occur within homogeneous groups. To some degree we all engage in this kind of unconscious or defensive thinking (Vedantam, 2010). This is why effective ILs continuously reflect on their professional practice and beliefs. They understand the value of thinking about their thinking as a tool for professional growth.

> *"It is not the most intellectual of the species that survives; it is not the strongest that survives; but the species that survives is the one that is able best to adapt and adjust to the changing environment in which it finds itself."* (Megginson, 1963)

SELECTING AND HIRING THE BEST

Selecting individuals whose personal beliefs are a good fit with those of the campus is one way to mitigate conformation bias. After synthesizing over 500,000 studies on influences that affect student achievement, Hattie reported that "excellence in teaching is the single most important influence on achievement." Of all factors that impact student learning, the teacher has the greatest effect (Hattie, 2003; Sergiovanni, 2000; Wong, 2009). It only follows that high priority should be given to hiring and developing the best. ILs should not merely attempt to fill a vacant position. As indicated earlier, there appears to be a "revolving door" hiring and rehiring process on some campuses that contributes to sluggish student progress.

Hence the goal should not be to hire but to hire well. Hire the "right person" (Collins, 2001). The "right person" believes in the human capacity to learn—get smarter. Remember the researcher John Hattie from chapter 2. He is credited with leading the most comprehensive study regarding factors that affect students' learning. His analysis included approximately 240 million students. He concluded, "Teachers' beliefs and commitments are the greatest influence on student achievement over which we can have some control" (Hattie, 2012, p.22).

In this regard, remember the Pyramid Approach urges us to seek to hire and develop ILs who possess a research-based belief system. It also matches people with campus needs. This minimizes hiring and rehiring for the same position. Thus, retention of ILs begins with an effective interviewing process that leads to hiring the right people. Here are some thoughts to keep in mind in assembling the right team.

Interviewing Process

First, ensure there is not already a capable person within the organization available to hire. "We're often attracted to the outsider because he seems nearly perfect, while in fact he has many flaws" (Sample, 2003, p. 127). Grow your own first and then look outside the organization. Once it is determined to post a position for hire, immediately begin collectively developing a profile of the skills and personality needed. Start developing this profile with people who are the closest to the vacant position. They know what skill sets are required for successful performance. An authentic interviewing process is essential.

Nepotism, cronyism, and favoritism are alive and well. Supporting a corrupt interviewing and hiring process undermines the entire credibility of the leadership and organization. It diminishes trust and sends an unequivocal message: we are not serious about the teaching and learning enterprise. We all know of people who alleged to have been offered a position prior to the position being advertised. If the hiring process is tainted, all the other instructional strategies will be severely compromised. Even when leadership has identified a person they want to hire but is required to advertise the position anyway, the hiring process must be objective and authentic. Simply put, hire the person whose skill sets best fit the position. Some will say this is common sense. Too often, "common sense is not so common." Hiring the best person raises an issue worthy of your consideration. Sample (2003) espouses that we generally hire people less talented than ourselves.

This problem becomes magnified if, for example, the person or team making the recommendation to hire is not considered very talented. The net result of this type of "hiring down" can become debilitating to the organization. While the collaborative process has proven to be the most effective, the campus instructional leader must reserve the option to make the final decision to hire.

Abraham Lincoln reportedly asked his cabinet members for their view on an issue he supported. After discussion, he called for a vote. All except Lincoln voted nay. Lincoln voted aye. He then stated "the ayes have it." Simply put, if the organization is unsuccessful in developing, recruiting, and hiring exceptionally capable people, synergy within the Pyramid will be misaligned.

Experience vs. Inexperience

Now that we have discussed the interviewing process, whom do we want to hire? Remember, we want to hire instructional leaders whose skill sets and belief systems are compatible with the organizational culture. Does this mean the person with the most experience is necessarily the more capable one? Some research studies show the most experienced is not the most capable. It turns out that many people not only fail to become outstandingly good at what they do, no matter how many years they spend doing it, they frequently don't even get any better than they were when they started. Occasionally people actually get worse with experience (Colvin, 2008, pp. 3–4). Consider the following when preparing to conduct an interview:

- The purpose of the interview is not to hire at all costs but to find a good fit, the right person for the position. Retention starts with hiring.
- Collaborating with the persons closest to the vacant position, develop a profile of the desired skill sets.
- Accurately describe the work environment and campus goals. Then solicit a response. This is not the time for deceptions. Otherwise, this position could be vacant again in the near future.
- Attempt to discern whether the candidate is an optimist or a pessimist. Research has revealed the former is positively correlated with student academic success.
- Share a hypothetical situation and ask how the candidate would respond. Be sure the scenario captures the key skills the team is seeking. Request the candidate read the Instructional Leaders Belief Statement. Ask for a reaction.

With regard to hiring, Angela Duckworth, at the University of Pennsylvania asserts, "First, when recruiting and selecting teachers, schools should consider that positive traits such as grit, life satisfaction, and optimism may be as important, if not more so, than traditional indicators of performance" (2009, p. 9). Grit is simply unyielding perseverance. I will say more about grit and its significance to student proficiency in the next chapter. But for now, Stronge and Hindman (2003) synthesized key hiring attributes of effective teachers. They recommend teachers who:

- possess prerequisites, qualifications, and credentials;
- are caring persons who possess a research-based belief system;
- have strong classroom management skills;
- set priorities, allocate time, and plan instruction for students' success;
- apply various teaching methods to meet the individual needs of students using guided practice and feedback;
- monitor learning and adjust instruction accordingly.

They assert that using current research regarding effective classroom ILs' characteristics enables the interviewing team to formulate more judicious decisions when making new hire recommendations.

DEVELOP BELIEVING TEACHERS

Professional Development

Roland Barth (1990) reminds ILs that all educators are educable, too. There are still educators behaving as though they learned everything they need to be successful when they were in college. And among those who recognize the importance of continuous professional growth, too many lament the lack of relevancy regarding these same professional development opportunities. The first mission of all professional development should be to demonstrate the relevancy of any given training process. I use the term process because deep and lasting improvement in one's professional practice takes time. "Mastery takes time, and teachers benefit when there is a sustained, multi-year commitment to training" (DuFour, 1998, p. 266).

In this chapter, I shared quotes from Alvin Toffler and Roland Barth. Now I would like to paraphrase these quotes to shed light on what I have come to realize is one of the central questions for professional growth practitioners and their participants: To what degree can all ILs learn, unlearn, and relearn? This is a question that deserves critical examination by everyone who recites the mantra: "All children can learn." Think about this three-part question for a moment. The first and third parts are not as difficult as the second part.

There is a distinction between this process, which deals with professional practice and the unlearn-relearn cycle, which focuses on one's professional beliefs. How many times have you learned something for the first time, let's say hitting a softball, a golf swing, or a new dance? Now imagine the softball or golf coach or one of your relatives explains you are performing the new sport or dance steps incorrectly. Your coaches or your relatives explain this is the correct way to perform. Did you find it difficult to discard old practices that had become ingrained into your performance? One might say I am explaining the obvious. However, when we examine professional development designs, what is apparently obvious is not so obvious in too many cases. ILs should remember it takes time and assistance (instructional coaches) to transition from learned to unlearned and finally learn again to reach a new performance level.

The fact that it can be difficult to learn, unlearn, and relearn is supported by neurological research. Daniel Coyle, author of *The Talent Code*, interviewed Dr. George Bartzokis, a professor of neurology at UCLA. Dr. Bartzokis reports myelin is "the key to talking, reading, learning skills, being human." Myelin is a substance that wraps neurons and makes them work more efficiently. It isn't static at birth. That is, it isn't distributed in finite quantities. It can be nourished and cultivated such that it grows (Coyle, 2009). Coyle explains, "The more we fire a particular circuit, the more myelin optimizes that circuit, and the stronger, faster, and more fluent our movements and thoughts become" (2009, p. 32).

With regard to learn, unlearn, and relearn, Coyle notes, "Like a highway paving machine, myelination happens in one direction. Once a skill circuit is insulated, you can't un-insulate it except through age or disease. That's why habits are hard to break" (2009, p. 44). In a very real sense, then, one can't "unlearn" what you already know, but over time you can learn a new way, and learn to use that rather than the old way.

One way to devote enough time and support for professional growth efforts to successfully augment ineffective practice is to commit to them on an ongoing basis, not as a special event. As mentioned earlier, "lesson study," as done in Japan, is an excellent practice to infuse into the culture of the campus. If we are going to close the student proficiency gap, we must first close the IL proficiency gap.

Professional learning teams provide opportunities to engage in continuous professional growth. DuFour espouses, "Although many school personnel are unaware of, or are inattentive to, emerging research and standards, educators in a professional learning community make these findings the basis of their collaborative investigation of how they can better achieve their goals" (1998, p. xi). With regard to applying what we know about professional improvement, a recent study reveals the majority of classroom ILs believe content-related professional development opportunities are very beneficial. Classroom management, special education, and limited English training were considered areas of need. Also, it appears approximately fifty hours of professional training are needed in a given area to substantially improve teaching skills. Classroom ILs feel they have little input in determining what the focus of professional growth efforts should be (Darling- Hammond, 2009).

Can You Coach?

If the right people are not on the bus when it leaves, develop them while the bus is in route. The more one knows, the more he can accomplish; "it follows that the most effective steps an organization can take to build innovation will include helping people expand and deepen their knowledge of their field" (Colvin, 2008, p. 162). The process of professional growth should include a coaching component that facilitates the learning of new skills (DuFour and Eaker, 1998). How professional growth activities are selected and presented determine their effectiveness.

Recall Eliza Doolittle in George Bernard Shaw's play. What transforms a flower girl into royalty is how she is treated. Instructional leaders should be aware of the Pygmalion effect when coaching for professional growth. The same principle applies whether we are helping children or colleagues to develop. Bum Phillips, the former professional football coach, was asked how you win. He replied, by getting average players to play good and good players to play great. That's how you win. Capable ILs are able to accomplish this same level of professional development on campuses. Relationships, trust, and beliefs about others matter.

Douglas McGregor, an MIT professor, developed the principles of theory X and theory Y in the 1960s. Theory X embraces the notion that people are inherently indifferent. They need a fire held to their feet to stimulate their best performance. Conversely, theory Y espouses that people are intrinsically motivated. Theory Z, developed by William Ouchi is very similar to theory Y. It postulates that trust coupled with a collaborative and supportive culture creates an environment where individuals exert their maximum effort. Coaching philosophy communicates we are a team. We share failures and successes together. Whitmore (2002) reveals that in performance coaching programs, he asks participants what percentage of peoples' potential is generally manifested in the workplace. The answers vary from single digits to 70 percent. The average, however, is 40 percent. Then he asks, what indicators you have observed that help to form your opinions? People generally report that the level of performance of these same persons outside the workplace and how they perform in a crisis suggests they possess untapped potential.

Finally, he asks what impedes their performance. The management styles of the company and the lack of encouragement and opportunity are frequent responses. What are your assumptions regarding colleagues? Whatever you believe about them will surely be reflected in your interactions with them. Thus your actions, positive or negative, will generate a consequent response. Beyond individual and group perceptions, the effective staff development process encompasses five key components (DuFour, 1998):

- Clarification and definition of the theory supporting the practice
- Demonstrations
- Guided practice
- Immediate feedback regarding participants' effort
- Continuous coaching

Additionally, coaching is a conversational tool that helps identify problems and possible actions that lead to improvement. Hence, when engaging in professional coaching, clear professional goals and targets designed to improve practice and students' proficiency should be collaboratively established. For example, Jim Knight suggests using the following questions (2007, p. 92):

- What are the rewards you experience as a teacher?
- What are your professional goals?

- What obstacles interfere with you achieving your professional goals?
- What are your students' strengths and weaknesses?
- What kinds of professional learning are most/least effective for you?

All outstanding coaches understand the relationship between committing to team and individual goals and seeing them come to fruition. Vince Lombardi, perhaps the greatest football coach ever, states, "The quality of a person's life is in direct proportion to their commitment to excellence, regardless of their chosen field of endeavor." Tom Landry says, "Setting a goal is not the main thing. It is deciding how you will go about achieving it and staying with that plan." Coaching has three basic components. The coach:

- engages in planning conversations
- observes teaching and
- conducts reflecting conversations (Knight, 2007).

The coach collects data during observations to be used later during a reflecting conversation about what happened. This new knowledge is used to improve professional practice. Non-authoritarian, open-ended, and clearly-communicated questions associated with a heightened sense of listening, reflecting, and self-directed learning is the hallmark of an effective coaching model. When coaches listen authentically to the coached, they, the coached, gradually begin to listen to themselves. Authentic listening means to listen without bias and to listen with care as well as empathy. We should practice listening. When the coach models effective listening and reflecting skills, the coached also improves in these areas. The coach attempts to reframe the situation for the person coached.

Many times stories are used to accomplish this goal. Stories influence because listeners continually reflect on them. That is, they replay them many times after the original presentation (Simmons, 2007). The coach is always positive and stories facilitate this process. They make it easier to communicate the truth to the coached without appearing abrasive or dogmatic. Stories do for the truth what sugar does for lemon juice and water.

The premise is for the coached person to take responsibility for his own professional development. This kind of professional growth paradigm shifts professional learning from one-shot training sessions off-campus to continuous growth opportunities on-site. The classroom and campus become laboratories for getting better. Initially, coaches attempt to ascertain the knowledge level and concerns of the coached.

Reflective practice is a very powerful method to facilitate this process and most people do this anyway. ILs generally reflect on lessons taught as well as comments and decisions made. They often, though, do not utilize those same reflections to improve professional practice. Coaching increases the opportunity to reflect and act upon those reflections. The coaching process can be time intensive, but it works. Confucius is reported to have said, "Give a person a fish, you feed him for a day; teach him how to fish, you feed him for a lifetime." This is the goal of coaching—to feed them for a lifetime.

Induction and Retention

In addition to hiring and investing in the professional development of classroom ILs, attention should be given to their retention rate. The National Commission on Teaching (2003) has criticized the turnover rate for ILs and revealed that it is the catalyst of the teacher shortage. The problem is not that too few teachers are entering the profession, but that too many are leaving it for other jobs. America's schools, in 1999–2000, hired 232,000 teachers who had not taught the previous year; but the next school year 287,000 teachers left the profession. That is a 24 percent deficit in one year. And on Title I campuses, the attrition rate is approximately a third higher than the rate for all teachers. While the classroom IL dropout rate varies over time, a review of research studies in 2011 showed that the new IL attrition rate remained at approximately 40 to 50 percent within five years. That is, roughly half of new classroom ILs leave the profession within five years (Di Carlo, 2011). The nation cannot achieve high quality teaching for every child unless these ILs can be kept in the classroom (NCTAF, 2003).

ILs should shift their focus from how many classroom ILs will need to be hired to how the number of ILs leaving the campuses can be curtailed. In this regard, ILs will do well to consider installing an induction program as a part of a comprehensive school-wide professional development effort. Most campuses have mentoring programs that at best provide an orientation to the campus and assign a buddy to answer questions when possible.

Mentoring is not the same as induction. Wong (2009) points out that mentoring focuses on survival and induction focuses on comprehensive professional growth. Three central components comprise all effective induction programs: 1) they are comprehensive, are supervised, and have many people supporting their implementation; 2) they are coherent, with relevant activities presented sequentially; and 3) they are sustained over several years.

Without a comprehensive induction program, beginning classroom ILs are much more likely to leave their current campus after the first year and eventually more likely to leave the profession altogether (Smith and Ingersoll, 2004).

As I have prepared alternative certification ILs to attain their state license, they have consistently reported, "I am frustrated because I am not sure what they want me to do. My mentor is too busy with her own class to assist me. Next year I will have a better understanding of what is expected." Surely the obvious benefits of implementing an induction program will lead more ILs to consider embracing it. Currently, there seems to be a national trend in this direction.

While induction initiatives are headed in the right direction, critical questions still remain. How many ILs participate? Are they high quality programs? Do they improve ILs retention rate and student achievement? Based upon a national study (Review of State Policies on Teacher Induction) conducted by the New Teacher Center (NTC), we have some answers.

Here is what we know: In 1987–1988, the typical classroom instructional leader had fifteen years of experience; by 2007–2008, the most common IL was in her first year of teaching. This is a result of baby-boomers retiring, K–12 enrollment increasing, and the high attrition rate of new ILs. In 2010–2011, there were twenty-seven states that required some form of induction or mentoring. That is the good news. The bad news is that the quality of many programs is suspect.

For instance, the same NTC study reported that not one single state has perfected its induction policy to ensure high quality impact and multiyear support for all beginning ILs. Even worse: some programs were underfunded and some classroom ILs reported they were not formally assigned a mentor or enrolled in an induction program even though it was indicated in their policy.

The NTC defined high quality to mean multiple year induction for campus and classroom instructional leaders. The study concluded high quality induction programs accelerate professional growth; thus making the ILs more effective at improving student achievement and decreasing their attrition rate. Other studies (Ingersoll and Strong, 2011) describe high-quality induction as having a subject area mentor with a common planning or collaboration period and meeting regularly with one of the campus ILs.

COLLABORATION VS. MERIT PAY

Time allocated for ILs to plan and collaborate regularly is essential. And it too, similar to induction, accelerates professional growth while at the same time enhances opportunities for academic success. It seems everyone agrees quality induction and planning are essential. Studies suggest the problem is these professional tools are not woven into the fabric of schooling on many U.S. campuses; or at least to the extent they are in other high performer countries.

For instance, in Japan for more than 140 years classroom ILs have shared a common collaborative and nurturing work space known as the teachers' room or *shokuin shitsu*. It is a large room in which each IL has a desk. The ILs' desks are arranged by grade levels or subject areas taught. Experienced ILs are strategically assigned seats next to new and first year ILs. This common area is used to meet daily.

Whenever they are not in the classroom ILs can be found in the *shokuin shitsu* building social capital with each other, sharing and critiquing lesson plans, and collaborating about effective professional practice. The assistant principal also has a desk at the front of the room. The campus IL, too, can be found frequently visiting among the ILs in this room. The teachers' room is the glue that holds the team together and it helps keep everyone focused (Ahn, 2014).

Moreover, ILs in Japan teach about two months longer than teachers in the United States; however, they have approximately 40 percent more time to prepare lessons and plan with their team members (Sato and McLaughlin, 1992). Mourshed (2010) after reviewing the literature of high performing school systems around the world concluded the one common thread they share is a commitment to team collaboration. In contrast, the Gates Foundation reported that classroom instructional leaders in the United States plan and collaborate approximately 3 percent of their day. They spend the majority of their time planning, teaching, and examining their professional practice in isolation.

Further, the annual MetLife Survey of the American Teacher reported that in 2009 as much as 68 percent of instructors had more than an hour per week to engage in planned collaboration with colleagues. By 2012, only 48 percent of classroom ILs had an hour or more designated for this type of valuable collaboration. In that same year, MetLife revealed approximately 65 percent of classroom ILs reported that time for professional development and planning opportunities with colleagues had either decreased or stayed the same during the past twelve months.

Merit pay is an initiative that has goals similar to those of high quality induction and planning efforts—high academic achievement for students. However, the method is different and it is this approach that can cause unintended results. At the outset, we should know performance pay is not a novel approach.

In fact, its use can be traced as far back as the mid-1800s in England (Murnane and Cohen, 1986; Ravitch, 2013). Even then there were allegations of cheating and students cramming. Nearly three decades later, it was abandon and deemed a failure. By 1918 this practice resurfaced: approximately 48 percent of school districts implemented what they termed "merit based" pay. But as in the past, the practice slowly dwindled until only about 4 percent of school district with three hundred or more students continued its use.

In the late 1950s after Sputnik and again in the 1980s responding to the "A Nation at Risk" report, there was renewed interest in merit pay. However, before the end of the 1980s only 1 percent of the nation's teachers worked in merit pay districts. These types of pay for performance systems general end within six years.

Notwithstanding, districts are increasingly considering or implementing merit pay programs in part because they have been incentivized by well-intended philanthropists and the U.S. Department of Education Race to the Top lucrative grants. Proponents, in addition, assert merit pay programs have the capacity to motivate ILs and improve achievement.

Their reasoning, however, flies in the face of teachings from Edward Deming. The renowned business consultant was himself an opponent of merit pay. He believed it promoted individual goals rather than the goals of the overall organization. Ironically what is intended to improve students' achievement may in fact stifle it.

I fear the implementation of such pay incentives undermines collaboration and achievement. The goal of policymakers and instructional leaders should be to foster teamwork and group celebration. What about the music, art, and physical education instructors as well as others whose students do not receive standardized assessments? How will they be affected? These types of concerns among ILs do not cultivate meaningful collaboration.

There are two essential lessons we can draw from research studies regarding merit pay: (1) While research studies have produced mixed results, merit pay is not a silver bullet; to date, there is not widespread evidence that it improves student achievement and (2) It does not promote synergy among instructional leaders as do high quality induction programs and adequate collaborative planning times. There is a need for policymakers and instructional leaders to align professional practice with current research in this area.

Research-Based Instructional Leader

So far, I have attempted to paint a profile of research-based instructional leaders. They are able to adapt and adjust to new research-based teaching information, strategies, and methods. They efficiently navigate the unlearn-relearn cycle, and as a result they reject "bell curve" teaching. They excel, at various times, at both coaching and being coached. Thus, they are able to internalize the Instructional Leader's Beliefs Statement and recite it with complete conviction.

In addition to these research-based instructional leader characteristics, Carol Steele has identified thirteen characteristics of master classroom ILs. She refers to those who possess these traits as inspired teachers. These ILs have acquired a wealth of knowledge about teaching. They also make informed instructional modifications based on students' feedback and reactions to lessons. These inspired teachers are proclaimed, by her, for the following:

- Knowing the Subject—We cannot teach what we do not know.
- Using Knowledge of Teaching and Learning—This skill is more than simple awareness of teaching methods and control techniques. It is also utilizing information on planning and instruction.
- Solving Instructional Problems—Solutions to problems that relate to curriculum and instruction are a constant concern of expert teachers. Unlike novices or less expert colleagues, inspired teachers solve problems all the time—before teaching, while teaching, and after teaching.
- Improvising—Inspired teachers can comfortably use the Socratic Method or other highly interactive approaches because they can draw from their broad and deep understanding of subjects.
- Managing a Classroom—They sense the reasons behind students' behaviors and adjust their teaching to increase the likelihood that learning will occur.
- Interpreting Events in Progress—Experts use more elaborate mental models to guide their teaching, and more often think about their teaching process while they are doing it.
- Being Sensitive to Context—They make continual adjustments to balance the complexities that connect these factors, aware that one size never fits all.
- Monitoring Learning—Expert teachers are flexible in how they move toward instructional goals.
- Testing Hypotheses—Experts concentrate on identifying a problem before they advance hypotheses or attempt solutions.
- Demonstrating Respect—Respect is one aspect of caring.
- Showing Passion for Teaching and Learning—Inspired teachers are committed and passionate about both teaching and encouraging student learning.
- Helping Students Reach Higher Levels of Achievement—Thanks to the efforts of outstanding teachers, students see that their own effort affects outcomes.
- Helping Students Understand Complexity—The best teaching allows students to mull over facts, synthesize their meaning, and form their own interpretations based on those facts. National Board for Professional Teaching Standards (2000)

Characteristics of Effective Campus ILs

To the degree ILs appreciate the significance interdependence plays among colleagues within organizations, success is more likely to occur. The following story illustrates this point: A naval academy pilot flew many dangerous missions in Vietnam. He was eventually shot down but safely parachuted to the ground. He was held captive until the war ended. Years later at a restaurant a stranger asked his name. After sharing his name, the gentleman stated I know you. The pilot inquired, how do you know me? I was the one who prepared and packed your parachute in Vietnam, replied the stranger. Their goals and efforts were interconnected. The same is true in education. For example, research indicates the campus IL's impact on students' learning is second only to the classroom IL. I believe sometimes they are equally significant.

For instance, a new classroom IL may not perform to her capacity because she did not have the support and assistance of an effective induction program or similar kinds of assistance. There are many variables out of her control. Conversely, the campus IL does not teach students. Regardless of the programs and support provided to staff, the campus IL ultimately depends on the effectiveness of classroom ILs. Hence, their goals and efforts are interconnected—collective instructional leadership. They need each other to experience real and sustained success. I identify ten campus ILs' characteristics that embrace this realization. Campus ILs

- are believers in human capacity
- make "all" students' academic proficiency the mission of the campus
- promote effort-based principles
- promote collective instructional leadership (they trust and can be trusted)
- make safety and a caring campus climate a priority
- ask the right questions and act upon findings using systems thinking
- make courageous decisions
- listen and communicate effectively—they care
- are positive, resilient and persevere—they possess "grit"
- are knowledgeable

Interdependence Recognition Gap

Peter Senge (2012) believes there is an unsustainability gap. Our present way of life on a global scale; he explains, is unsustainable. More countries are gaining a higher level of education and becoming industrialized. His point is globalization has shrunk the world community such that what happens in faraway lands has a direct impact on the entire world community. We live in an ever increasing interdependent society. And yet we behave as though we do not recognize it.

Take for example, a pound of food travels 2,000 miles or more to reach American grocery store shelves. Some children think their food comes from the grocery store. And many children and adults have no concept of foods that grow only during particular seasons. This is because they can purchase these foods year-round. As a result, they are virtually unaware of the world's interdependence.

I see a similar disconnect between what we know works in education and our daily professional practice. Think about the story you just read: the naval pilot and the person who prepared and packed his parachute. Their goals and behavior made them interdependent. One could not become completely successful without the other experiencing the same.

The need for this very same symbiotic relationship exists within the education system, but we behave as though we do not recognize it. There appears to be an interdependence recognition gap within education practice. Reflect upon the plant research conducted by Wilson and Swenson in chapter 1; or Muir's study regarding the value of selecting group traits over individual characteristics. Both studies underscore the positive impact effective teams can have on organizational success. Hence, team collaboration time should be increasing.

Yet, the MetLife Survey showed time allocated for team collaboration is decreasing.

Recall the U.S. Department of Education's findings regarding the use of merit pay to recruit high performing educators to low performing campuses. Overall, it did not work. Still, some policymakers continue to promote merit pay as a "silver bullet."

Conversely, rather than engage in practices that yield little benefit or possibly prove to be counterproductive, policymakers should allow educators more quality time to collaborate in teams and participate in high value induction programs. These methods

- improve student achievement
- reduce IL's attrition rate
- enrich professional growth
- promote shared purpose and collective responsibly
- enhance trust among staff.

Further, we know that high performing countries generally allocate more time for regular team collaboration than U.S. school systems, and that merit pay generally does not promote the sharing of ideas, trust, and authentic collaboration.

So why, in education, do we continue methods that do not work at the exclusion of what does work? Perhaps the answer is that some are slow to accept change while others are reticent to accept the "bare facts." That is, they are hesitant to accept research findings they dislike. In this instance, however, there appears to be another reason—an interdependence recognition gap. See Figure 3.3.

Notwithstanding budget challenges which often drive policy, policymakers and ILs should acquire a greater appreciation for the extent to which actions or inactions of each individual are intertwined with achieving the goals of the entire organization. Virtually everything in education should be executed with this realization in mind. Since the report "A Nation at Risk" there has been clear evidence that an ever increasing level

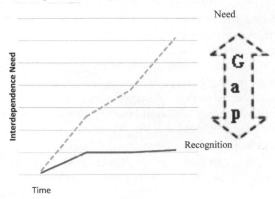

Figure 3.3. Interdependence Recognition Gap

of interdependence awareness in schooling is needed. And to the degree we realize it and act accordingly, achievement will improve.

Consider the level of interdependence required to successfully institutionalize quality time for team collaboration: to share methods, to offer support, and to model lessons and discuss and analyze student progress. What about collaborating not only within the same grade level but with upper and lower grade levels, and with those on other campuses (elementary, middle, and high schools)? And what about induction programs too?

Clearly, efficient teams are needed more than ever. Nevertheless, at the same time, widespread acceptance of the type of interdependent culture now required to effectively education every child goes unheeded.

There is, indeed, an interdependence recognition gap. Too many in education do not recognize how much the success of schooling relies upon mutual assistance, support, and cooperation among all individuals. This is so partly because there are those who mistakenly believe they can accomplish organizational goals by achieving individual objectives. They are trapped by their own flawed thinking.

It was reported Henry Ford once stated, coming together is a beginning; keeping together is progress, and working together is success. Below is an acronym that illuminates this point.

T = Together
E = Everyone
A = Achieves
M = More

WE HAVE HAD OUR FIFTY YEARS

Colvin (2008) explores our thinking about talents and intellect and how it can be traced back at least 2,600 years ago, to the *Odyssey* and the *Iliad*. Demodocus attributes the ability to sing well to the wishes of Zeus or the muses (his nine daughters). He contends this type of thinking in a general sense still exists, this belief that wherever excellent performance comes from it surely does not have its geneses in hard work, deliberate practice, and perseverance. "It turns out that our knowledge of great performance, like our knowledge of everything else, has actually advanced quite a bit in the past couple of millennia. It's just that most of the findings haven't made their way into people's heads. Scientists began turning their attention to it in a big way about 150 years ago" (Colvin, 2008. p. 6).

This same phenomenon regarding a lag in the acquisition and adoption of new knowledge occurred during the century following the death of Nicolaus Copernicus, who published *On the Revolutions of the Celestial Spheres* in the middle sixteenth century, offering a revolutionary paradigm for viewing the universe. He postulated that the sun, not the earth, rested at the center of the universe. His ideas were not accepted by many, even in the circles of learning, for well over 100 years.

Lewis Terman's research further highlights how intractable beliefs sometimes become. Terman, a professor at Stanford, had a special interest in intelligence testing and the behavior of people who scored extremely well on them. He is credited with having developed the Stanford Binet. In 1921, he began one of the most comprehensive studies of highly intelligent people to date. He recruited approximately 1,500 participants. They were selected from a pool of 250,000 potential candidates who had been nominated by their elementary teachers.

The nominated group was then administered an intelligence examination. Those who scored in the top 10 percent were tested again to prune the group and the remaining group was tested a final time. Terman selected his "Termites" (the name given to the group) from this final group. As indicated, the average IQ is considered 100. The "Termites" scored between 140 and 200. Albert Einstein's IQ was reported to be 150.

Terman began a lifetime of cataloguing the experiences of his subjects. He recorded their educational, professional, and personal experiences in a document he titled "Genetic Studies of Genius." Terman postulated the higher one's IQ, the more successful she should become. However, disappointingly, Terman concluded that "intellect and achievement are far from perfectly correlated" (Gladwell, 2008, p. 90). The majority of the Termites had ordinary careers and some had careers that Terman himself considered failures (Gladwell, 2008).

The Termites provide another example in the age-old debate nature vs. nurture. Nature is undeniably a factor in human development but it is not the complete story. Nurture, in many instances, plays an equal or more significant role in one's ultimate outcome in life. Most instructional leaders are already aware of Terman's conclusion that IQ is not the determining factor in the future success of individuals. Think about the people in your high school graduating class. Were the people considered the smartest always the most successful?

To illustrate this point, two students that were in the pool of 250,000 Terman selected from, but were not selected by him, won the Nobel Prize—William Shockley and Luis Alvarez. No Termite received such distinction (Gladwell, 2008). Remember, for the purposes of ILs, students just have to be "smart enough." For some, this landmark study still has not put to rest the belief that "bell curve" teaching is anachronistic.

In the final analysis, instructional leaders must confront the following questions: Who are you? What do you believe? Is your practice congruent with your espoused professional beliefs? Are you in the category of an innovator, early adopter, early majority, late majority, or a laggard? What you believe guides your professional practice. It is extremely difficult to transform practice without first embracing a belief system to base it on. In the medical profession, the average time that passes between a conclusive finding and its widespread application is five years; in education, the comparable number is fifty years (Danielson, 2002, p. 30).

In education, we have had our fifty years to transform our belief system, and when we do alter our beliefs, transformative professional practice will not be far behind. I am convinced that our beliefs are prerequisites for what every IL espouses: "All children are educable."

Plato, in the *Republic*, underscores the challenge nonbelieving ILs face. The allegory of the cave is considered by many to be Plato's most famous work. In it, he explains that there are people chained to a wall in a cave. There is a hole in the wall. A fire casts shadows of persons walking outside the cave on the inside wall. Since these experiences shape the belief system of the cave inhabitants, they consider the shadows to be real people. One cave dweller manages to free himself and leaves the cave. Initially, the sun blinds him because he has never experienced direct sunlight. Upon meeting the people outside, he is informed that the shadows are not real people but only reflections. He does not readily accept this explanation. I imagine he is going through the unlearn-relearn cycle. Over time, he embraces his newly acquired knowledge.

Now comes an equally challenging experience. He returns to the cave to share his new belief system with his colleagues. You can imagine their reaction. The cave dwellers have a different perspective because they possess a different knowledge base. What can this insightful cave dweller say? What can he do to alter the belief system of the other cave dwellers? This is our challenge. We must be willing to explore new concepts and ideas if we are to grow intellectually and professionally. With regard to acknowledging students' intellectual capacity to learn, again we have had our fifty years. This same challenge confronts ILs in every district and on every campus. Their belief system can be compared to the cave dwellers not venturing outside their familiar surroundings.

There has to be an organizational mission to "take off their chains" regarding beliefs about students' intellectual capacity to become proficient with rigorous curricula, starting with ourselves first and foremost. When students are exposed to a rich, challenging environment with instructional leaders who believe they have professional skills to grow dendrites while fostering effort-based principles, students will become significantly smarter. Believe it!

REFLECTIVE THOUGHTS

What are your thoughts and beliefs regarding the following statements and how are they manifested in your daily practice?

- Are you a believer in growing dendrites, or a nonbeliever?
- Are you an informer or influencer?
- What are your thoughts regarding "bell curve" teaching?
- Why do you think the Ms. Allisons in other classrooms are so successful when their colleagues seem to struggle with similar kinds of students?
- Can you tell an effective story?
- What is your reaction to the Instructional Leaders' Belief Statement?
- Does the Pygmalion effect exist? If it does, how can it be countered or exploited?
- How willing are you to unlearn and relearn?
- Do we always hire people less talented than ourselves?
- Is lesson study a fad or is it here to stay?
- Can you coach?

BARE FACTS

- Beliefs matter!
- One person can alter the beliefs of many.
- Stories work; lectures don't.
- Nepotism, cronyism, and favoritism are alive and well.
- Experienced does not mean efficient.
- Innate ability and environment both impact students' learning.
- Students are smart enough to demonstrate proficiency with rigorous college preparatory curricula, or can become smart enough.
- Students can literally get smarter.
- Either you believe all students have the capacity to learn challenging curricula or you don't—there is no middle ground.

- One's belief system trumps high expectations.
- In education, we have had our fifty years to transform our belief system, and when it does happen transformative professional practice will not be far behind.
- Merit pay does not promote synergy among instructional leaders as do high quality induction and collaborative planning times.
- There is, indeed, an interdependence recognition gap.
- When students are exposed to a rich, challenging environment with instructional leaders who believe they have the professional skills to grow dendrites while fostering effort-based principles, students will become significantly smarter. Believe it!

REFERENCES

Ahn, R. (2014). How Japan supports novice teachers. *Education Week*.

Bandura, A. (1986). Social foundations of thought and action. Englewood Cliffs, NJ: Prentice-Hall.

Barth, R. (1990). *Improving schools from within*. San Francisco, CA: Jossey-Bass.

Begley, S. (2007). *Train your mind, change your brain*. New York: Ballantine.

Binet, A. (1975). *Modern ideas about children*. San Francisco, CA: San Francisco State University.

Christakis, N. A., and Fowler, J. H. (2009). *Connected*. New York: Little, Brown and Company.

Collins, J. (2001). *Good to great*. New York: HarperCollins.

Colvin, G. (2008). *Talent is overrated*. New York: Penguin Group.

Comer, J. P. (2008). An open letter to the next president. *Education Week, 27*(19), 25, 32.

Covey, S. (2008). *The speed of trust*. New York: Free Press.

Coyle, Daniel. (2009). *The talent code*. New York: Random House.

Danielson, C. (2002). *Enhancing student achievement*. Alexandria, VA:ASCD.

Darling-Hammond, L. (2009). "Professional learning in the learning profession." The School Redesign Network at Stanford University.

Di Carlo, M. (December, 18, 2011). "Do half of new teachers leave the profession within five years?" National Policy Education Center. Retrieved from http://nepc.colorado.edu/blog/do-half-new-teachers-leave-profession-within-five-years.

Doidge, N. (2007). *The brain that changes itself*. New York: Penguin Group.

Duckworth, A. L., and Quinn, P.D. (2009a). Development and validation of the Short Grit Scale (Grit-S). *Journal of Personality Assessment, 91*, 166–74.

Duckworth, A. L., and Quinn, P.D. (2009b). Positive predictors of teacher effectiveness. *Journal of Positive Psychology*, 1–8.

DuFour, R., and Eaker, R. (1998). *Professional learning communities at work, best practices for enhancing student achievement*. Bloomington, IN: National Educational Service.

Dweck, C. S. (2006). Mindset: The new psychology of success. New York: Random House.

Edmonds, R. (1979). Effective schools for the urban poor. *Educational Leadership, 37*(15–18): 20–22.

Ericsson, K. A., Krampe, R. Th., and Tesh-Romer, C. (1993). The role of deliberate practice in the acquisition of expert performance. *Psychological Review, 100*, 363–406.

Fullan, M. (2001). *Leading in a culture of change*. New York: Jossey-Bass.

Fullan, M. (2010). *All systems go: The change imperative for whole systems reform*. Thousand Oaks, CA: Corwin Press.

Fullan, M., and Hargreaves, A. (1996). *What's worth fighting for in your school*. New York: Teachers College Columbia University.

Gardner, H. (2009). *Multiple intelligences around the world*. San Francisco, CA: Jossey-Bass.

Garner, E. (Oct. 25, 2005). "The Pygmalion effect." Retrieved June 26, 2009, from http://ezinearticles.com/?The-Pygmalion-Effect&id=86460.

Gladwell, M. (2008). *Outliers: The story of success*. New York: Little, Brown and Company.

Hattie, J. (October, 2003). "Teachers make a difference: What is the research evidence?" University of Auckland, Australian Council for Educational Research.

Hattie, J. (2012). *Visible learning for teachers: Maximum impact on learning*. New York: Routledge.

Ingersoll R., and Merrill, L. (2010). Who's teaching our children? *Educational Leadership, 67*(8), 14–20.

Ingersoll R., and Strong, M. (2011). The impact of induction and mentoring for beginning teachers: A critical review of the research. *Review of Educational Research, 81*(2), 201–33.

Jensen, A. (1980). *Bias in mental testing*. New York: Free Press.

Jensen, E. (1998). *Teaching with the brain in mind*. Alexandria,VA: ASCD.

Jensen, E. (2006). *Enriching the brain*. San Francisco, CA: Jossey-Bass.

Knight, J. (2007). *Instructional coaching*. Thousand Oaks, CA: Crown Press.

Kohn, A. (Sept. 27, 2000). Standardized testing and its victims. *Education Week.*

Kubler-Ross, E. (1969). *On death and dying*. New York: Macmillan.

Marzano, R. (2003). *What works in schools: Translating research into action*. Alexandria, VA: ASCD.

McConnell, J. V. (1983). *Understanding human behavior*. New York: Holt, Rinehart and Winston.

Megginson, L. C. (1963). Lessons from Europe for American business. *Southwestern Social Science Quarterly, 44*(1): 3–13.

Mourshed, M., Chijioke, C., and Barber, M. (2010). *How the world's most improved school systems keep getting better*. London: McKinsey and Company.

Murnane, R. J., and Cohen, D. K. (1986). Merit pay and the evaluation problem: Why most merit pay plans fail and a few survive. *Harvard Education Review, 56*(1), 2.

National Commission on Teaching. (2003). National Teaching on America's Future. http://nctaf.org/wp-content/uploads/2012/01/NCTAF-Cost-of-Teacher-Turnover-2007-full-report.pdf.

Nehring, J. (2007). Conspiracy theory: Lessons for leaders from two centuries of school reform. *Phi Delta Kappan, 88*(6) pp. 425–432.

Nelson, M. R. (2005). *Bill Russell: A biography*. Westport, CT: Greenwood Publishing Group.

New Teacher Center. (2012). Review of State Policies on Teacher Induction. www.newteachercenter.org. Retrieved February 3, 2014.

No dream denied: A pledge to America's Children. (2003). Washington, D.C.: National Commission on Teaching and America's Future.

Patterson, K., Grenny, J., Maxfield, D., McMillan, R., and Switzler, A. (2008). *Influencer: The power to change anything*. New York: McGraw- Hill.

Ravitch, D. (2013). *Reign of error*. New York: Random House.

Ridley, M. (1996). *The origins of the venture*. Harmondsworth, England: Penguin Books.

Rogers, E.M. (1995). *Diffusion of innovations*. (4th ed.). New York: The Free Press.

Rogers, E.M., and Shoemaker, F. F. (1971). *Communications of innovations: A cross-cultural approach*. New York: Free Press.

Rosenthal, R., and Jacobson, L. (1968). *Pygmalion in the classroom*. New York: Holt, Rinehart and Winston.

Sahlberg, P. (2010). *Finnish lessons*. New York: Teachers College Press

Sample, S. (2003). *Contrarian's guide to leadership*. San Francisco: Jossey-Bass.

Sato, N., and McLaughlin, M.W. (1992). Context matters: Teaching in Japan and in the United states. *Phi Delta Kappan, 73*(5), 359–68.

Senge, P. (2012). *Schools that learn*. New York: Random House.

Sergiovanni, T. (2000). *The lifeworld of leadership*. San Francisco: Jossey-Bass.

Seung, S. (2012). *Connectome*. New York: Houghton Mifflin Harcourt Publishing Company.

Simmons, A. (2007). *Whoever tells the best story wins*. New York: American Management Association.

Steele, C. F. (2009). *Inspired teacher*. Alexandria, VA: ASCD.

Stigler, W. J., and Hiebert, J. (2009). *The teaching gap*. New York: Free Press.

Smith, T. M., and Ingersoll, R. M. (2004). What are the effects of induction and mentoring on beginning teacher turnover? *American Educational Research Journal, 41*(3), 681–714.

Stronge, J. H., and Hindman, J. L. (2003). Hiring the best teachers. *Educational Leadership, 60*(8), 48–45.

The MetLife Survey of the American Teacher: Collaborating for Student Success. (2009). Retrieved February 3, 2014.

The MetLife Survey of the American Teacher: Challenges for School Leadership. (2012). www.metlife.com/teachersurvey. Retrieved February 3, 2014.

Tolstoy, Leo. (1894). *The Kingdom of God is Within You*. Chapter III. http://www.kingdomnow.org/winyou03.html%20 (e-transcribed in 2002).

"Tom Landry Quotes." Quotes.net. STANDS4 LLC, 2014. Retrieved January 18, 2009 from http://www.quotes.net/quotations/tom%20landry.

U.S. Department of Education. National Mathematics Advisory Panel. Retrieved July 28, 2014 from http://www2.ed.gov/about/bdscomm/list/mathpanel/report/final-report.pdf.

Vedantam, S. (2010). *The hidden brain*. New York: Random House.

" Vince Lombardi Quotes." Quotes.net. STANDS4 LLC, 2014. Retrieved July 28 2014. http://www.quotes.net/authors/Vince Lombardi.

Watson, P. C. (1971). Natural and contrived experience in a reasoning problem. *Quarterly Journal of Experimental Psychology, 23*, 63.

Wei, R. C., Darling-Hammond, L., Andree, A., Richardson, N., Orphanos, S. (2009). Professional learning in the learning profession: A status report on teacher development in the United States and Abroad. Dallas, TX: National Staff Development Council.

Whitmore, J. (2002). *Coaching for performance, growing people, performance and purpose*. London: Nicholas Brealey Publishing.

Willingham, D. (2009–2010). Ask the cognitive scientist. *American Educator, 33*(4) 14–19.

Wolf, T. H. (1973). *Alfred Binet*. Chicago: University of Chicago Press.

Wong H. K. (2009). New teacher induction: The foundation for comprehensive, coherent, and sustained professional development. In H. Portner, *Teacher mentoring and induction: The state of the art and beyond* (pp. 41–58). Thousand Oaks, CA: Corwin.

REFLECTIVE THOUGHTS

_____

_____

_____

_____

_____

_____

_____

_____

_____

FOUR

Increase All Students' Efforts with $E=mc^2$

Construct your determination with sustained effort, controlled attention, and concentrated energy. Opportunities never come to those who
wait; they are captured by those who dare to attack. —Paul J. Meyer

The goal of using $E=mc^2$ as an analogy is to cause us to think differently
about motivation and effort as it relates to students, leadership, and human behavior in general. I want to convince the reader that this scientific
expression can be used effectively to advance effort-based learning principles. Albert Einstein explains his most popular scientific expression in
this way:

> It followed from the special theory of relativity that mass and energy
> are both but different manifestations of the same thing—a somewhat
> unfamiliar conception for the average mind. Furthermore, the equation
> E is equal to mc-squared, in which energy is put equal to mass, multi-
> plied by the square of the velocity of light, showed that very small
> amounts of mass may be converted into a very large amount of energy
> and vice versa. The mass and energy were in fact equivalent, according
> to the formula mentioned above. This was demonstrated by Cockcroft
> and Walton in 1932, experimentally. (From the soundtrack of the film
> *Atomic Physics*)

Chapter 4

TRY HARDER

We will return to the $E=mc^2$ analogy and its connection to effort-based principles and how it can be applied in the classroom, a little later. For now, though, let me say I first learned the power of these effort-based principles on the practice field. I recall my first year as a high school teacher. I had just graduated from college and was assigned a coaching position I had not applied for.

When my players did not perform well, I would direct them to redo what they just unsuccessfully performed. If that did not work, I would repeat my previous direction. Only this time, I would say the same thing louder. "Try harder! Let's go!" I didn't see any improvement. So I thought surely threats would help. I yelled, "You all don't want to win! You won't be on this team long if you don't give a better effort!" After about a week of unsuccessful coaching, it dawned on me that coaching was nothing but a method of teaching. So I stopped yelling and threatening and began teaching. I employed these teaching methods:

Set Goals

First, we sat down and began to talk about our future as a team. I did a lot of listening—even apologized for my coaching style. Then it was my turn to speak. I looked them in their eyes and expressed with absolute conviction that they had talent, but we had a long way to go if we were going to have a successful season. I explained the level of play I expected was at the all-district or all-state level. Some looked convinced while others looked doubtful. I closed by communicating our goals were very lofty but achievable if we focused and worked hard.

Demonstration and Feedback

Beginning the next practice, I always asked the best players to demonstrate new skills for the rest of the players. Then everyone took turns demonstrating his level of competence compared to the team's standard. I offered suggestions on how to improve. When we viewed videos of our games, I highlighted what our players did well and what I expected them to do better. I also acknowledged their focus and effort. In addition, I would point out what the other team's best player did well. In retrospect, I think they began developing an image of excellence in their minds.

Scrimmage or Evaluation

A scrimmage is an opportunity to practice in a game-like situation. The concept of a scrimmage can be applied to any endeavor. After a scrimmage, I would ask: What do you think you did well? What did you do wrong? Why did you do that? What could you have done? They were able to evaluate their own performance and generally took responsibility for their errors and improvement.

Motivation

Now when I said: "Try harder! Let's go! You can do it!" These same words carried a different meaning and engendered positive emotions and responses. I also continued to praise their effort.

Connections

The players quickly made the connections between effective practice and excellent performance. It seemed that because they were focused and worked very hard (deliberate practice), their performance significantly improved, and because their performance improved, they worked much harder, believing all the time that they could get even better. Upon reflection, I realized something unexpected had occurred. The players began devoting a disproportionate amount of time to practicing the skills they had not fully developed compared to practicing skills they had already mastered.

Self-Motivation

I noticed the players began practicing before and after the official practice. This was not required. They understood the team could win but only if they performed at their peak level and that they could only achieve this exceptional level of performance by fully engaging in practice and deliberating on it.

Coaching Is Teaching

Here is the interesting part about this experience: not only did my players benefit from my newly acquired insight, but the students in my classroom did as well. Notice how compatible these same coaching principles are to the classroom. For one to become significantly good at almost anything is extremely difficult without proper guidance and coaching.

ILs should apply these same effort-based principles in the classroom daily—first by setting high goals. By motivating students to understand with appropriate feedback, concentrated effort, and persistence, academic success will soon follow.

Teaching and Leading Embrace Coaching Principles

My experience as a coach has implications for all instructional leaders. The concepts of effective coaching can be applied successfully in education. Most top-performing organizations have exemplary programs to guide, coach, and develop their employees.

Coaching is not something that occurs only when a problem surfaces. ILs should embrace the notion that coaching is an effective method of interacting with others, in ways that build trust and competence. With increased experience and the aid of ILs and coaches, the developing individual is able to internalize methods for assessing improvement and can thus monitor the effects of their own practice (Colvin, 2008; Ericsson et al., 1993).

There is a clear connection between coaching and effective practice. Superior athletes have talent, but that is not what separates them for the crowd. What distinguishes them from others is their exposure to quality coaching, effective practice, and commitment to improve. That's an important concept for us to remember. The most important attribute of successful coaches is their unwavering belief that the team will prevail. Once this positive attitude is ingrained in the coach, it appears to permeate the thinking and behavior of the team.

Think about your own life experiences. If you were a member of the choir, orchestra, debate team, soccer team, or any other competitive team, you understand the importance of the coach or leader demonstrating that she believes the group has the capacity to perform well.

I actually observed a coach once who explained that his players would lose the game but he was confident that the other team would not embarrass them. He explained that they would be able to leave the competition with their heads up and their dignity still intact.

Quality coaches do not concede any competition before it is played. Can you imagine a classroom instructional leader or a campus instructional leader echoing similar sentiments in a meeting with regard to student proficiency? "Teachers, we all know the challenges we face given the kinds of students we have on this campus. So let's just roll up our sleeves and do the best we can. And at the end of the school year, regardless of our students' academic achievement results, we will be able to hold up our heads with dignity." This type of helpless defeatist mindset does not have to exist.

All students possess intellectual energy that as of yet has not been fully tapped on many campuses. The research is overwhelming and profoundly convincing; poor student achievement is not rooted in a lack of pedagogical knowledge. We in education know what works. As indicated earlier, it is an obsolete belief system that serves as a vehicle for perpetuating the status quo. Researchers questioned a group composed primarily of educators to ascertain whether they thought singing, composing, and playing concert instruments require a gift or talent. Seventy-five percent of the participants said, yes, a gift was required.

The researchers concluded, however, that "One factor, and only one factor, predicted how musically accomplished the students were, and that was how much they practice" (Colvin, 2008, p. 18). It is time for instructional leaders, students, and parents to accept the advice offered by Plato in his allegory of the cave. Before some ILs can experience the success they seek, they must first take off their shackles and liberate themselves from the kind of thinking Menelaus and Agamemnon accepted a couple of millennia ago, that the muses are responsible for the achievements of others. The E=mc² analogy can provide another way to explain successful performance and provide a new mindset regarding effort-based principles that lead to success.

Letters to Presidents

On August 2, 1939, Albert Einstein expressed these thoughts in a letter to President Franklin D. Roosevelt. "Certain aspects of the situation which has arisen seem to call for watchfulness and, if necessary, quick action on the part of the Administration. I believe therefore that it is my duty to bring to your attention the following facts and recommendations." Einstein considered his message to the president to be of the highest national importance. He was calling attention to what he perceived to be an immediate threat to the security of America. There are scholars who see similarities between Einstein's concerns of decades ago and concerns of today. In 1939, Einstein was referring to international competition on the battlefield.

Today, scholars are equally concerned about international competition, but this time the concerns are centered on what happens within the classrooms of America compared to those in competing nations. Recall in an open letter written to the president of the United States by Dr. Comer. I shared portions of it with you in a previous chapter. In America, we have heard the clarion call before: in 1957, with the Russian Sputnik launch; in the 1960s, with the Coleman report; in the 1980s with "A rising tide of mediocrity"; and again at the turn of the twenty-first century with "No Child Left Behind." Most would agree that in the case of the Sputnik launch, America responded "with all deliberate speed" and prevailed.

Since that time, reasonable people can agree or disagree about how well America has responded to previous challenges from other nations to its international status in education. Nevertheless, according to Robert Compton and colleagues, once again America's international preeminence is being challenged. He makes the case in *Two Million Minutes*, a documentary, that American schools are not adequately competing with those in China and India. The documentary chronicles the lives of two high school students in the United States, India, and China.

Two million minutes is the amount of time that expires from the end of eighth grade to high school graduation. Compton argues, "When it was Finland who was winning, it wasn't such a concern. But now that our K–12 students are being outperformed academically by China and India, the two highest populated countries in the world with the fastest growing economies and with cultures that embrace intellectual challenge, it is cause for serious concern."

He continues, "Most worrisome, is that few Americans are even aware that India and China, with a combined 2.3 billion people, have over 400 million students in K–12 education compared to our 53 million. Our knowledge of these two cultures is seriously out of date and that has to change. Our economic future depends on it." The film shows that compared to China and India, in the United States, fewer hours are devoted to academic studies and more time is spent on extracurricular activities. The theme of *Two Million Minutes* is that community leaders, parents, students, and ILs should refocus and redouble their efforts to improve student academic achievement levels in American schools.

I propose that one way to significantly improve students' academic achievement level is to fully understand, teach, and apply effort-based teaching and learning principles. And perhaps the most famous formula in the world can be utilized to facilitate the realization of this noble and lofty goal. Albert Einstein's famous scientific expression has played a significant role in developing successful responses to many unique challenges in technology and medicine. Perhaps with the assistance of this same formula, $E=mc^2$, we will experience equally dramatic results for encouraging the use of effort methods in education. Symbols can effectively capture the essence of ideas and concepts. By doing so, these same symbols facilitate the comprehension and implementation of otherwise complex ideas.

Steven Sample, the tenth president of the University of Southern California, declares: "Effective leaders are able to create, manipulate and exemplify not only stories but symbols, slogans, and mantras as well. All of these help define in the minds of followers the essence of the leader's vision and his character" (2003, p. 148).

It is my desire that $E=mc^2$ will do for effort-based instruction and learning what the Nike symbol has done for sneakers, what acronyms have done for the names of verbose divisions and organizations, and what mnemonics have done for memorizing lengthy bits of important information. Most students, parents, and educators are familiar with this formula but few can accurately explain its meaning.

Suppose students, including elementary students, were able to articulate the fundamental principles of this expression. How many students might develop an interest in math or science because of its ubiquitous application throughout grade levels? And for instructional leaders, $E=mc^2$ can become one symbol that helps change minds away from "bell curve" instruction, and help lead to a paradigm shift that embraces effort-based instruction and learning.

BIOGRAPHY OF E=MC²

David Bodanis (2000) offers a chronology of this most famous scientific expression and explains its meaning in easily understood language. He explains that Antoine Laurent Lavoisier conducted an experiment to determine whether old metal sealed in a container and heated or burned to increase the rate at which the metal would rust would weigh more or less. After allowing the metal to cool, he weighed it and also measured the amount of air that might have escaped. He was so surprised with the results that he repeated the experiment several times, achieving the same result. The rusted metal did not weigh less nor did it weigh the same; it weighed more than its original weight.

Lavoisier measured the amount of weight the metal gained. Then he measured the air in the container and discovered it had decreased in weight by the exact amount the metal had gained weight. What happened? Some of the gasses in the air had attached to the metal. What he had demonstrated was that matter could transform from one form to another. This was considered a major discovery in the 1700s.

Let's look a little more at how this works. Bodanis explains "c" is the speed of light and was probably used because *celeritas* is a Latin word meaning "swiftness." He continues: "The speed of light becomes the fundamental speed limit in our universe: nothing can go faster" (p. 51). Energy and mass were thought to be separate entities for centuries. Einstein demonstrated that there could be a transfer between energy and mass. Finally, "c² is a huge number. In units of mph, c is 670 million, and so c² is 448,900,000,000,000,000" (p. 53). Hence, "A very little mass gets enormously magnified whenever it travels through the equation and emerges on the side of energy" (p. 69). One might reason this expression is not so simple to comprehend. That's why the concept that we want to hold onto regarding effort-based instruction is that in physics, a little mass can yield a huge amount of energy and similarly, in education, a little motivation can inspire a huge amount of effort.

USING E=MC² AS AN ANALOGY IN EDUCATION

Bodanis (2000) explains E=mc² represents Energy equals Mass times the Speed of Light (c) squared. Simplified, this merely means that the mass of any object multiplied by the speed of light squared reveals the amount of energy it possesses if converted to energy. "E" is the vast domain of energies, and "m" is the material stuff of the universe. But "c" is simply the speed of light." Because the speed of light is such a large number, this means a very small amount of mass when multiplied by this large number squared, yields a phenomenal amount of energy (p. 37). The release of such massive amounts of energy can obviously be used for productive or nonproductive purposes. It is like all other discoveries; its application determines its usefulness. For example, fire can be used for good or bad purposes.

Remember, of course, that our purpose for calling attention to this famous expression is not to fully comprehend its scientific properties, but to use its fame to spread the principles of effort-based thinking and teaching. We can refer to it as the "smart formula."

It is my hope that this formula will keep in the forefront of educational discourse what really matters most with regard to the development of high achievers: effort and persistence. A practical analogy of this formula's original application and effort-based instruction and learning can be explained (see table 4.1).

Using $E=mc^2$ in physics	Using $E=mc^2$ in education
➤ Energy and mass are the same. Energy transforms itself into mass and mass transforms itself into energy. One begets the other.	➤ Effort and motivation are the same (effort converts into motivation and motivation converts into effort). Another way to express this interaction is to say effort transforms into motivation and motivation transforms into effort. One begets the other.
➤ The speed of light provides a bridge for mass to transform into massive energy.	➤ Concentration (focus) provides a platform for motivation to transform itself into effort.
➤ Mass times the speed of light squared (mc^2) releases extraordinary energy.	➤ Motivation times concentration squared (mc^2) can generate extraordinary effort.
➤ All three, energy, mass, and the speed of light squared, are required to unleash massive energy.	➤ All three—effort, motivation, and concentration (focus)—are required to generate effective effort (Weiner, 1980).
➤ The central insight is a small amount of mass can be converted into massive energy.	➤ The central insight is a small amount of motivation can be converted into a great deal of concentrated effort (deliberate practice).

Table 4.1. $E=mc^2$ Analogy — The Smart Formula

Figure 4.1. The Smart Formula

For our educational purposes, E=mc² can be taken to mean that effective fffort on students' part (E) can be achieved when a small amount of motivation (m) causes students to concentrate (c) on their learning in guided and focused ways (c²). This way of looking at this is important because it connects motivation and effort, not motivation and proficiency. Effort is the gold standard for academic proficiency. It underscores what impacts learning the most and de-emphasizes "bell curve" thinking and teaching. Bobby Knight, the famous college basketball coach, is reported to have stated: "The will to succeed is important, but what's more important is the will to prepare." E=mc² revealed profound insights in physics. I believe it can do the same for effort-based teaching and learning principles, by helping focus attention onto it.

I recommend teaching this effort-based formula to ILs, students, and parents. You can refer to it as the "smart formula." If students were asked whether they understood the bell curve or grading on a curve, many of them will be able to articulate that a few students receive "As" and "Fs" while most students receive average grades. This explains why some students, instructional leaders, and parents are potentially at risk. Too many still embrace a faulty belief system that suggests some students have the "right stuff" and other students do not.

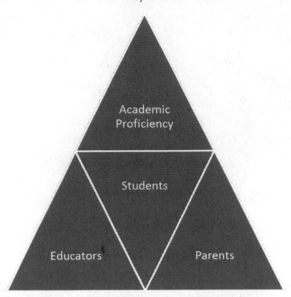

Figure 4.2. Teach the smart formula to educators, students, and parents.

Applying Attribution Theory

Attribution theory attempts to explain the world and to determine the cause of an event or behavior. Fritz Heider first wrote about attribution theory in 1958 in his book, *The Psychology of Interpersonal Relationships*. It is worth noting that Heider's work was published more than fifty years ago. Bernard Weiner (1980) was one of the first to relate attribution concepts to education. His attribution theory is one of the most celebrated educational theories of the second half of the twentieth century.

This theory provides a mental framework that puts students and instructional leaders in control of learning and teaching, exactly where they should be. To believe otherwise promotes frustration and anxiety within the classroom. Psychologists have explained this is why some people fear flying. They are normal well-adjusted people yet their emotional state changes when flying because when flying, one relinquishes complete control to pilots and air traffic controllers. How unsettling it must be for some students and instructional leaders who believe their fate is determined by the luck of the draw, because they believe ultimately they have little control over human capacity.

I submit that when we change our beliefs we will change our professional practice, thus unleashing the full human potential and thirst for learning. Attribution theory assumes that people attempt to determine why they behave as they do. This theory also postulates that one attempts to maintain a positive self-image. For example, if one performs well, he will take credit for his success. However, if one performs poorly, he is likely to blame others. What is even more debilitating is when students blame themselves for their poor performance after asserting, "I did my best." Recall Bill Russell's childhood. He had already encountered multiple failure experiences when his coach saw something in him that Russell perhaps did not see in himself.

Some students really do not know how to apply effective effort to be academically proficient. This situation sheds light not only on the skill level of students, but also on that of instructional leaders as well. Attribution theory is mainly about motivation and the perceived cause of prior achievement. The most important factors affecting attributions are as follows:

- First, the cause of the success or failure may be internal or external. In other words, we may succeed or fail because of circumstances we believe have their origin within us or because of ones that originate in our environment.
- Second, the cause of the success or failure may be either stable or unstable. If we believe the cause is stable, then the outcome is likely to be the same if we perform the same behavior on another occasion. If it is believed to be unstable, the outcome is likely to be different on another occasion.
- Third, the cause of the success or failure may be either controllable or uncontrollable. A controllable factor is one that we believe we ourselves can alter if we wish to do so. An uncontrollable factor is one that we do not believe we can easily alter.

The central concept of attribution theory is that one's motivation level is directly related to his perceived likelihood of success or failure. That is, if one believes he cannot successfully complete a task, he is not likely to give his best effort to succeed. Remember $E=mc^2$, a little motivation can generate phenomenal effort. The four components of successful task completion are:

- Ability
- Task Difficulty
- Luck
- Effort

ILs should have an operational definition of effort. Effort is effectively applying concentrated persistence to an academic task. Students should be taught that perseverance cannot be defeated. They should come to realize that no one successfully completes every academic task in his desired amount of time, but appropriate methods and persistence, along with concentrated effort, offer a one-way highway to success.

ILs should remember that failure begets failure. The goal of effective teaching is to challenge students at a level just below their maximum skill level. Recall that Bloom's research revealed effort and perseverance were the keys to achievement—not natural talent (McConnell, 1983).

Listen and Work Hard

I recall that as an elementary campus instructional leader, our school motto was: "Listen and Work Hard." Working hard is a character trait of successful people. Alan Schoenfeld, a university math professor, developed a computer program to teach algebra concepts.

One student, a nurse in her mid-twenties, was videotaped attempting to solve an algebra problem. Initially, she was puzzled as to what procedure would lead to answering the problem successfully. Even though she was confused, she remained focused and persistent. Twenty-two minutes later, she solved the problem. Schoenfeld laments that the problem in eighth grade mathematics is that most eighth grade students would have probably given up after two minutes of unsuccessfully solving the problem. He tested this belief by asking high school students how much time and effort they would exert to solve a math problem before throwing in the towel. Thirty seconds to five minutes was their response. The average time expressed was two minutes.

The video was one of Schoenfeld's favorites because it demonstrated the "secret to learning mathematics" (Gladwell, 2008, p. 245). His student brainstormed. She went over the same problem many times. She thought out loud. She was persistent. She simply did not give up. She knew there was something wrong with her analysis about how to draw a vertical line, and she would not stop until she was absolutely sure she had it right (Gladwell, 2008). I submit this type of persistence should, and can, be effectively taught in our classrooms.

I have come to understand that with too many students there is an academic tug of war between students and classroom instructional leaders. These types of students are attempting to demonstrate how little they know. This might sound surprising to some, but I am sure many instructional leaders are very familiar with what I am describing. These types of students attempt to convince ILs how little they know to cause ILs to reveal the correct answer. During this tug of war, ILs encourage students to think critically and persevere, while at the same time students in various ways communicate, "I don't understand; just give me the answer."

Schoenfeld provides a possible solution to this type of student resistance to commit to complex problems that are void of easy solutions. He teaches problem solving where the focus "is to get his students to unlearn the mathematical habits" that are counterproductive and replace them with more efficient ones (Gladwell, 2008, p. 246). He accomplishes this by giving students complex assignments that will require two weeks to complete. He then tells them that many of them will wait until the second week before they begin working on them. He cautions the students that their lack of commitment is a plan for failure—that successful completion of the assignment will require concentrated effort (E=mc²) for two weeks.

Here is the most liberating portion of this story. We sometimes think of being good at mathematics as an innate ability. You either have 'it' or you don't. But to Schoenfeld, it is not so much ability as it is ones mindset; you master mathematics if you are willing to try. Success is a function of persistence and resolve and the willingness to work hard. (Gladwell, 2008, p. 246).

In Japan, the emphasis is on effort and deep comprehension of mathematical concepts. Students are not rushed through classroom content because of rigid timetables tied to scope and sequence calendars that allow for little flexibility. As in Schoenfeld's class, these students in Japan might devote an entire class period to solving one problem.

Students taught in this manner come away with a deeper understanding and armed with many strategies for solving problems. After years of this kind of learning the average Japanese student performs better than the top 5 percent of U.S. students in mathematics (Darling-Hammond, 1997, p. 52). Notwithstanding the inherent challenges that accompany the standards era, ILs would indeed benefit from identifying ways to incorporate more in-depth effort-based teaching into their classrooms.

As with my first coaching experience, when students make the connection between effort and excellent performance, both increase. That is, as effort increases, performance improves and as performance improves, effort increases. Thus, E=mc² is being effectively applied. A small amount of motivation can yield a phenomenal amount of effort. Believe it. It works. To illustrate this point, recall the Trends in International Mathematics and Science Study (TIMSS) is given every four years to middle school and elementary students worldwide. All students taking this examination are required to answer a detailed questionnaire with approximately 120 questions. As a result, some students do not complete the entire questionnaire. A university professor, Erling Boe, discovered something interesting about this laborious questionnaire. That is, it could be rank ordered based on the average number of answers completed by each student's country. Then this rank ordered list could be compared to the rank order of countries based on average students' performance in math.

Here is the shocker. The two lists are identical. The performance of students listed by countries could be determined without administering one TIMSS examination. Just by analyzing which countries had the highest rate of students who were willing to persevere and complete the very lengthy survey, it could be accurately predicted which countries would score highest on the math exam (Gladwell, 2008). Again, we would know exactly where each country would rank based on the survey without students answering one math problem. Think about how profound this revelation is for instructional leaders

Let's apply this same effort-based concept on all our campuses. We would then be able to predict that those students enrolled in classrooms with a strong effort-based philosophy ($E=mc^2$), would, other things being equal, have a higher student achievement rate than students enrolled in classrooms where a "bell curve" philosophy is being practiced. Can you guess the five countries at the top of the TIMSS math list for 2007 and 2011? Singapore, South Korea, China (Taiwan), Hong Kong, and Japan are the top five countries (National Center for Education Statistics; Gladwell, 2008).

These top ranked, high performing nations seem to agree that the formula for academic success is having a rigorous curriculum, high expectations and a laser like focus on galvanizing student effort. Let's examine one of them, Korea, to better understand how rigor on steroids really looks—the good, the bad, and the ugly.

RIGOR ON STEROIDS

During 2010–2011 school year, Amanda Ripley (2013) followed three U.S. foreign-exchange students who attended high school in Korea, Finland, and Poland. She interviewed officials in each country as well as the three foreign-exchange students. Here is what she discovered about the Korea education system.

In class, students are graded on a curve and only 4 percent of them can get the top score in spite of how hard they worked. High school classes end at approximately 4:00 p.m. "After classes, the kids cleaned the school, mopping the floors, wiping the chalkboards and empting the garbage" (p. 56). Work is at the center of Korean school culture, including the unpleasant kind, and no one is exempt.

At 4:30, students return to their classes to begin test-prep for the college entrance exam. Afterwards, they eat dinner in the school cafeteria. Yes, dinner. And for Korean students, a typical day of school does not stop here. Now it is time for *yaja*. This is a two hour independent study period that is supervised by teachers. At roughly 9:00 p.m., students finally leave the campus. But not all students return home to their parents immediately. Most, seven out of ten, report to *hagwons*. *Hagwons* are private tutoring academies; this is where the real learning takes place. The teachers are very capable and highly paid. They teach until curfew; otherwise students would continue to study. Yes, curfew. By law teaching and studying must stop in the *hagwons* by 11:00 p.m. This gives students time to hurry home to sleep and be prepared to complete the same schedule the next day, returning to school by 8:00 a.m. *Hagwons* have even made their way into the United States. Koreans attending elite American universities receive tutoring and support in these institutions.

Oh, what about sports? There are very few sports teams if there are any at all. Basically, studying is their extracurricular sport. In Korea, students go to school nearly twelve hours a day when we consider the *yajas* and *hagwons*. And there's more. These students already attend school nearly two months longer than U.S. students. In Korea, school seems to never stop.

So what are the results of all their efforts to improve students' academic achievement? As recently as the 1950s most Koreans were illiterate and today, they are among the leading nations in academic achievement: Studying, high expectations, hard work, and learning at high levels are woven into the fabric of their culture.

Schools have one clear goal and that is ensuring all students master highly challenging academic content. Many believe it is a bridge to success—overcoming national poverty and illiteracy. High performing countries like Korea do not engage in "bell curve" teaching. Finland, another high performing nation, for instance, has a high special education population, one of the highest in the world. However, Finnish "Teachers considered most special ed students to have temporary learning difficulties, rather than permanent disabilities" (Ripley, 2013, p. 164). It is this type of mindset that is central to the accomplishments of education powerhouses and Korea is one of its leaders.

Notwithstanding the celebrated success of their educational system, some in Korea are not impressed. They point to the obvious stress and strain this type of educational system has perpetrated on some students and even parents—an unhealthy preoccupation with test scores. They seem to be addicted to competing for rank on exams, almost as much as they focus on the learning itself.

Thus, there is a need for balance as we drive students toward education excellence. Offering alibis for some students, lowering expectations for others, and denying there is a real need for improvement within particular areas of the U.S. educational system serves only to perpetuate the status quo. For instance, a survey of international and U.S. foreign-exchange students revealed that both groups agreed school was easier in the United States than school abroad (Ripley, 2013). In addition, a similar survey revealed thirty-five countries scored above American students in math. Yet, U.S. students were more likely to report they earned good math grades than students in thirty-seven other countries (OECD, PISA, 2012). These data raise one obvious question. How much rigor is required in U.S. schools to earn excellent grades?

THE AFFLUENZA MINDSET

In various ways, U.S. students seem to be at the opposite end of the rigor and hard work continuum compared to some high performing nations.

We all, students, parents, and ILs must accept some responsibility for the current state of affairs as it relates to developing and maintaining rigor in every classroom. Accountability and authentic praise may well be diminishing. Consider that on many sports teams, children expect awards regardless of their poor performance or lack of hard work. It is not uncommon for all members of teams to receive trophies or medals. Do they all deserve the gold? What about the bronze or the silver medal? Are there valuable lessons to be learned from losing and winning? The trophy and medal industrial complex must be flourishing. Is praise used too often, even when it is not earned? The psychologist Carol Dweck at Stanford University cautions that nonstop praise can become counterproductive— it diminishes effort.

There is even a disease used to explain why some students are not motivated to work hard and achieve their full potential in school—affluenza. It is a complex psychological concept. Essentially, it is a false sense of entitlement as well as an inability to delay gratification. It is not an official disease. Currently, this term does not appear in the *Diagnostic and Statistical Manual of Mental Disorders* (DSM) (this manual list the official classification of mental disorders).

Affluenza is generally thought of as a wealthy person's disease. Children who grow up in an environment where they believe they themselves are not really accountable for their actions or inactions because their parents have wealth and power are vulnerable to this disease. There are varying degrees of wealth; hence, I believe students from all economic strata can develop a sense of entitlement or "it is someone else's fault" attitude.

Thus affluenza is a mindset rather than some arbitrary amount of wealth. Moreover, these students typically have poor impulse control. An Atlanta psychologist, Mary Gresham (2013) has conducted research in this area to demonstrate how this type of thinking affects some of our students. Students were given a set of serious school infractions (caught for the third time with alcohol on campus or plagiarizing) and asked whether they thought their parents would object or not if the school attempted to punish them. Some students indicated that their parents would object.

A few research studies warn that the use of red pens by classroom instructional leaders can hurt the feelings of certain students and using them may induce ILs to give lower grades (Dukes and Albanesi, 2012; Bartlett, 2010). Maslow was correct. Striving to achieve self-actualization is essential. School centered instruction is vital too. And schools need caring ILs.

But do we have to exchange high self-esteem for high self-efficacy and hard work? I recommend ILs explore methods that nurture all three. We should strive to find a state of equilibrium between some of the extreme practices within the Korean education system and some of the easygoing practices in the United States. In short, all students can and should be taught the value of effort, motivation and concentration—E=mc².

Teaching students directly or indirectly to fanatically compete for rank points and to be first in class at all cost can create difficulties. In this type of education system, regardless of the country, the goal of winning can superseded real learning eventually. Consider the story of the Zen Master, for instance, and a discussion he had with one of his students. A conscientious student wanted to become a Zen Master. So he asked the Zen Master, How long would it take to become excellent? The Zen master answered, "Five years" if done correctly. The student, looking disappointed asked: Suppose I worked really fast. Then how long would it take me to become a Zen Master? The Zen Master replied, "Ten years." The frustrated student tried one last time to explain his plan for high achievement. You don't seem to understand, he said. My goal is to be first, at the top of my class and I am willing to work really fast and really hard. Doing it that way, how long will it take to achieve my goal? "Fifteen years" the Zen Master stated. Why so long he asked? It seems the faster I work, the longer it takes to accomplish my goal. Why?

The Zen Master responded: "Because you will have one eye on completing the task and that leaves only one eye for learning." Students must have both eyes on learning.

Grades can be tricky if we are not careful. While they are beneficial and necessary, they can stifle intrinsic motivation. This has been demonstrated in considerable research studies. That is, some students shift their focus from deep learning to attaining grades or the highest rank number. Assessed later, all too often, we discover that their working knowledge or skill level is not congruent with the grade they received earlier.

It is time to reexamine how extensively we are promoting authentic rigor and perseverance in our schools and communities. ILs should be proactive when developing a campus culture that encourages hard work. Through the use of technology, PTA meetings, parent workshops and the like, ILs should assist parents, students, and colleagues with understanding the academic benefits of students acquiring delayed gratification skills.

As indicated in Korea, some students have become fanatical and obsessed with scores and rankings; to a point they have lost sight of the real purpose of learning. Recently, however, they have come to recognize a need to moderate their thinking in this regard. For example, Korea has borrowed, in part, from the U.S. university admission system in that students are admitted on criteria other than test scores only. We can do the same by maintaining what we know works; borrowing what is good from high performing countries and rejecting what we know is detrimental to the wellbeing of children.

RIGOR AND HARD WORK

Angela Duckworth and Carol Dweck share fascinating studies about what works in regard to how rigorous methods and hard work yield favorable results. After examining the effectiveness of effort-based principles, Duckworth (2009a) postulates that beyond IQ and talent, there is something else responsible for individual success. She refers to that something else as "grit." Grit is defined as using passion and perseverance to achieve long-term goals. She declares, "Nobody is talented enough to not have to work hard." She developed the "Grit Scale," which through a questionnaire, measures the degree of passion and determination one possesses. Participants were asked to indicate to what degree they disagreed or agreed with a list of similar questions: "I aim to be the best in the world at what I do. I have overcome setbacks to conquer an important challenge." The Grit Scale is online for anyone to take. She used the Grit Scale to predict successfully which West Point cadets would remain beyond the summer program.

The Grit Scale was equally successful with spelling-bee students. ILs should be aware of two important findings: One—even though grit is positively correlated with success, it is not positively correlated with IQ. That is, just because one scores higher on IQ tests does not necessarily mean he will be more successful than a grittier person who has a lower IQ score. And two—grit can be taught.

To illustrate its teachableness, Carol S. Dweck (2006), a psychologist at Stanford University, conducted a study of fifth grade students. She first administered an IQ assessment to a random sample of them. After receiving the results, researchers commented to one group of students, "You must be smart." The researchers then commented to the other group of fifth graders, "You must have worked really hard."

Next, the researchers gave an eight-grade IQ assessment to both groups. Dweck observed students who were praised for their effort persevered while students praised for their intelligence quickly became discouraged. Finally, Dweck administered another grade appropriate IQ test.

Here is what is profoundly interesting about her research. The students that were praised for their effort increased their intelligence score by 30 percent while those students who were praised for their intelligence had a 20 percent drop on their score. That is why I recommend saying to students, "The smartest works the hardest." When ILs embrace a research-based belief system as well as effort-based principles, students will naturally begin to believe differently and learn more efficiently. Grittiness is a characteristic we all should seek to acquire, ILs and students alike.

Another example of the results of hard work is Supreme Court Justice Sonia Sotomayor. She was a nominee to the United States Supreme Court in the summer of 2009. Her father died when she was just nine years old; thereafter, she was raised by her mother. Yet because of perseverance (E=mc²), Judge Sotomayor graduated with an AB, summa cum laude, from Princeton University in 1976 and received her JD from Yale Law School in 1979, where she was an editor at the *Yale Law Journal*. She credits her phenomenal academic success to hard work. Below are excerpts from her opening statement before the Senate Judiciary Committee.

> On her own, my mother raised my brother and me. She taught us that the key to success in America is a good education. And she set the example, studying alongside my brother and me at our kitchen table so that she could become a registered nurse. We worked hard. I poured myself into my studies at Cardinal Spellman High School, earning scholarships to Princeton University and then Yale Law School, while my brother went to medical school. Our achievements are due to the values that we learned as children, and they have continued to guide my life's endeavors. I try to pass on this legacy by serving as a mentor and friend to my many godchildren and students of all backgrounds. (Supreme Court Justice Sonia Sotomayor)

EFFECTIVELY TEACHING EFFORT

The quickest is the smartest! Cowboys understood the distinct advantage of being a quick draw. This kind of "quick draw" thinking, however, is pervasive in classrooms today. Many students correlate quick responses in the classroom with high intelligence.

They extend this type of analysis to completing class projects and assignments; that is, if it takes a long time for me to complete assignments, I must not be smart. Therefore, why should I continue to overexert myself when apparently I was not born with the "right stuff"? These types of students would much rather be lazy than dumb—we all would.

To perpetuate this unfortunate myth, some students engage in a cover-up of sorts. These students understand the relationship between effort and academic success yet they cover up their efforts and perseverance from other students because, again, if they are devoting significant amounts of time to their studies, they must not be very smart. Otherwise, they would not have to study so hard.

This kind of thinking has actually been documented by Dweck (2006). She asked persons ranging from elementary school age to young adulthood: "When do you feel smart?" The persons who embraced "bell curve" thinking responded: "It's when I don't make any mistakes." "When I finish something fast and it is perfect." Conversely, those persons embracing effort-based concepts responded: "When it's really hard, and I try really hard, and I can do something I couldn't do before" (p. 24).

ILs should discourage the former kind of analysis and encourage the latter.

In fact, according to Stigler and Hiebert (2009), the latter is exactly what occurs in most Japanese classrooms but the opposite is true in many U.S classrooms. For instance, some U.S. ILs consider confusion and frustration exhibited by students in class to be problematic. Students are taught and expected to respond to questions quickly.

To illustrate this point, imagine students being taught how to add and subtract fractions with unlike denominators (1/3+3/7). They would probably be shown how to add fractions with like denominators first (1/4+2/4), then shown how to add simple fractions with unlike denominators (2/2+3/4) and finally students would be asked to solve more complex problems (1/3+3/7). During this entire process, students are warned about common errors and provided opportunities to practice procedures. When students appear confused, some ILs immediately provide assistance. What message do students receive? "The IL does not think I can reason my way to the correct answer."

Conversely, instructors in Japan apparently possess a different belief system. They use confusion and frustration to reinforce effort principles while at the same time teach concepts. They believe students learn best when they struggle with problems; the quickest is not the smartest. Students are encouraged to discuss their thinking and use their acquired knowledge in order to make sense of the information they will receive later. Students struggle, making mistakes and learning from them is thought to promote deep and lasting understanding in Japan. This method makes students smarter.

On some campuses, we have to make being smart cool again. It is well documented that some students are ridiculed for being smart. Moreover, ILs should strive to make effort-based principles cool as well. In other words, students should come to understand that effort and smart coexist. In fact, concentrated effort causes one to become even smarter than before.

Ericsson (1993), in a landmark study, revealed what it takes to develop phenomenal talents. "Deliberate practice is above all an effort of focus and concentration" (p. 70). His research study points out that it takes ten thousand hours of concentrated effort ($E=mc^2$) to develop phenomenally elite performing skills. He even studied the lives of Mozart and other great performers and reached the same conclusion. It takes ten thousand hours to acquire elite status. And as the amount of time and deliberate practice decreases, so does the quality of the performance. Just another example that success is found in one's blood, sweat, and tears, not in genes.

In addition, ILs can explain to students that not all of them have equal background knowledge and experience, and that these varying previous experiences cause students to begin each school year at different starting points. If experienced ice skaters and novices are in the same training session, one should not consider one group more gifted than the other. They possess different background knowledge and experiences. Thus, they are at different skill levels. With appropriate training, concentrated effort, and persistence, over time both groups should achieve comparably well. Their achievement level is related to their commitment.

This is how it is in the classroom. Students answer questions at different rates and begin each school year with differences in the quality of prior knowledge and experiences. Notwithstanding, ILs should operate from the premise that they all are smart enough to become proficient with rigorous curricula. The notion that quick responses are analogous with quality thinking and high achievers is not useful. Some of the best minds engage in a process rooted in hard work and effort. This process includes curiosity, brainstorming, pondering, thinking, rethinking, checking, and rechecking possible solutions. Classroom ILs promote this kind of effort-based process ($E=mc^2$) by asking students similar questions: Do these assignments reflect your best work? How can you improve your work? How much time did you devote to this assignment?

Also, instructional leaders might make similar types of comments, such as: I will give you a moment to think before you respond. Discuss your thoughts with a classmate before you respond. Take your time before responding; you will not receive credit for answering first. I am looking for thoughtful responses. Nick Imoru of Esteem Motivation, Inc. illustrates the effectiveness of effort with a story about Thomas Edison.

Never Give Up—Thomas Edison

Thomas Alva Edison had only three months of schooling before he was considered by his teacher to be "too stupid to learn" and was sent home. Nancy Edison, his mother, was very annoyed at his teacher for saying this, and decided to teach Thomas herself. However, she did encourage him to be self-educated, and he spent most of his time in the library reading books, especially scientific books. His mother later bought him the *Dictionary of Science*, and he read it all. Before Thomas Edison was ten, he had already read *History of England, Decline and Fall of the Roman Empire, History of the World*, Burton's *The Anatomy Of Melancholy, The Age of Reason*, and a number of works on practical chemistry. When he was ten years old, he set up his own chemical laboratory in the basement of his house.

Life for Thomas was not an easy one, so when he was twelve, he took a job as a newspaper boy. He sold newspapers, candy, books, fruits, and other snacks to train passengers. At fifteen, he purchased a small printing press located at the train station. His turning point came when he rescued the son of the railway stationmaster. To show his appreciation to Edison, he taught Edison the art of telegraphy. When he was seventeen, Thomas became one of the most expert telegraph operators. This is a man who had been written off by his schoolteacher.

Edison continued to spend time and money on self-improvement, and as a result, he gained the equivalent of many college degrees, although he had only three months of formal education. Edison realized his limitations and used the brains of others. He had a pool of sixty-one talented people, including chemists, engineers, model makers, scientists, mathematicians, and skilled mechanics.

During his lifetime, he patented more than 1,100 inventions. One of his inventions was the electric light bulb. He succeeded in finding a suitable substance to make a light bulb filament out of, only after failing more than ten thousand times. As a result of this incredible persistence, Thomas Edison invented something that changed the world and technology forever—the light bulb. He installed a lighting system in New York and lit it up. Everyone thought that Thomas was a wizard, and gave him the name "Wizard of Menlo Park."

Friends, you may get a lot of negative feedback from others, and so much happens in life to block the road you wish to travel. But never give up! Stay at it, just like Edison did. In the fullness of time, you will achieve success, and maybe even arrive at greatness, where the whole world will celebrate you. You have to understand that there are no shortcuts to building a life of substance. It's an on-going process. It takes time, real effort, and a desire to become more than you already are. It's a worthy challenge. Education alone will not make you successful, although it does help. Edison was successful because he was creative and had a strong willingness to learn new things.

He had a mastermind alliance with a group of experts to bridge his weakness. He was also persistent in whatever he did. When he failed ten thousand times to perfect the electric light bulb, he did not treat it as ten thousand failures. To Edison, he found ten thousand ways that did not work! Yes, it is up to you! Do not forget, your future is not a function of your current circumstances. With effort you can change it, and be the master of your destiny.

Stories like this one, poems, and lyrics to motivational songs can be read to students to highlight the connection between effort and successful performance. Here is an example, from Napoleon Hill, author of *Think and Grow Rich*: "Effort only fully releases its reward after a person refuses to quit."

When I first read this story about Edison, the reference to failure captured my attention. Students should come to understand there is nothing bad about failure. It is the acceptance of failure that is bad. For example, if students conclude they failed, this indicates they know they didn't understand or give their best effort, and that their failure is temporary. On the other hand, if they reason "we are failures," this is debilitating. Obviously, these two groups possess drastically different belief systems.

As indicated earlier, students should understand that persistence cannot fail in the long run. In Silicon Valley, short-term failure is expected. It is a vital part of the learning process. Technology innovators use their failures as platforms that ultimately lead to success.

A 1997 newspaper article appeared in the *Chicago Tribune*. It is from a commercial Michael Jordan made where he states: "I've missed more than nine thousand shots in my career. I've lost almost three hundred games. Twenty-six times I've been trusted to take the game winning shot and missed. I've failed over, and over and over again in my life. And that is why I succeed." This type of thinking and persistence can and should be taught.

Teach Differently

When we begin to teach differently, students will practice learning differently. It would help students if instructional leaders thought differently regarding effort. For example, what if effort ($E=mc^2$) were thought of as a discipline to be taught from pre-kindergarten through the twelfth grade, just as we teach mathematics or literacy?

Too many view effort-based concepts as a family value that should be taught exclusively at home. I say this because if effort principles work, and we believe they work, then why haven't we taught them in our classrooms? One classroom or a few ILs teaching effort-based principles is insufficient. There has to be a system-wide approach to their application.

If effort principles are not taught at home, teach them at school. If they are taught at home, reinforce them at school. Talk to any coach, choir, or band director, or perhaps the drama or art instructors—they can all teach effort concepts. Some might reason that I have enough to teach without adding something else. Effort principles can and should be taught simultaneously with required curricula.

Teach students to think differently about their brain. Explain the brain is like the neurological muscle in one's body. The more they exercise it in the right way the stronger and more efficient it becomes. The exercise their brain responds to is concentrated effort. As indicated in the previous chapter, this analogy is supported by neurological research. Also, exploit every teachable moment to establish effort principles. Create a culture that values effort. If it is visible in your eyes, if it is what you believe, students feel it and understand it. Table 4.2 delineates a list of IL effort-based behaviors.

An effort-based IL:

> Believes all students are smart enough to demonstrate proficiency with rigorous curricula

> Re-teaches and reassesses

> Rewards students' effort

> Accepts responsibility for student academic progress

> Maintains positive attitude

> Teaches students, not content

> Attends to students' differences

> Ascertains what motivates students; each one is different

> Attempts to minimize classroom disruptions

> Accepts responsibility for student behavior in classroom

> Is eager to share and learn from colleagues

> Makes the classroom come alive

> Has students who demonstrate significant academic progress

> Doesn't give up on students

Table 4.2. IL Effort-Based Behaviors

It is the preponderance of these effort-based behaviors as well as their collective effect on students' academic learning that separates the effort-based teacher from the normal distribution teacher.

Motivation Can Be Increased

Motivation is a goal-orientated behavior in that it leads one to becoming committed to effective effort. There are two types of motivation: extrinsic and intrinsic. Extrinsic motivation is effective in some instances; that is, motivation outside of the student's person. Award assemblies, recognition lists, and class stickers would fall in this category. Student characteristics such as age, gender, and personal interests should be considered. Some school districts have resorted to giving students money in exchange for good grades; to date, it has not worked.

In fact, some research reveals extrinsic rewards can stifle motivation for students who already have demonstrated interest in an activity. Mark Lepper, a Stanford University professor, observed that when students were taught the internal value of learning, intrinsic motivation was enhanced. Conversely, when the learning environment was reduced to merely a hurdle to overcome, the purpose for learning was undermined (1998).

Extrinsic motivators do not have to be elaborate. Sometimes just a smile, a nod, or an affirmation will prove to be very effective in terms of motivating students. A caring IL is always motivational and is more likely to connect with students. Students are like adults in that they are motivated when they are engaged and interfacing with others, so group them when appropriate. It is human nature to seek some degree of control. Offer students choices and observe their motivational level heighten. Learning can and should be fun and enjoyable. Using curiosity to set the stage for a lesson, or participating in academic games, captures the attention and interest of students. All praise is not equal. Research has established it should be specific and sincere.

Both extrinsic and intrinsic motivation can be utilized effectively; however, research indicates intrinsic motivation is more likely to sustain itself. Intrinsic motivation is within one's person. Studies have demonstrated it has a higher correlation with high achievers than does external motivation. Success itself is the best intrinsic motivator. As they say, "Nothing succeeds like success." Again, ILs should set the learning threshold just below students' maximum skill level, so students can experience success. In this process, goal setting is the key to stimulating motivation. This ensures students are challenged to get better, and at the same time experience success. It is at this critical juncture that $E=mc^2$ comes into play.

Students who initially might be slightly motivated after experiencing success become even more motivated. Then a spiraling effect occurs. "Thus their well-founded belief in their own effectiveness helps give them the crucial motivation to press on, powering a self-reinforcing cycle" (Colvin, 2008, p. 120). There is phenomenal power in this process. Believe it. No one knows what the limits of academic development are. Since we have established what methods reinforce intrinsic motivation, building and nurturing students' self-efficacy should be the goal of all ILs.

Rather than saying, "You are really smart," it may be more effective to say, "Because of your focus and perseverance you are performing really well." Recall Carol Dweck's research. Perhaps what educators and parents have been saying to motivate students has in fact been counterproductive. Preoccupation with "bell curve" thinking and behaviors stifles motivation. This new insight deserves individual reflection and group discussion and implementation among ILs. It should be implemented on campuses and within communities.

Now, let us turn to the question of what are the professional characteristics of ILs that enable them to set off this internal motivational chain reaction in students that include motivation, effort, and finally improved performance. The answer is simple. They can be found embedded within the concept of deliberate practice itself. It is what ILs believe and do that ignite a spark that ultimately develops into an inextinguishable blaze of curiosity.

As William Arthur Ward expresses it, "The mediocre teacher tells. The good teacher explains. The superior teacher demonstrates. The great teacher inspires." A prerequisite for all students achieving at high levels is ILs first believing they have the skills to teach demanding curricula successfully and, second, believing students possess the capacity to learn it.

Concentration

Sometime I wonder whether sustained focus is becoming a lost art. Engaging in more than one activity at once and making quick decisions appear to be the norm for adolescents and adults alike; it is called multitasking. Technology could facilitate increasing students' intellectual prowess yet at the same time contribute to their inability to effectively focus and concentrate—if we are not careful to assist them in developing an appreciation for sustained focus. We are so preoccupied with celebrating multitasking that we are losing our capacity for deep focus (Jackson, 2008). It is not uncommon to observe students listening to music, text messaging, eating, and doing their homework all at the same time. Notwithstanding various learning styles, there appears to be a need to assist students with sharpening their focus.

Just as we have learned to multitask, we can and must learn to improve purposeful concentration. This term means to focus, concentrate, ponder, or think with an academic purpose. ILs should use it and similar terms to underscore what it takes to learn at high levels. But how can we specifically teach students to do this well? Walter Mischel's (1990) studies might assist in this regard. He examined the process that enables preschoolers to delay gratification for a greater reward. His study is known as the "marshmallow experiment."

Toddlers were promised another marshmallow if they could wait twenty minutes before eating the first treats. Obviously, some waited and others could not resist the temptation of immediately enjoying marshmallows. Subsequent to the initial experiment, both groups of students were observed into their teenage years.

The preschoolers who were able to delay gratification, compared to their impulsive counterparts, demonstrated superior personality traits as adolescents based on surveys of parents and teachers. The patient group also performed better on college entrance exams. In particular, the patient group was able to concentrate better than the impulsive group of students.

Mischel studied preschoolers and adolescents. But what about adults: Does possessing self-discipline during childhood benefit adult behavior? Moffitt's (2010) and his colleagues addressed this question. They followed one thousand children from birth until thirty-two years of age. They wanted to know, like Mischel, whether self-control predicts important adult outcomes.

After removing students who were later diagnosed with attention-deficit hyperactivity disorder, the researchers reported: Children with low self-control had poorer health, were more economically unstable, had more single-parent child rearing, and more criminal convictions than participants with higher self-control.

In addition, these researchers asked a different question, one that is of particular interest to ILs: What would happen if we were able to intervene and improve the self-control of some participants? While the design of their study did not include an intervention, they were able to answer this question by administering an instrument that was highly correlated with self-control. Interestingly, after identifying participants who improved their self-control over time, they noticed that those same participants also had better outcomes by age thirty-two.

Similar results have been established with other marshmallow-type studies that have been conducted with older students and even young adults. Take the California State University study, for example, which underscores the negative impact task-switching can have on one's ability to focus on a single task for an extended period of time. In 2011, 185 students were randomly selected to view a lecture on video. During the video, students were texted four, eight, or no times at all.

The texts had nothing to do with the exam and students were asked to respond promptly. Students who waited five minutes or more or who did not receive a text at all scored one letter grade higher than those students who responded within five minutes. Students who demonstrated greater self-discipline were less likely to text.

Another study showed it is not uncommon for thirteen to eighteen year olds to use up to six types of media at one time. These students don't want to miss out on anything and as a result, many lack effective focus and concentration. The brain can only attend to one thing at a time. Steven G. Yantis, a brain researcher at Johns Hopkins University, asserts not only can we not multitask, it takes longer to complete task correctly when we attempt it.

Simply stated, attempting to multitask can have an adverse effect on learning. This problem is exacerbated with students who have attention deficient disorders or who are hyperactive. Those who practice task-switching frequently perform better than those who do it sparingly; however, both groups are less effective compared to those who focus on one task at a time (Sparks, 2012).

These types of studies have been replicated. One even concluded that self-discipline is a better predictor of students' proficiency than IQ (Duckworth, 2005). It appears when adults model self-discipline, meditation, quiet-time, and the like, students are more inclined to do likewise. Armed with this knowledge, ILs and parents should consider ways to improve students' self-discipline and similar qualities. It has been demonstrated they have a positive impact on one's ability to concentrate and focus.

Not only does self-discipline improve concentration, educational psychologist Kathie Nunley (2010) reports there is a section of the brain that is responsible for sifting through stimuli and deciding what we will focus on or ignore.

Further, there is a hierarchy of importance that determines what gets our attention. Four main categories spark our attention. They are listed in order of importance:

- Physical needs
- Novelty
- Self-made choices
- Your name

ILs who embrace this hierarchy of attention should be able to improve the academic focus of their students. Ignoring these focus factors is to accept the status quo regarding students who, for reasons previously delineated, find it difficult to concentrate for extended periods of time.

Purposeful Concentration

Let's drill a little deeper into this notion of purposeful concentration and its benefits by answering the question below:

- A bat and a ball cost $1.10 in total. The bat costs $1.00 more than the ball.
- How much does the ball cost?
- What answer did you give?

According to Shane Frederick (2005), an assistant professor at the Massachusetts Institute of Technology, the most frequent response given during his research study was 10. He developed what is known as the cognitive reflection test (CRT). It is highly correlated with college entrance examination results. That is, those who perform well on his exam perform equally well on university entrance exams, and conversely, those who do poorly on college qualifying tests show a comparable decline in scores with the CRT.

He distinguishes between two types of thinking processes. The first is spontaneous and "does not require or consume much attention" (p. 26): for example, recognizing a familiar person. The second type of mental operation requires "effort, motivation and concentration." Sounds like the E=mc² formula.

Returning to the baseball question; the answer that requires the least amount of effort, motivation and concentration is wrong. Ten is incorrect. Upon reflection, we can readily see that the difference between $1.00 and 10 cents is only 90 cents, not a dollar. Recognizing this distinction solves the problem. Taking time to focus and concentrate while at the same time resisting the temptation to be impulsive as some of the multitasking groups did earlier, should facilitate more thought provoking analyses. The ball costs 5 cents.

Frederick demonstrated the CRT measured impulsivity and lack of focus; first, by observing the response 10 on the answer sheet of the participants and second, by noticing that some of the persons who answered 5 had scratched out 10 before answering correctly. Another interesting aspect about Frederick's research is that participants who answered the question incorrectly had no idea they were wrong.

Those who inaccurately answered 10 estimated 92 percent of participants would answer the question correctly while those who answered 5 predicted 62 percent would respond accurately. Similarly, in too many classrooms, because of inadequate focus and concentration on details, students do not recognize their errors. They think their responses are correct. There is a real need for ILs to guide students' growth in this area.

What can ILs conclude from Fredrick's research? (1) As stated, there is a need to improve students' focus. (2) Higher performing students appreciate the significance of purposeful concentration. And (3) these skills can and should be developed in our schools.

Below is an opportunity for you to apply E=mc² for yourself. I want to convince you, if you are not already, of its viability. Once you are convinced, explain to students E=mc² is the "smart formula" and what you want them to understand is that a small amount of motivation can be converted into a great deal of concentrated effort (deliberate practice). Improving these skills, effort, motivation, and concentration (focus) will enable them to become more academically successful in school as well as other endeavors. When it is clear students are not applying these three academic skills, ask them: Are you using the "smart formula?"

The CRT was administered to more than three thousand persons over a two year period of time. There are only three questions on the entire exam. The other two are below and I have provided the answer for one of them in the Reflective Thoughts section. I would like you to discuss the answer to the third question with colleagues and friends—use the "smart formula."

- If it takes 5 machines 5 minutes to make 5 widgets, how long would it take 100 machines to make 100 widgets?
- In a lake, there is a patch of lily pads. Every day, the patch doubles in size. If it takes forty-eight days for the patch to cover the entire lake, how long would it take for the patch to cover half of the lake?

Deliberate Practice

Turning to the issue of deliberate practice: concentration (focus) is the key component of effective practice; it is necessary to maintain full attention during the complete period of deliberation (Ericsson, 1993, p. 366). The goal of ILs as it relates to concentrated effort should be to assist students with understanding and fully appreciating the differences among work, play, and deliberate practice.

They are distinctly different. Work's primary distinction is that services are generally rendered for pay. Play has no particular goal and is inherently fun. Conversely, deliberate practice includes activities that have been specially designed to improve one's level of performance (Ericsson, 1993). Deliberate practice is so taxing that it can be sustained only for a limited time without leading to exhaustion or "effort constraint" (Ericsson, 1993, p. 369). The most challenging facet of deliberate practice is mental, not physical. The key, again, is to maintain concentration and deliberate practice at a very challenging yet achievable level (Colvin, 2008).

Research overwhelmingly confirms that consistently challenging students to get better reaps extraordinary benefits. Moreover, feedback supports and sustains deliberate practice. Without proper and timely feedback, students give up and stop caring. Under these conditions, efficient learning is almost impossible for even highly motivated students (Ericsson, 1993). Essentially, deliberate practice is focused practice and effort. It is a means to an end. The result can be very invigorating, even though the means can be rather taxing.

Practice without guidance and assistance by the classroom IL is anything but deliberate practice, especially in the initial stages of learning. Students can be released gradually to engage in independent practice only after essential concepts and principles are understood. It should be noted, concerning feedback, that students should use critical thinking skills as a form of feedback. As Richard Paul (2005) points out, students should be taught the skill of thinking about their thinking while they are thinking, thus providing their own feedback that ultimately improves learning.

Repetition is another feature of deliberate practice. Remember, this type of repetition builds on concentration. The student is fully attending to improving performance, not simply engaging in rote repetition. This is a key distinction between practice and deliberate practice.

This type of concentration is analogous to starting a fire by focusing sunlight through a magnifying glass. A great deal of sunlight falls to the earth every day; however, it is diffused. The magnifying glass concentrates (focuses) the sunlight in a way that harnesses its full potential. Concentration within the context of deliberate practice ($E=mc^2$) has a similar effect. During practice, one practices what he has already mastered, while deliberate practice shifts attention to getting better by moving up one notch, practicing new concepts.

Deliberate practice is not necessarily enjoyable. Individuals are motivated to engage in it because they recognize how deliberate practice improves performance (Ericsson, 1993 p. 372). Again, the major components of deliberate practice are focus (concentrated) effort, feedback, and repetition. Because of this kind of academic engagement, students eventually learn to monitor their own performance and, most importantly, they develop an efficacious attitude. When this occurs, effort increases significantly as well as their academic performance. At this point, the principles of $E=mc^2$ are being utilized efficiently.

While there is potential promise in using Einstein's renowned formula $E=mc^2$ ("smart formula") to change minds about human capacity and promulgate effort-based principles in schools, some may explore other symbols and slogans to galvanize support among educators and parents for its widespread use. In any event, students would benefit from the teaching of effort-based principles school wide.

REFLECTIVE THOUGHTS

What are your thoughts and beliefs regarding the following statements and how are they manifested in your daily practice?

- Is your belief system more congruent with the bell-curve philosophy or the $E=mc^2$ philosophy?
- Are you willing to re-examine your core belief system regarding effort and student academic proficiency?
- Does your current belief system support exceptional student academic achievement?
- How do you teach effort-based principles?
- Do they all deserve the gold?
- How can you utilize the expression $E=mc^2$ to promote effort-based principles? (The answer to the CRT question is 5.)

BARE FACTS

- $E=mc^2$ can and should be effectively applied to advance effort-based principles.

- Teaching and leading embraces coaching principles.
- The quickest is not the smartest.
- Students must have both eyes on learning.
- In some ways, our students seem to be at the opposite end of the rigor and hard work continuum.
- We indeed already know more than we need to know to ignite high student achievement for all.
- To increase student effort, tell them, "I noticed you worked really hard."
- Before some IIs can experience the success they seek, they must first take the shackles off and liberate themselves from the kind of thinking Menelaus and Agamemnon accepted a couple millennia ago—the muses are responsible for the achievements of others.

REFERENCES

American Rhetoric. (2009). Sonia Sotomayor *Opening Statement to the Senate Judiciary Committee* Retrieved August 14, 2009 from http://www.americanrhetoric.com/speeches/soniasotomayoropeningstmt.htm.

Atomic Physics, soundtrack. Copyright © J. Arthur Rank Organization, Ltd., 1948. Sterling, PA: Image © Brown Brothers.

Bartlett, T. (2010). The Terror of the Red Pen. *The Chronicle of Higher Education*, August 10. http://chronicle.com/blogs/percolator/the-terror-of-the-red-pen/26120.

Bodanis, D. (2000). *E=mc². A biography of the world's most famous equation.* New York: The Berkley Publishing Group.

Colvin, G. (2008). *Talent is overrated.* New York: Penguin Group.

Compton, R. (2007). *Two million minutes.* Documentary film.

Coon, D. (1986). *Introduction to psychology: Exploration and application.* St. Paul, MN: West Publishing Company.

Darling-Hammond, L. (1997). *The right to learn.* San Francisco, CA: Jossey-Bass.

Duckworth, A. L., and Quinn, P.D. (2009a). Development and validation of the Short Grit Scale (Grit-S). *Journal of Personality Assessment, 91,* 166–74.

Duckworth, A. L., and Quinn, P.D. (2009b). Positive predictors of teacher effectiveness. *Journal of Positive Psychology, 19,* 1–8.

Duckworth, A. L., and Seligman, M. E. P. (2005). Self-discipline outdoes IQ in predicting academic performance of adolescents. *Psychological Science, 16*(12), 939–44.

Dweck, C. S. (2006). *Mindset: The new psychology of success.* New York: Random House.

Dukes, R.L., and Albanesi, H. (2012). Seeing red: Quality of an essay, color of the grading pen, and student reactions to the grading process. *The Social Science Journal, 49,* http://dx.doi.org/10.1016/j.soscij.2012.07.005.

Einstein, A. (1939). Letter to President Roosevelt. Retrieved July 7, 2009 from http://hypertextbook.com/eworld/einstein.shtml.

Ericsson, K. A., Krampe, R., Th., and Tesh-Romer, C. (1993). The role of deliberate practice in the acquisition of expert performance. *Psychological Review, 100,* 363–406.

Frederick, S. (2005). Cognitive reflection and decision making. *Journal of Economic Perspectives, 19,* 25–42.

Gladwell, M. (2008). *Outliers: The story of success.* New York: Little, Brown and Company.

Gresham M. (2013). *Is affluenza a real disorder*? http://atlantafinancialpsychology.com/2013/12/affluenza-real-disorder/.

Hill, N. (2004). *Think and grow rich: The 21st-century edition, revised and updated* . High Roads Media.

Jackson, M. (2008). *Distracted*. New York: Prometheus Books.

Lepper, M. (1998). Intrinsic versus extrinsic motivation: Further thought on turning "play " into "work" and "work into "play." http://www.puki.org/socialpsyc/lepper.html.

Mischel, W., Shoda, Y., and Peake, P. K. (1990). Predicting adolescent cognitive and self-regulatory competencies from preschool delay of gratification: Identifying diagnostic conditions. *Developmental Psychology, 26*(6), 978–86.

McConnell, J. V. (1983). *Understanding human behavior*. New York: Holt, Rinehart and Winston.

Moffitt, T. (2010). A gradient of childhood self-control predicts health, wealth, and public safety: http://www.pnas.org/content/suppl/2011/01/21/1010076108.DCSupplemental/sapp.pdf.

Nunley, K. (2010). "Keeping pace with today's quick brains." Retrieved November 5, 2013, from http://Help4Teachers.com.

OECD (2012), *Education at a Glance 2012: OECD Indicators*, OECD Publishing. http://dx.doi.org/10.1787/eag-2012-en.

Paul, R. (2005). *Critical thinking: Tools for taking charge of your learning and your life*. Upper Saddle River, NJ: Prentice Hall.

PISA 2012 Results. http://www.oecd.org/pisa/keyfindings/pisa-2012-results.htm.

Ripley, A. (2013). *The smartest kids in the world*. New York: Simon and Schuster.

Sample, S. B. (2003). *The contrarian's guide to leadership*. San Francisco, CA: Jossey-Bass.

Sparks, S. D. (2012). Studies on multitasking highlight value of self-control. *Education Week, 31*(31), pgs. 1, 13.

Stigler, J., and Hiebert, J. (2009). *The teaching gap*. New York: Simon & Schuster.

Weiner, B. (1980). *Human motivation*. New York: Holt, Rinehart, and Winston.

Weiner, B. (1986). *An attributional theory of motivation and emotion*. New York: Springer-Verlag.

Whitmore, J. (2002). *Coaching for performance, growing people, performance and purpose*. London: Nicholas Brealey Publishing.

REFLECTIVE THOUGHTS

_____

_____

_____

_____

_____

_____

_____

_____

_____

_____

_____

_____

_____

FIVE

The Apex: Where All Students Achieve at High Levels

Some people see things, and they say, 'Why?' Other people see things that never were, and they say, 'Why not!' —George Bernard Shaw

GETTING TO THE FIFTH LEVEL

Once I attended a retirement dinner where the retiree stated he was a fan of old cowboy movies. He explained, "After the good guy beats up the bad guys and cleans up the town, he always rides off into the horizon. And I always wondered where he went; now I am about to find out."

Erik Erikson, in *Identity and the Life Cycle*, delineated eight stages of life. He discusses the importance of positive self-reflection after retirement. This is addressed in the eighth stage. After discussing the previous seven stages of the life cycle, he postulates that in this final stage, one looks back on his earlier experiences with happiness and a sense of satisfaction or a sense of despair and regret. The conclusion one draws will significantly influence his self-image and behavior (Erikson, 1994). In other words, in later life, one reflects on previous experiences. These reflections, positive or negative, affect one's self-perception.

If you have ever attended a retirement dinner, you know it is a special time for the honoree. Generally, all the family members and coworkers attend. Wonderful remarks are given, some true and some embellished. Gifts fill a designated area. The highlight comes when the honoree receives a retirement plaque and offers farewell remarks. The plaque will have a beginning time and ending time engraved on it. Now, according to Erikson, comes the critical and sobering period in everyone's life.

During this stage of life, one engages in self-reflection. On every plaque, there is an imaginary symbol between the beginning and the ending dates. I can imagine each person reflecting upon what is between those two dates. Not everyone will see a dash. When you are holding your plaque and rewinding your career multiple times, which mark will you see on your plaque?

- A Dash—The dash symbolizes the feeling that I had a sense of urgency about my daily work. I was a leader because I helped create the organizational mission and then consistently followed it. I made a difference in the lives of students and colleagues. I saw success in students who didn't see it in themselves. I persevered! I never acquiesced!
- A Question Mark—The question mark highlights the question, was I successful? Did I keep my eyes on the prize or did I allow myself to be derailed early in my career? Why didn't I believe more in the abilities of others and myself? Notwithstanding all of the social ills in society, how many more students and colleagues could I have possibly helped if I had only believed and persevered?
- A Period—The period illustrates that I did it my way, period. I attended staff training sessions, read the research, and heard what my colleagues had to say in team meetings; however, I knew what I wanted to do and that is exactly what I did. Perhaps I could have experienced more success, but I didn't.
- An Ellipsis—The ellipsis indicates, I wish I had more time so that. . . .

Again, which symbol will you see on your retirement plaque? If you walked away from instructional leadership today, which symbol would you expect to see on your service plaque? All of us who enter the field of education do so because we want to make a difference in the lives of our students. We believe that we can make a difference. At the end of our careers, we hope to experience that sense of satisfaction that comes from knowing we were successful in our job. What we realize along the way, however, or sometimes not until our retirement, is that the journey is not about our success—but about their success. We are successful as instructional leaders only if our students succeed because of our efforts. The following story tells how one teacher made a difference in the life of one student—and how he made a difference in her teaching career.

Elizabeth Silance Ballard first published this fictional story in 1976 in *Home Life* magazine (2008). The story is about an elementary teacher whose name is Mrs. Thompson. Her story begins as follows:

Teddy's letter came today and now that I've read it, I will place it in my cedar chest with the other things that are important to my life. "I wanted you to be the first to know." I smiled as I read the words he had written, and my heart swelled with a pride that I had no right to feel.

Teddy Stallard. I have not seen Teddy Stallard since he was a student in my fifth-grade class, fifteen years ago.

I'm ashamed to say that from the first day he stepped into my classroom, I disliked Teddy. Teachers try hard not to have favorites in a class, but we try even harder not to show dislike for a child, any child.

Nevertheless, every year there are one or two children that one cannot help but be attached to, for teachers are human, and it is human nature to like bright, pretty, intelligent people, whether they are ten years old or twenty-five. And sometimes, not too often fortunately, there will be one or two students to whom the teacher just can't seem to relate.

I had thought myself quite capable of handling my personal feelings along that line until Teddy walked into my life. There wasn't a child I particularly liked that year, but Teddy was most assuredly one I disliked.

He was a dirty little boy. Not just occasionally, but all the time. His hair hung low over his ears, and he actually had to hold it out of his eyes as he wrote his papers in class. (And this was before it was fashionable to do so!) Too, he had a peculiar odor about him that I could never identify.

Yes, his physical faults were many, but his intellect left a lot to be desired. By the end of the first week I knew he was hopelessly behind the others. Not only was he behind, he was just plain slow! I began to withdraw from him immediately.

Any teacher will tell you that it's more of a pleasure to teach a bright child. It is definitely more rewarding for one's ego. But any teacher worth his or her credentials can channel work to the bright child, keeping that child challenged and learning, while the major effort is with the slower ones. Any teacher can do this. Most teachers do, but I didn't. Not that year.

In fact, I concentrated on my best students and let the others follow along as best they could. Ashamed as I am to admit it, I took perverse pleasure in using my red pen; and each time I came to Teddy's papers, the cross-marks (and they were many) were always a little larger and a little redder than necessary. "Poor work!" I would write with a flourish.

While I did not actually ridicule the boy, my attitude was obviously quite apparent to the class, for he quickly became the class "goat," the outcast—the unlovable and the unloved.

He knew I didn't like him, but he didn't know why. Nor did I know—then or now—why I felt such an intense dislike for him. All I know is that he was a little boy no one cared about, and I made no effort on his behalf.

The days rolled by and we made it through the Fall Festival, the Thanksgiving holidays, and I continued marking happily with my red pen. As our Christmas break approached, I knew that Teddy would never catch up in time to be promoted to the sixth-grade level. He would be a repeater.

To justify myself, I went to his cumulative folder from time to time. He had very low grades for the first four years, but no grade failure. How he had made it, I didn't know. I closed my mind to the personal remarks.

First Grade: "Teddy shows promise by work and attitude, but he has a poor home situation."

Second Grade: "Teddy could do better. Mother terminally ill. He receives little help at home."

Third Grade: "Teddy is a pleasant boy. Helpful, but too serious. Slow learner. Mother passed away end of the year."

Fourth Grade: "Very slow but well behaved. Father shows no interest."

Well, they passed him four times, but he will certainly repeat fifth grade! Do him good! I said to myself.

And then the last day before the holidays arrived. Our little tree on the reading table sported paper and popcorn chains. Many gifts were heaped underneath, waiting for the big moment. Teachers always get several gifts at Christmas, but mine that year seemed bigger and more elaborate than ever. There was not a student who had not brought me one. Each unwrapping brought squeals of delight and the proud giver would receive effusive thank-yous.

His gift wasn't the last one I picked up. In fact it was in the middle of the pile. Its wrapping was a brown paper bag, and he had colored Christmas trees and red bells all over it. It was stuck together with masking tape. "For Miss Thompson—From Teddy."

The group was completely silent and I felt conspicuous, embarrassed because they all stood watching me unwrap that gift. As I removed the last bit of masking tape, two items fell to my desk. A gaudy rhinestone bracelet with several stones missing and a small bottle of dime-store cologne—half empty. I could hear the snickers and whispers, and I wasn't sure I could look at Teddy.

"Isn't this lovely?" I asked, placing the bracelet on my wrist. "Teddy, would you help me fasten it?" He smiled shyly as he fixed the clasp, and I held up my wrist for all of them to admire. There were a few hesitant oohs and ahhs, but, as I dabbed the cologne behind my ears, all the little girls lined up for a dab behind their ears.

I continued to open the gifts until I reached the bottom of the pile. We ate our refreshments until the bell rang. The children filed out with shouts of "See you next year!" and, "Merry Christmas!" but Teddy waited at his desk. When they had all left, he walked towards me clutching his gift and books to his chest. "You smell just like Mom," he said softly. "Her bracelet looks real pretty on you, too. I'm glad you liked it." He left quickly and I locked the door, sat down at my desk and wept, resolving to make up to Teddy what I had deliberately deprived him of—a teacher who cared.

I stayed every afternoon with Teddy from the day class resumed on January 2 until the last day of school. Sometimes we worked together. Sometimes he worked alone while I drew up lesson plans or graded papers. Slowly but surely he caught up with the rest of the class. Gradually there was a definite upward curve in his grades.He did not have to repeat the fifth grade. In fact, his final averages were among the highest in the class, and although I knew he would be moving out of the state when school was out, I was not worried for him. Teddy had reached a level that would stand him in good stead the following year, no matter where he went. He had enjoyed a measure of success and as we were taught in our education courses: "Success builds success."

I did not hear from Teddy until several years later when his first letter appeared in my mailbox.

"Dear Miss Thompson,

I just wanted you to be the first to know. I will be graduating second in my class on May 25 from E High School.

Very truly yours, Teddy Stallard"

I sent him a card of congratulations and a small package, a pen and pencil set. I wondered what he would do after graduation. I found out four years later when Teddy's second letter came.

"Dear Miss Thompson,

I was just informed today that I'll be graduating first in my class. The university has been a little tough but I'll miss it.

Very truly yours, Teddy Stallard"

I sent him a good pair of sterling silver monogrammed cuff links and a card, so proud of him I could burst!

And now—today—Teddy's third letter:

"Dear Miss Thompson,

I wanted you to be the first to know. As of today I am Theodore J. Stallard, MD. How about that???!!! I'm going to be married on July 27 and I'm hoping you will come and sit where Mom would sit if she were here. I'll have no family there as Dad died last year.

Very truly yours, Ted Stallard."

I'm not sure what kind of gift one sends to a doctor on completion of medical school. Maybe I'll just wait and take a wedding gift, but the note can't wait.

"Dear Ted,

Congratulations! You made it and you did it yourself! In spite of those like me and not because of us, this day has come for you. God bless you. I'll be at that wedding with bells on!!!"

***

So you see the success of ILs and students is intertwined. One cannot experience success without the other. Even though this story was written decades ago, its central premise still rings true today. ILs must first care whether all students succeed; and second, they must believe that they and their students possess the capacity to prevail. I should note, sympathy is not the type of care students need.

Mrs. Thompson's professional reflections and ultimate transformation made a difference in her life and her student. Teddy and Mrs. Thompson learned from each other. She taught him that, in spite of adversities, he was important, capable, and should never give up—grit. Likewise, he taught her to give all students her best. For many ILs, this should not be very difficult to do.

As I indicated at the outset, teaching ultimately becomes a calling. All children have a unique quality. It is the ability, over time, to capture the heart of adults. Because ILs interact with students daily, this is a well-established fact among educators. For those who doubt it, just observe ILs who occasionally lament the diminished efforts or poor quality of assignments produced by some of their students. These same ILs will immediately come to the defense of their students if someone else utters the same remarks. The bottom line is success does beget success, for ILs and students. Conversely, experiencing persistent failure overtime is debilitating, unnecessary, and unacceptable. This is why making a difference in the life of one student, does not, by itself, satisfy our calling to be successful instructional leaders. We must all strive to apply effective techniques—ones that not only work for one or two or three students, but also for the full spectrum of students. That means implementing "theories of action" that are applicable to all students, in all schools and districts.

A THEORY OF ACTION

Hargreaves and Fullan describe what a theory of action in schools is by declaring, "There are three conditions a theory must meet to be called a theory of action: First, it must meet the 'system' test. Do the ideas stand a chance of addressing the whole system, not just a few hundred schools here and there? Second, the theory must make a compelling case that using the ideas will result in positive movement. We are, after all, talking about improvement—transitioning from one state of being to another. Third, such a theory must demonstrably tap into and stimulate people's motivation" (2009, p. 275).

The Instructional Leadership Pyramid (ILP) embraces all three of these theoretical conditions. Its fundamental premise is rooted in its systemic approach. That is, the Pyramid can be applied district wide. It is applicable in small and large districts alike. Its principles can and should be utilized in rural, urban, and suburban schools.

I am convinced, when applied appropriately, the Pyramid will indeed advance professional practice and significantly improve student academic achievement regardless of the demographic makeup of the campus or district. Additionally, the ILP makes a convincing case that something is missing in the application of educational practice. Many of the critical missing pieces can be found within the ILP.

Recall the question posed decades ago by Ron Edmonds: If we already know more than we need to be successful in schooling, then why haven't we experienced the outcomes we desire? There are two answers to this question. The ILP addresses both of them.

As indicated earlier, too many ILs do not accept what we know from educational research and some who do, incorrectly apply it in schools; that is, they fail to see the interconnectedness of research methods and programs and they lack a strategic and systematic plan to apply those same methods and programs.

The ILP addresses this issue by first refusing to use euphemistic language when discussing the belief system of practitioners. For example, the ILP makes the case that "high expectations" have outlived their usefulness. At best, this phrase "high expectations" has become a platitude; at worst, it has become a euphemism for accepting some students' failure to learn.

I assert that the time has arrived where ILs must stand and declare whether they are believers or non-believers in the capacity of all humans to learn what they need to know. One may take the position that beliefs are subjective. Other than the individual himself, who really knows what one believes? A reliable indicator of ILs' beliefs regarding human capacity is how they respond to their own failures and to those of students. Do these ILs resort to using campus learning disabilities when they do not realize the academic proficiency results they desire? And what recommendations do they make when students experience failure?

I submit one's beliefs are accurately manifested in one's professional practice. That is, do they embrace "J curve" or "bell curve" teaching? I should offer a cautionary note: not every ineffective practitioner is a non-believer in human capacity. There are multiple reasons for deficient professional practice.

For example, poorly implemented induction programs, and professional development efforts that are not supported over time, as well as a lack of the kind of coaching opportunities that can lead to improved practice are some reasons. In addition, when professional growth opportunities and campus support are not aligned with the stated mission of the campus, professional practice tends to be less effective.

The ILP calls attention to all of these areas and more. Over time, however, after considering multiple indicators, a clear picture begins to emerge concerning one's professional belief system. Even at this point, the ILP offers strategies and concepts to align one's beliefs with what truly is the common denominator when it comes to experiencing students' high academic achievement. It is beliefs and effort, not the "right stuff" that matters.

In addition to aligning one's belief system with current research, there has to be a framework to effectively apply what works. The ILP provides such a platform. So, indeed, the ILP will cause schools and districts to improve student proficiency. The ILP is comprehensive with multiple components; however, just embracing research-based beliefs and effort concepts alone, are more than enough to significantly advance schooling.

In addition, stimulating people's motivation can cause impressive results. Motivation is Hargreaves' and Fullan's third criteria for a theory of action. The challenges in schooling are enormous. In some schools and districts, resources are inadequate. The turnover rate in too many schools is prohibitive to progress. Some communities are struggling with inadequate health services and unemployment. Since schools and districts are microcosms of the larger community, many of these same community issues naturally exist within the walls of schools.

Therefore, ILs are eager to find possible solutions to these longstanding social ills that could ultimately threaten the preeminence of America. The Pyramid offers a pathway to addressing many of the impediments to experiencing "all students achieving at high levels." This is motivation enough for instructional leaders to begin applying the ILP process.

Concerning pathways, in the introduction I used a recipe analogy to describe the ILP. For clarity, in this final chapter, I will use finding one's directions as an analogy. The ILP is not a global positioning system (GPS). The effective school characteristics, outlined in chapter two, provide that type of detailed guidance.

The Pyramid framework is more like a compass. While there is a great deal of latitude within the Pyramid, the direction it does provide is significant. There is a profound difference between traveling east when one's stated goal is to travel north. The Pyramid offers a practical research-based framework to stay on course for continuous improvement. Owens and Valesky (2007) underscore the value of such a framework or theory. They report:

> The alternative to using theoretical knowledge is to scurry through the maze of professional leadership practice mindlessly hoping to take the right action but guessing all the way. In that sense, there is perhaps nothing more practical than good theory, for it provides the foundation for taking appropriate action in a busy, complex world where few problems are truly simple, where time is chronically short, and where any decision usually leads only to the need for further decisions. (p. 72)

Educational Leadership National Standards

In addition to embracing a theory of action, the Pyramid is aligned with the six standards of the 2008 Interstate School Leaders Licensure Consortium (ISLLC). The ISLLC and the National Policy Board for Educational Administration, along with a nationally renowned research panel, updated the Educational Leadership Policy Standards. These national standards reinforce the belief that instructional leaders' primary responsibility is to improve teaching and learning for all children.

The following organizations and councils are members of the National Policy Board for Educational Administration (NPBEA): American Association of Colleges for Teacher Education, American Association of School Administrators, Association for Supervision and Curriculum Development, Council of Chief State School Officers, National Association of Elementary School Principals, National Association of Secondary School Principals, National Council for Accreditation of Teacher Education, National Council of Professors of Educational Administration, National School Boards Association, and University Council for Educational Administration.

Table 5.1 lists Educational Leadership Policy Standards, published by the Interstate School Leaders Licensure Consortium (ISLLC) 2008, as adopted by the National Policy Board for Educational Administration. These standards represent the broad, high priority themes that education leaders must address in order to promote the success of every student. These six standards call for:

Standard 1: An education leader promotes the success of every student by facilitating the development, articulation, implementation, and stewardship of a vision of learning that is shared and supported by all stakeholders.	**Standard 4:** An education leader promotes the success of every student by collaborating with faculty and community members, responding to diverse community interests and needs, and mobilizing community resources.
Function:	**Function:**
A. Collaboratively develop and implement a shared vision and mission B. Collect and use data to identify goals, assess organizational effectiveness, and promote organizational learning C. Create and implement plans to achieve goals D. Promote continuous and sustainable improvement E. Monitor and evaluate progress and revise plans	A. Collect and analyze data and information pertinent to the educational environment B. Promote understanding, appreciation, and use of the community's diverse cultural, social, and intellectual resources C. Build and sustain positive relationships with families and caregivers D. Build and sustain productive relationships with community partners

| Standard 2: An education leader promotes the success of every student by advocating, nurturing, and sustaining a school culture and instructional program conducive to student learning and staff professional growth.

Function:

A. Nurture and sustain a culture of collaboration, trust, learning, and high expectations
B. Create a comprehensive, rigorous, and coherent curricular program
C. Create a personalized and motivating learning environment for students
D. Supervise instruction
E. Develop assessment and accountability systems to monitor student progress
F. Develop the instructional and leadership capacity of staff
G. Maximize time spent on quality instruction
H. Promote the use of the most effective and appropriate technologies to support teaching and learning.
 I. Monitor and evaluate the impact of the instructional program | Standard 5: An education leader promotes the success of every student by acting with integrity, fairness, and in an ethical manner.

Function:

A. Ensure a system of accountability for every student's academic and social success
B. Model principles of self-awareness, reflective practice, transparency, and ethical behavior
C. Safeguard the values of democracy, equity, and diversity
D. Consider and evaluate the potential moral and legal consequences of decision-making
E. Promote social justice and ensure that individual student needs inform all aspects of schooling |
| Standard 3: An education leader promotes the success of every student by ensuring management of the organization, operation, and resources for a safe, efficient, and effective learning environment.

Function:

A. Monitor and evaluate the management and operational systems
B. Obtain, allocate, align, and efficiently utilize human, fiscal, and technological resources
C. Promote and protect the welfare and safety of students and staff
D. Develop the capacity for distributed leadership
E. Ensure teacher and organizational time is focused to support quality instruction and student learning | Standard 6: An education leader promotes the success of every student by understanding, responding to, and influencing the political, social, economic, legal, and cultural context.

Function:

A. Advocate for children, families, and caregivers
B. Act to influence local, district, state, and national decisions affecting student learning
C. Assess, analyze, and anticipate emerging trends and initiatives in order to adapt leadership strategies |

Table 5.1. Educational Leadership Policy Standards: ISLLC 2008. As Adopted by the National Policy Board for Educational Administration

The ISLLC standards were developed by the Council of the Chief State School Officers (CCSSO) and member states. Copies may be downloaded from the Council's website at www.ccsso.org.

HOW TO APPLY THE INSTRUCTIONAL LEADERSHIP PYRAMID

As noted earlier, Abraham Maslow theorized a hierarchy of human needs. It focuses on lower needs of human beings and progresses to higher levels of concern. Maslow reasoned until lower needs are met, it's very difficult for human beings to satisfy higher ones.

In a similar way, I view organizations as living organisms. They all have needs. And unless their essentials are addressed, organizational systems are not likely to function at their optimal level. This is particularly true of school campuses and school districts. Further, the notion of viewing organizations as living organisms is not necessarily novel. But what is exceptional is combining this living organism metaphor with a research-based framework that is designed to guide professional practice and increase student achievement.

Think about the Pyramid as having five levels, with each level being used to build to the next level, beginning with Level One. The Pyramid aligns theory with professional practice. It strives to take what we know and provides a practical framework to effectively apply it.

For example, every college basketball team has a playbook. Every play in it is designed to score points; however, that is the way it is designed to work, but it does not always happen as planned. Why? Because there are five defensive players on the other team, it matters which play is called, who is executing it, and what the circumstances are at the time it is attempted. And so it is when applying educational research methods. The process is as important as the research methods themselves.

This insight is at the heart of the ILP. Based on more than twenty-five years of observations as a teacher, principal, assistant superintendent, educational consultant, and university assistant professor, it seems to me that the system many instructional leaders employ when applying research-based methods is analogous to pulling the winning ticket from a hat.

The ILP is different. It calls attention to the need for a systematic framework that recognizes the interconnectedness among and between research methods. It makes the case that instructional leadership is more than having at one's disposal a collection, or a hodgepodge, of research strategies. It matters which methods are implemented, and it matters, just as much, when and how they are used. At this point, I would like to highlight each level of the Pyramid and briefly discuss its rationale.

Level One

The focus of Level One is on team culture. In the standards era, I have observed the preoccupation with analyzing student achievement data. To be sure, this is a worthwhile and necessary practice. It should not, however, preempt establishing a foundation for students' academic success built on instituting a safe, caring, and trusting team culture.

One word captures the essence of Level One: culture. Culture drives professional practice. Recall the comment made to me as a new campus instructional leader: "On this campus, you improve or you move." When sufficient time, thought, collaboration, and implementation are given to Level One principles of the campus, the effective implementation of higher level principles are more likely to be achieved. Conversely, campuses struggling with Level One principles are not likely to celebrate Level Five successes.

Level Two

The focus of Level Two is on identifying and implementing appropriate school-wide instructional strategies. School-wide instructional strategies do not seek to standardize the delivery of campus instruction. The goal of these instructional strategies should be tailored to what works for each individual campus.

When making this determination, everything should be on the table for discussion. That includes the physical, social, and psychological needs of students as well as their academic needs. District and community resources should be given ample consideration. Priority should be given to those strategies that yield the most benefit in terms of students' development. The key factor is that every campus should have broad support for school-wide instructional strategies delineated in some document—for example, a campus handbook or strategic plan.

Remember the basketball analogy. It matters which play is called, who is executing it and what the circumstances are at the time it is attempted. Every play that is called is not always run appropriately; or worse, some plays that are called are never attempted. In any organization, a critical mass is required to reach a tipping point. Just having campus strategies on shelves in classrooms or in offices serve no meaningful purpose for anyone. The campus-wide strategies must be applied correctly in a consistent and efficient fashion. Hence, the process matters. A systematic process should be employed to identify and implement appropriate strategies. Level Two of the Pyramid offers a process that can be used to achieve this.

Level Three

The focus of Level Three is on the belief system of instructional leaders. One might be inclined to postulate that if campuses began by developing research-based beliefs, Level One and Level Two of the Pyramid would not be necessary. Perhaps that's true; however, if beliefs were easy to change, we would have already realized the kind of student success everyone seeks.

Therefore, while we are aligning our beliefs with professional practice, support systems should be instituted that will foster and support research belief systems. Level One and Level Two principles provide such support. Level Three attempts to align beliefs with research-based professional practice by first facilitating one's transformation through the unlearn-relearn cycle, and second, by hiring persons who already possess this kind of research-based thinking.

Level Four

The focus of Level Four is on what matters most in schooling—effective effort. Once ILs ensure students are provided an opportunity to learn appropriate knowledge, effort becomes the prerequisite for achieving success in learning rigorous academic curricula. It is the type of effort applied (E=mc2), not genes, that matters most in the learning process.

My analogy to Einstein's most famous mathematical expression is intended to be used as a catalyst to generate and heighten the interest of instructional leaders, students, and parents in applying effort-based concepts. This needs to be jumpstarted—a renaissance is needed. Once ILs become believers, it is much easier to teach effort-based principles. Students will believe it because the instructional leader believes it. It is very difficult to teach anything one does not unequivocally believe.

Recall when Troy Aikman was in the huddle and he turned to Michael Irvin and said, "I am coming to you no matter what." Michael said Troy looked him and the others in the huddle in their eyes while making those comments. Do you think Michael thought Troy believed he, Irvin, would catch the pass? Troy was also saying to the others in the huddle that he believed that they would block so that he would have time to throw the pass. So it is in the classroom. Students know whether ILs are believers or pretenders. Think about William Glasser's comments to me regarding classroom management. He stated that to exert effective classroom management skills, the classroom IL must first be believable. Students have a sixth sense about sincerity. Their behavior is, to a large degree, dependent on what they sense ILs think about them. The point is that a research-based belief system precedes effectively applying effort-based principles within the classroom. Attempting to reverse the order misaligns the principles of the Pyramid. This does not mean that effort-based principles cannot be implemented until one fully embraces research based belief principles. It simply means that when the desired students' academic achievement level is not realized, reexamining the research-based beliefs of the organization and individual members is an excellent place to begin exploring possible solutions.

Level Five

Level Five is a bar that constantly rises. Therefore, as student proficiency increases, so does the Level Five threshold. And perhaps that is as it should be. There seems to be unlimited capacity to the human intellect.

So that's the Instructional Leadership Pyramid and how it can be applied for advancing the teaching and learning enterprise. I offer it as a theoretical framework to apply best practices. In its absence, ILs are left with the current practice of using guesses and hunches regarding the application of research-based knowledge. Synergy exists among all levels of the Pyramid.

It is impossible to consider each level in isolation. All four levels should be applied at various rates, depending on the circumstances of individual campuses. It embraces systems thinking. The overriding concept of the Pyramid is first, to understand the significance of firmly establishing a safe, caring and trusting team culture, and second, to understand how to achieve the same. Campus-wide strategies, research-based belief system, and effort-based methods will follow. This framework provides a way for schools to get better.

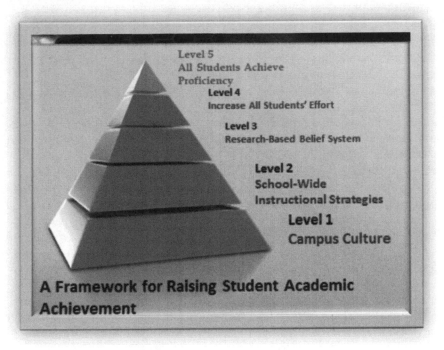

Figure 5.1. Instructional Leadership Pyramid

YOU ARE IN CONTROL OF YOUR DESTINY

The belief system one embraces guides professional practice. We have looked at a model that demonstrates how ILs can take control of their own and their students' destinies. This model illustrates the beliefs instructional leaders hold for themselves and students. The beliefs they hold in both areas significantly influence professional practice.

In the table below, the first letter symbolizes the beliefs instructional leaders hold regarding their beliefs about their own pedagogical skills and the second letter represents the beliefs instructional leaders hold regarding their beliefs about students' academic prowess. For instance, (HH) illustrates instructional leaders who possess a high (H) belief system for themselves, high self-efficacy and a high (H) belief system for students. They believe that, exposed to a rich academic environment, students have the ability to increase their intellectual capacity. Campus instructional leaders should come to know these four types of classroom ILs and plan accordingly. It should be noted, however, that campus ILs fall into one of these four categories as well.

Research-Based Belief Model

Instructional leader	High Beliefs	Low Beliefs
Students	High Beliefs	Low Beliefs

Table 5.2. Research-Based Belief Model

- HH—These instructional leaders possess a high sense of professional effectiveness, along with the belief that effort based practices work. They fully embrace the belief that students, through the effective application of $E=mc^2$ principles, can indeed become smarter. They believe smart is not something one is born with; it can be acquired. These instructional leaders believe they hold destiny within their own hands.
- HL—These instructional leaders possess a high sense of their own professional effectiveness when working with certain kinds of students—those whom they perceive to have been born with the "right stuff." As their perceptions of students' abilities decrease, so does their effectiveness—the Pygmalion effect. These instructional leaders often communicate their preference to work with specific students who demonstrate certain kinds of characteristics.

- LH—These instructional leaders recognized the intellectual potential of their students; however, they doubt their when engaged with rigorous curricula. The problem here is generally not a lack of knowledge of one's content area but a deficiency in teaching methods, strategies, and classroom management techniques. Through coaching, induction, professional learning teams, and aligned professional development, these ILs often possess the potential to become very successful.
- LL—These instructional leaders were referenced earlier. They doubt their own ability and the ability of their students. They generally feel extremely frustrated and overwhelmed. They frequently engage in using organizational learning disabilities as reasons for their problems. That is, they believe some external force is responsible for their success or failure in the classroom. The learning environment they create in their classrooms is most debilitating to students and requires immediate corrective action. Research has consistently revealed that students coming from this type of environment are profoundly disadvantaged in subsequent years.

I began by asserting that two essential questions would be explored and answered. These questions have been answered. Now it is your time to act. I further stated that the ILP will pull the cover off and expose the "bare facts" regarding these questions and shed light on a comprehensive synergistic approach that corrects misconceptualized and misapplied professional practices. The "bare facts" have been exposed and possible solutions offered. To restate: We cannot achieve what we don't believe. The Instructional Leadership Pyramid provides a pathway to all students' academic success.

I challenge everyone who reads this book to reanalyze the "bell curve" paradigm and to begin thinking differently about both ILs' effectiveness and students' capacity to learn rigorous content. Indeed, ILs are the solution but only when they take action. And those who are slow to act or may be content with the status quo should reflect upon Walt Kelly's cartoon character Pogo: "We have found the enemy and he is us."

The good news is that instructional leaders are in control of their own destiny. There is no credible reason for them to succumb to the debilitating effects of campus learning disabilities. To be sure, the challenges are great in the schooling enterprise, considering all the social ills of our larger society. However, the Instructional Leadership Pyramid provides a comprehensive, synergistic, research-based framework, that when effectively applied to the unique circumstances of individual campuses, provides enduring solutions.

Above all, the evidence is resoundingly consistent and clear as it speaks to the predominant impediment to students' demonstrating proficiency with demanding college preparatory curricula. It says the predominant hindrance to all students achieving at high academic levels is not innate ability but the inability of some instructional leaders to embrace the most current research regarding this issue. All students are smart enough. Believe it!

REFLECTIVE THOUGHTS

What are your thoughts and beliefs regarding the following statements and how are they manifest in your daily practice?

- What are your thoughts regarding the applicability of the ILP?
- How might the ILP be applied effectively on your campus?
- Of the four categories delineated within the research-based belief model, which one most accurately describes you?
- Which symbol will you see on your service plaque and why?
- When you recite the ubiquitous phrase, "All youth are educable," what do you really mean?

BARE FACTS

- You will see one of four symbols on your service plaque.
- You will experience more personal fulfillment if you see a dash.

REFERENCES

Ballard, E. S. (2008). *Three Letters from Teddy and Other Stories*. Timberlake, NC: Righter Publishing Co., Inc. From *Home Life*, March 1976. Copyright 1976, The Sunday School Board of Southern Baptist Convention (now LifeWay Christian Resources of the Southern Baptist Convention). All rights reserved. Used by permission of the author.

Council of Chief State School Officers. (2008). Interstate School Leaders Licensure Consortium (ISLLC) Standards for School Leaders. Washington, DC: Author.

Erikson, E. (1994). *Identity and the life cycle*. New York: W.W. Norton and Co.

Hargreaves, A., and Fullan, M., eds. (2009). *Change wars*. Bloomington, IN: Solution Tree.

Owens, R. G., and Valesky, T.C., (2007). *Organizational behavior in education*. Boston, MA: Pearson Education, Inc.

REFLECTIVE THOUGHTS

_____

_____

_____

_____

_____

_____

_____

_____

_____

_____

_____

Index

About the author

George Woodrow Jr., EdD, instructs university students studying education leadership in Dallas, Texas. He heads an education consulting firm: The Instructional Leadership Pyramid Institute, LLC. It offers staff and parent training. In addition, he is the author of three books. *The Pyramid Approach: A Framework for Raising Student Academic Achievement* is his latest. His practitioner experience includes serving as principal of elementary, middle, and large high schools and as an assistant superintendent. At the university level, his areas of expertise include organizational change and instructional leadership. He can be contacted at instructional-leadershippyramid.com or 1-800-301-2215.